MARY LEAKEY

Disclosing the Past

MARY LEAKEY

Disclosing the Past

DOUBLEDAY & COMPANY, Inc.
Garden City, New York 1984

Copyright © Sherma B.V. 1984

This book was designed and produced by
The Rainbird Publishing Group Limited
40 Park Street, London WIY 4DE
for Doubleday & Company, Inc.
Garden City, New York

All rights reserved. No part of this publication
may be reproduced or transmitted, in any form
or by any means, without permission.

First edition published in the United States of America 1984

Library of Congress Cataloging in Publication Data

Leakey, Mary D. (Mary Douglas), 1913–
    Disclosing the past.   *224/25*

    Includes index.
    1. Leakey, Mary D. (Mary Douglas), 1913–
    2. Anthropologists—Africa—Biography.
    3. Fossil man—Africa.   I. Title.
GN21.L372A33 1984   306'.092'4[B]   84-10189
ISBN 0-385-18961-3

*301.092
Leak*

Text set by Tradespools Limited, Frome, Somerset
Photographs originated by N.S. Graphics Limited, London
Printed and bound by Mackays of Chatham, Kent, England

Contents

List of Illustrations

To the Dalmatians, past and present, who have
so greatly enriched my life with their
companionship, intelligence and loyalty.

Acknowledgments

Few autobiographies are entirely the work of one person and I, like others before me, owe a debt of gratitude to the many people who have helped me.

Firstly my thanks go to my son Richard, for suggesting that I write the book in the first place and for his support and encouragement throughout the project.

My thanks also to the many kind friends in Africa, Europe and America who have given so generously of their time and patience to answer questions and dig deep into their memories in search of forgotten dates and places, and missing links in the story.

To Chris Parker go my special thanks for her typing skill, unbelievable speed and unfailing cheerfulness in the face of hand-written inserts and last-minute alterations.

And most of all my thanks are due to Derek Roe, who undertook the daunting task of helping me get the whole story down on paper. With the possibility in mind that one day my life story might be written, I had – over the past several years – taken to jotting down memories as they came to me. The result was a sizeable pack of index cards arranged in no particular order. From these, Derek has helped me piece together the full story of my personal and professional life.

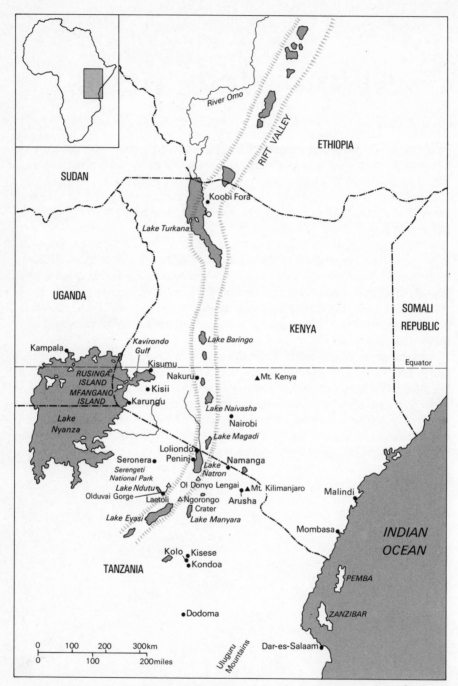

Mary Leakey's Africa, with places and features mentioned in the text.

By way of prelude

HOW ON EARTH does one get talked into these things? Mind you, publishers will talk one into anything, but I still cannot regard myself as the autobiography-writing type: this is the first paragraph, and I'm already regretting it. It always struck me as rash and arrogant to feel that one's life story was worth inflicting on other people. Those who really care know all they need to know already, and why should I share personal details with the rest? Thus would have spoken the Mary Leakey of ten years ago, certainly, and perhaps also of five years ago, but by then perhaps not quite so inflexibly. Now, as I reach seventy, I'm prepared to be convinced that not all of it *is* my own to keep locked away. The finds made by an archaeologist are not his or hers to retain for personal pleasure. Least of all should the really important discoveries remain private property. I am lucky enough to have been involved for half a century with work, mostly in East Africa, that very much belongs to everyone, since it concerns the human origins that are common to the whole human race. Most of my writing is concerned with the highly technical exposition of the main individual finds: hominid fossils, early stone implements, animal bones and all aspects of their archaeological and geological context. That, of course, is fine for the specialists in these fields who are my colleagues, but it may not be much good to the rest of the world, to whom the information also belongs. I well know what an appetite there is all over the world for the human story told in simple terms, and also for the story of the research and of the people who take part in it.

The last thing I ever wanted to be was a public figure or a star of the television screen or lecture platform. For many years I would have done anything to avoid lecturing in public: the very idea terrified me. Latterly, however, public appearances, especially in the United States, have become a major and essential part of my work in raising the enormous amounts of money required these days to finance archaeological research in remote areas. I have now, to my amazement, come to terms with lecturing to large audiences, and even find it exhilarating, though not even for the sake of the many kind friends I have made in the process will I pretend that I have actually come to enjoy the endless repetitive travel and the crowded receptions that are part of the same trips. Yet even those have helped to change a lot of my thinking. I can see now that large numbers of people really would like a book of this kind. And I must admit that my life has been far from ordinary.

In any case, autobiographical writing seems to be a trait in the Leakey family. Louis started early, publishing a first volume of his memoirs, *White African*, in 1937, when he was only 33, and many of his later writings contain a clear autobiographical element. He actually handed in the completed text of a second volume, *By the Evidence*, shortly before he died, and had planned a third volume in due course. My second son Richard, still in his late thirties, has recently completed *One Life*, an account of himself up to the time of a serious illness in 1979, the fatal consequences of which were averted only by major surgery. My other sons, Jonathan and Philip, have not yet succumbed to writing their life stories, but each would have plenty to write about and maybe one or both will set it all down one day. I hope the world will not feel it already has a surfeit of Leakey books: at least we have somehow all managed to do different things.

But when all that has been said, the task remains of telling the story and indeed of facing it myself when it is set out in some sort of order. You find poets and philosophers telling us of Man's unceasing search for his own identity and for self-knowledge. I'm not sure I believe them, though it sounds very impressive. How many of one's friends does one catch – say late at night when all the television channels have closed – explicitly engaged in the restless search for themselves? Where would they be looking, anyhow? Life is too full of the ceaseless struggle to bring projects to completion with inadequate resources; to extract from friends and colleagues the information they have promised, and to do what one has oneself promised them; and to cope with the unexpected obstacles of all kinds so lightly and liberally provided by fate. All I will say in advance is that perhaps my life divides into three reasonably clear parts. First there were the early years of my childhood and growing up, when I formed certain opinions and attitudes, likes and dislikes which have lasted ever since, and when I also learned various skills that were to stand me in good stead. This period ended fairly abruptly when I met Louis, who was to become my husband: the work and career on which he was already well embarked changed all my horizons. Because of him I went to East Africa, which otherwise I might conceivably never even have visited, though in fact it became my real and permanent homeland. So the second major period may simply be called 'the years with Louis', though so much varied life is packed into them that any single title must be inadequate. Louis died in 1972, and all that has happened since then has a similarly spurious unity as the 'post-Louis' period. Various friends have told me they see this as my emergence from Louis's shadow into my own proper share of the limelight. I'm not sure that I would entirely agree with that, but certainly there was no option for me but to take on the full official role of fund-raiser and director of the projects with which I was concerned, particularly the work at Olduvai with all the attendant publicity, which Louis to my horror had so carefully built up. No longer could I just live quietly at Olduvai and get on with my work. Besides, quite new research developments were in store which neither Louis nor I could have envisaged in 1972, notably the whole Laetoli operation, of which I shall have much to tell. Political changes were also to affect our traditional organization, and our mode of operating.

I'm sure that an autobiography, like any other book, needs a structure that holds it together, and these three stages should suffice. Archaeologists often divide things into three stages, usually 'lower', 'middle' and 'upper' if they are thinking stratigraphically. Afterwards, of course, they argue that the whole thing was continuous anyhow and that the divisions are arbitrary and for convenience only.

I
Childhood and forbears

LIKE EVERYONE ELSE I find it almost impossible to distinguish between what really are direct early memories of my own and the stories of my childhood that others have repeated so often that I have created my own visual impressions of the events and therefore think I am remembering them. Perhaps it doesn't matter very much that there is this division between fact and fiction for the early years, because although the details would be of interest they are not always of importance. My early years involved so much movement and so many temporary homes that I cannot hope to trace childhood friends of my own age, and the grown-ups of those distant days are all gone. For later stages of the story accuracy will be far more important.

I can almost look back on my first ten to fifteen years as if they were archaeological material to be studied: some clearly identifiable features, a pretty reasonable idea of the order of events and, of course, some gaps that will never be filled because the evidence just hasn't survived. Archaeologists must make the best and most complete story they can from the information available: no fabrication where there are gaps, but reasoned deductions; no dwelling at excruciating length on the unimportant details; absolute concentration on conclusions that are relevant to the cause and effect in the overall sequence to which the site belongs.

I was born Mary Douglas Nicol on 6 February 1913, in London. My father was Erskine Nicol, a painter, and my mother Cecilia, *née* Frere. For the sake of the genes, we need to look briefly further back. On my father's side, my grandfather was also called Erskine Nicol, and he too was an artist with R.S.A., A.R.A. and R.A.E. after his name. He enjoyed considerable success as a painter in oils and I think his paintings, often of Irish character scenes, are quite highly prized today. He was twice married, and his second wife, Margaret Wood, was my grandmother. She and my grandfather both died before I was born. My father's family was essentially Scottish and seems to have remained so in most of the marriages of the distant cousins, most of whom I hardly know except by name. But it should certainly be from the Nicol side that I inherited my talent for drawing, which was greatly to influence my career. I never had any formal instruction in drawing, but took to it naturally and with pleasure on my own initiative, from the age of about ten.

My mother's family, the Freres, came from East Anglia and I am directly descended from the eighteenth-century John Frere, who is famous in the history of British prehistoric archaeology for his recognition of stone implements, including hand axes, at Hoxne near Diss. The site is just on the Suffolk side of the county boundary; the Frere home was at Diss, a mile or so into Norfolk. It was in 1797 that John Frere wrote to the Society of Antiquaries about the flints that he had found at a depth of some twelve feet in the diggings of the local brickmakers. They were associated with large bones of extinct animals, and Frere argued that they were '... weapons of war, fabricated by a people who had not the use of metals.... The situation in which these weapons were found may tempt us to refer them to a very remote period indeed; even beyond that of the present world....' The letter was published in full by the Society in 1800, but the information it contained was virtually ignored for the next 60 years, because his interpretation of the finds was too radical, if not actually heretical. At that time most educated people believed literally in the Old Testament account of the Creation of the World. In any event honour has been restored; the excavations and researches at Hoxne by twentieth-century scholars have vindicated everything he wrote.

It would be tempting to stretch my faith in genetic inheritance to the point of claiming that my own interest in archaeology came naturally to me on the Frere side. I'm not prepared to do that, though it is interesting that my cousin Sheppard Frere is also an archaeologist, and retires this year from a chair at Oxford with a long and distinguished record of field-work and publication. I also approve thoroughly of the Frere tradition of being willing to put forward new and unwelcome views. Various nineteenth-century Freres fought hard against slavery, and there still exist three Freretowns, which were set up for freed slaves: one in Mombasa, Kenya, one in South Africa and one in India. Members of the family reached various high positions in colonial administration and there were several distinct African connections, which may or may not have assisted my taking so rapidly to East Africa as home. One Frere ancestor was made a baronet, but the last Sir Bartle Frere died in the 1930s, and the baronetcy is now extinct.

My maternal grandmother was Cecilia Byrne, devotedly Irish and devoutly Catholic, of whom I was very fond: she and the home where she lived with my mother's three unmarried sisters was one of the few stable and predictable elements in my world of childhood travel. She must, I suppose, bring an Irish element into my make-up. Possibly it is represented by my very blue eyes, which, like those of my son Philip and granddaughter Kyela, sometimes change their hue with changing moods.

There seems to have been little money in the Byrne family, but some of the Freres were wealthy. My Frere grandfather was Douglas Frere, and it is after him that I was christened Mary Douglas Nicol. Douglas Frere soon contrived to gamble his share of the Frere wealth away and died at an early age from TB in Switzerland. This left my grandmother almost penniless with four daughters to care for: my mother, and my aunts Mary (Mollie), Kathleen (Toudy) and Margaret (Marty). All the silver and my grandmother's jewellery had to be pawned or sold. There had been a large and beautiful villa in Italy, near Florence, where the family lived for much of each year: that too went, of course, and they returned to London to search for cheap rented accommodation, which they found first at Iverna Court off Kensington High Street and then at 17 Lincoln Street, off the King's Road in Chelsea. If these sound good addresses, it should be remembered that both areas were then far from the fashionable and trendy parts of London that they have since become. My three aunts first ran a shop selling hats in Beauchamp Place, and after that failed they directed their talents to the repair of antique tapestries, mainly accepting commissions from London art dealers. Of the four sisters, only my mother ever married. They were all good-looking, but she was easily the prettiest of the four, and very feminine. When she met my father she was working as the paid travelling companion of a rich friend. The family was never again even comfortably off, and I remember that from time to time the telephone was cut off because the bill had not been paid.

My parents' meeting took place in Egypt. My father had gone there to paint, and in fact painting was almost always the reason why he travelled anywhere: he would stay at some place until he had painted all that he wished and then move on, either to a new place to paint or until it was time to return to London to sell his pictures. This, of course, is why my own early years were so full of travel and short stays here and there in western Europe. It also meant that I never had a proper settled schooling, because we were never in the same place for long enough. My father's needs were simple and he could spend long periods travelling before his money ran out. In Egypt he actually spent four years living with the Bedouin, of whom he always spoke with great affection and admiration. I remember he often told of how the Bedouin had nursed him through typhoid by keeping him supplied with oranges, which they rolled to him through the flap of his tent. The Bedouin undoubtedly saved his life, although they would not approach him too closely for fear of catching his illness. Although herself never more than an amateur painter, my mother was always deeply interested in art and had studied it in the well-off days in Florence. It was a fair basis on which to start a friendship that ripened quite rapidly. After they were married, they lived on a houseboat on the Nile until I was expected, at which point they returned to London in time for my birth in a rented house in Trevor Square, Knightsbridge, early in 1913. My father certainly had not finished with Egypt, because he did not sell the houseboat when they left; but then the First World War broke out before he had a chance to return, and before the end of the war the boat had reluctantly to be sold after all.

My father took a deep interest in Egyptology and the archaeological work that was going on around him. He was fascinated by Egyptian mummies and by the rich objects from royal burials. Although his main thoughts were always for the aesthetic qualities of the material culture of the past, he was also interested in the process of their recovery, and often went to visit excavations in progress. In this way, with his open nature and capacity to make friends, he came to move easily in the circles of the leading Egyptologists and those working for them, and met most people of any significance. Among these were Howard Carter and Lord Carnarvon, later household names as the discoverers of the tomb of the Pharaoh Tutankhamun. At this time Howard Carter was still a junior employee of the Egypt Exploration Society, and his main work was as a draughtsman, which he did brilliantly. Occasionally he had reports to write up on small excavations or individual finds, and when it came to writing he had some problems and my father would often help him. I expect that at first it was simply as one artist helping out another, but their collaboration was certainly one reason for my father's deep and abiding interest in archaeological objects. The friendship with Howard Carter continued after my father left Egypt, and I remember his visiting us in England.

I can remember no details of the Great War, which broke out when I was still only one. The effect on London was hardly as direct as that of the early years of the Second World War and the Battle of Britain. But there must have been various practical difficulties for our family, and one of these was that my father could not travel abroad to paint; he had to follow his usual pattern of movements as best he could in Britain. He was for some reason not eligible for active service; perhaps it was simply on grounds of age, as he was already 46 in 1914. He did, however, join a reserve, which required occasional periods of duty, and I can remember seeing him in a military uniform of the period. But he was still able to spend plenty of time painting.

As somewhere where he could both paint and live, my father rented for us a small cottage at Hemingford Grey in Huntingdonshire, complete with pumped water and an outside earth closet. The cottage was an idyllic place, near the River Ouse. How well I remember the river-smell: even now the smell of a river and water weeds can transport me back to that place in a moment. I do not know whether the cottage still exists as I recall it, or whether it has been 'done up' to make someone a weekend cottage. I remember punting expeditions there, and water-lilies and marsh-marigolds. But we did not spend all our time at Hemingford Grey: there were frequent visits to London, and while there we stayed with my grandmother and my three aunts, at 17 Lincoln Street, in Chelsea. Since I was often to stay there in my later childhood at times when my parents were away, their house if anywhere was really home. Not surprisingly, my grandmother and aunts were delighted to have me and loved to spoil me: I was and indeed remained the newest and youngest thing in their small circle.

I cannot remember very much that belongs specifically to those first few years. The house in Lincoln Street was fairly large, with three floors and a basement. In passing, I know that even in the 1930s, when the area was coming into its own, the controlled rent was only £90 a year. What would it be today? But even that could only be scraped together with difficulty. For ordinary everyday wear I remember being dressed by my mother in linen smocks with conveniently large pockets – the equivalent of modern children's dungarees, no doubt. For anything that could be counted a special occasion she used to coax me into over-pretty dresses with ribbons and frills, which I hated. Even today my heart sinks when occasions demand that I must dress smartly rather than comfortably.

At this time there occurred my first encounter with the world of dogs, which has been so important to me throughout my life. It was with Jock, my aunts' smooth-haired Fox Terrier, who used to accompany my pram as far as the gardens near the Chelsea Royal Hospital when I was taken out for a walk. He would always return home alone, and then be at the gardens again faithfully to meet me on my return. My aunts were always fond of animals and had shared a tame fox when they were children in Italy. The house in London always had at least one dog and several cats, but Jock was the first for me. All the Nicols were animal lovers, with a strong preference for dogs, so here perhaps, like the ability to draw, there is something in my genes. I think, however, that since I came to Africa I and my family have comfortably outdone all my relations in the number and variety of our pets.

In those early days I was often the only child in a world of grown-ups. My father's brother Percy was the only close uncle, and he was a great favourite of mine. However, my father's sister Elizabeth, my aunt Bessie, was quite a different proposition from Toudy, Mollie and Marty. She was married, with a son in his late teens, and she had much stricter views on how I should be brought up, though I suspect she was in fact very fond of me.

Aunt Bessie used to come and stay with us at Hemingford Grey, and I regarded her visits with mixed feelings. For example, I had an infinitely precious teddy bear called Pimpy, more a companion and social equal than a toy. Pimpy was certainly my most treasured possession, and in order to discipline me Aunt Bessie would threaten to take him away, burn him or throw him in the river in order to make me behave as she saw fit. I developed considerable ingenuity in concealing Pimpy from her, but poor Pimpy lost out on the river trips, if she was there, because she more than once threatened to drown him if I did not behave. Aunt Bessie was extremely fond of birds, even to the extent later on of keeping an Australian cockatoo, which followed her around like a dog. For many years I could feel no enthusiasm for birds myself and I can only surmise that Aunt Bessie's love of birds was inextricably associated in my mind with her treatment of Pimpy. Later on, when I came to live at Olduvai, birds were to become one of my chief enthusiasms. It is remarkable for how long childhood likes and dislikes can influence one's adult life.

How very different were my mother's sisters: they were the kind of aunts that any child would have felt lucky to have. One very happy memory dating from about this time illustrates their goodness to me. I was staying at my grandmother's house in London over Christmas and, for all the charms of Pimpy, I had long wanted a real doll. My trio of kind maiden aunts knew this. From saved money they could ill afford, they clubbed together to buy a doll of great magnificence, with real hair and eyes that opened and shut, and then behind mysterious locked doors they set themselves to make her a complete trousseau, with no less than six different sets of clothing, including a gold-trimmed evening dress. On Christmas Day my joy was complete, and even after all these years I can recall the unbelievable happiness I felt that this elegant lady, possessing a wardrobe more lavish than any I had ever seen, should be mine.

For all the shortage of money, that was a happy household. Among themselves my aunts, and my mother if she were there, would speak Italian rather than English, their childhood language or a sign, perhaps, of the wrench it must have been to them all to leave the luxurious villa near Florence where they had been brought up. In contrast, my grandmother retained her Irishness in full measure. When I try to recall her visually, the memory that comes first is of her sitting in her favourite armchair dressed in a lilac tea-gown, long-sleeved and trimmed at the throat and cuffs with Irish lace. She was always kind to me and I used to enjoy our shopping trips together in the King's Road – except once each year, and that was when St. Patrick's Day came round. Then she would sally forth with me reluctantly in tow, wearing a large bunch of fresh shamrock which some relative would specially send over from Ireland for the occasion. She would ignore passers-by and treat the King's Road to Irish songs, notably *The Wearing of the Green*, sung loud and clear, while I wished myself dead or a thousand miles away. My grandmother also undoubtedly had the second sight. I usually regard such claims with the deepest suspicion, but in this case I am entirely convinced that it was so, and there were many examples. Perhaps the most remarkable came almost at the end of her life, when she had become quite senile. It had been anxiously and effectively concealed from her that I was to go out to Africa to join Louis, a move that the family viewed with real dismay. Yet when the time drew near she knew not merely that I was going away but also that I was going on a long journey overseas. There was no way she could possibly have overheard or found out.

My grandmother died early in 1937, very soon indeed after my departure for Africa; and when the Second World War broke out my aunts volunteered for work in censorship and were drafted to Liverpool. They left Lincoln Street before the bombing of London began in earnest, although they had some close shaves, and on one occasion just missed boarding a bus that was blown to pieces only a short time after. In Liverpool, the eldest, Mollie, caught pneumonia, followed by thrombosis, from which she never recovered. She died in 1940, at Steen Cottage in Hertfordshire, where she and my mother were living at the time. It was the cottage that Louis and I had first rented in 1936. After the war my aunts Toudy and Marty returned to London and, being still short of money, took a top-floor flat in Warwick Road, Earls Court. Marty died there suddenly after a thrombosis in 1958, and I suspect that the climbing of the long staircases to their not very suitable accommodation was the chief cause. This left Toudy completely alone and her life quite empty, and I am delighted to say that she accepted my invitation to come out and live with Louis and me in East Africa. She was with us both at our home in Langata, Nairobi, and also down at Olduvai; she was as lively as could be, went everywhere, saw and enjoyed everything and had a marvellous time. Thus she alone of the aunts saw at first hand the nature and chief backgrounds of my adult life. At least I was finally able to make to her that token repayment of hospitality for everything that I owed to them all from the early days. She was with us for about a year, apart from one final short visit to Ireland, before she died, well into her seventies.

2

First encounters with archaeology

WITH THE FIRST WORLD WAR OVER, my father soon settled into an annual pattern of painting abroad in Switzerland, France or Italy during winter and early spring, and spending the summer season in London because that was the best time to hold exhibitions and sell paintings, so raising enough money to repeat the cycle. His pictures sold well. The most typical are watercolours, gentle landscapes full of light, painted in such soft pastel shades that people who see them for the first time think they have faded in the sunlight. I have a roomful in my house at Langata in Nairobi and there are others in picture galleries in England and Scotland. He was a prolific painter, but I have no idea where the best collections of his work are now, or whether they ever come on the market or with what result if they do. His was a very distinctive style and his work may one day come back into fashion among collectors.

My mother and I would go along with him on these travels. Our journeys to and from England were by boat and train: my parents would sit up all night and I would be put to sleep on some arrangement of suitcases bridging the gap between the seats so that I could lie down. Thus it was that between the ages of eight and thirteen I visited Italy, Switzerland and several parts of south and southwest France. We would stay at some small hotel with minimal facilities, where often we would be the only guests. The value of the pound was high and that of the main European currencies low in those days, and it cost us very little to live. My father would paint by himself, in the mornings mainly, and my mother would look after me unless I had made any local friends with whom she felt able to trust me. As I grew older, my father and I increasingly spent the afternoons together on expeditions of our own.

My earliest memories are of Italy, and they are mostly indistinct and mainly unfavourable. My father was never a good linguist, and in Italy, as in France, my mother's fluent languages must have been a great advantage. Later, even after several visits to France, he had still not come to terms with speaking French, and my mother would interpret for him. Fortunately in this respect I took after her rather than him, and I quickly picked up quite a lot of Italian, though I deliberately let it go later because I didn't like Italy.

In Italy we were mainly in the north, at various villages. Some, I remember, had Etruscan tombs and other relics. We also stayed at Spoleto, where there was a brief but quite sharp earthquake, the only substantial one I have ever been in. My memory of it is vague, but I recollect loud rumblings and cracking noises of what sounded like thunder within the hotel where we were living, followed by a lot of shouting and excitement. I don't think anyone was hurt, but some buildings were damaged and I was frightened. This by itself might have been enough to put me off Italy, but there was more and worse to come. Once, when we were on a family picnic by a river, I saw Italian boys pulling the legs off live frogs for no reason but to amuse themselves. I was absolutely horrified and became completely frantic. I begged my father to stop them, but as I remember the boys paid no attention either to my mother's remonstrances or my father's evident anger. The day ended in rage and tears, and from that time I never wanted to visit Italy again. On the credit side I retain a clear memory of beautiful clumps of wild cyclamen flowering in the hill country of northern Italy. Their scent and colour and the shapes of the flowers delighted me. I was also very much addicted to Italian ice cream and Italian cherries, and indeed there is a lot to be said in favour of both; but as a result of eating one or the other I nearly died. It happened when we were visiting Florence on the way home, and there I went down with a very serious attack of dysentery. My father, who had an exhibition to arrange and open, had to continue the journey to England alone while my mother stayed with me. She told me afterwards that I did indeed nearly die. At last, in desperation, she took me back to London by train, ill as I was, and there I rapidly and completely recovered. All things considered, the Italian visit cannot be regarded from my point of view as a success.

It was during this otherwise unmemorable stay in Italy that I had my first reading lessons, when my father decided it was time I learned to read. And so it was, for I was seven or eight at the time. He started me straight off on *Alice in Wonderland* and *Robinson Crusoe*. This strategy paid off, fortunately: I picked up the idea quickly and from that time I read eagerly any book I could get my hands on.

I am a little uncertain as to the exact order of the next visits. If my father did not like a place from the painting point of view he would move on rapidly, so that we sometimes had more than one base in the same year. I know that we had one brief visit to Switzerland, but I can remember little or nothing about it and I assume therefore that it was short and probably came next after the unsatisfactory Italian trip. All our other stays were in France and I believe that together they add up to the most important and influential part of my upbringing. Certainly I remember far more about them than anything else of that period of my life, including the intervening times in London. I have taken every opportunity (too few, alas) to revisit France, and I know that if I could not live in the wilds of East Africa, south or southwest France is where I would wish to spend my days, in one of those little villages that have often managed to remain quite unspoilt. Louis and I took our own children there in due course: Jonathan, the eldest, first came alone with us when he was ten, in 1950, just about the age of my own first visits, and later we took the whole family there on a camping holiday. Much more recently, in the autumn of 1982, I took the opportunity provided by a human palaeontology conference at Nice to make a short stay in France, with nostalgic visits to some of the childhood places. It's a dangerous thing to do, since one risks finding places much changed and so shattering fragile memories that cannot be repaired, but in fact for the most part I found that my memories had not played me false and that most of my childhood haunts were as delightful as ever.

Our first stay in France was at Biarritz. I did in fact attend a kindergarten school there with French children, and I think it was the first time I had to speak French. As children often do, I accepted this as quite natural and soon became fluent. I also recall walks along the sea-shore, and collecting shells. A longer and better-remembered stay was at the little village of Saint-Guillaume le Désert, in Hérault, Languedoc, not far from Montpellier; such a beautiful place, full of that aromatic scent of wild flowers and herbs mingled that is like nothing else I have ever encountered. There were rocky gorges to explore among the limestone hills that are everywhere in southern France. I also made a friend of my own age. If this were a biography rather than an autobiography, Emile would doubtless be written up as my first boyfriend, and tremendous importance attached to him; but it really wasn't so. I was nine or ten and Emile perhaps a year older, and he just happened to be a boy. We were inseparable and did everything together, and of course all our talk was in French.

I was always happy in my father's company. He was a big man, strongly built and must have been nearly six feet tall. He had grey hair, a beard and moustache. Like many painters, he was not in the least concerned with his personal appearance and, whether painting or not, would dress in the oldest and untidiest clothes that my mother would let him get away with. He was a highly intelligent man, perhaps a bit on the serious side, but full of wide-ranging interests in people, animals and flowers and places and subjects of all sorts. I think I should have developed such interests myself in any case, but I'm sure the process was hastened and guided into particular paths by the time we spent together in the afternoons and to some extent too by the long after-dinner conversations he so much enjoyed, and to which I would listen avidly. At Saint-Guillaume he continued what might loosely be described as my formal education by teaching me a little mathematics: fractions, I particularly recall. In my own grandchildren's world, maths seems a very different matter, and calculators are now such an ordinary part of daily life. I even have one myself, and cannot imagine existence without it when it comes to dealing with ordinary figures. You may conclude that my father did not achieve as much for me with fractions at Saint-Guillaume as he had in Italy with *Alice* and *Robinson Crusoe*.

The rest of our visits to France were to one or another part of the southwest. My father knew from various friends that the villages and countryside there were eminently paintable, and of course they had long been attracting artists. But I think he was also glad of a chance to see the already famous Upper Palaeolithic cave paintings of the area, both as a painter and as one with a genuine interest in everything archaeological, dating back to his days in Egypt if not before. We must have been on our outward journey when we stayed a night at Sarlat, the principal market town of the Dordogne, where we met M. and Mme. Masbrenier and their teenage daughter. My parents, of course, got talking with them and it was on their advice that we visited the villages of Domme and Les Eyzies, with a stay in between at La Roque Gageac. To Les Eyzies we went twice, but Domme came first because that was where the Masbreniers themselves lived, in a small manor house. The whole region is full of Palaeolithic sites, including some of the most famous in all France.

At Domme the Masbreniers became our firm friends. I was constantly in and out of their house, living virtually as a member of their family. Our stay, however, was not a long one, and I remember it took place over Easter, because children from the village were making their First Communions. This I took note of because my mother was determined that I should be brought up as a good Catholic, as her own mother of course expected. My memories of La Roque Gageac, a village close to Domme on the Dordogne River, are summer memories, of great heat and of the blissful coolness of bathing in the river. We stayed here long enough for me to have my first ever kitten – a little white scrap of a thing that I found abandoned in a cornfield. I saved its life by drip-feeding it milk from a pen-filler, aided and advised by my mother, and it was mine long enough for me to see it begin to flourish and to adore it, so that the heartbreak came in full measure when the time came to leave it behind. I did return there in 1982, and the little village was much as I remembered it, nestling against its protecting cliff.

It was at Les Eyzies that I first began to come consciously in contact with Palaeolithic archaeology. As a family, we spent two successive winters there, and later, after my father's death, I was taken back there by

Uncle Percy for a summer holiday, when I learned to swim in the Vezère River. For the winters at Les Eyzies we stayed at the little Hotel Lesvignes, which offered the simplest of facilities and had floors of bare, scrubbed boards. In 1982 I saw that it had been enlarged and glorified into a Hotel Les Glycines, which to me seemed pretentious and uninviting. My father painted as usual, and we went to see all the cave art we could, at sites including Les Combarelles, Font de Gaume, La Mouthe and Cap Blanc, the site of the famous frieze of sculptured horses. I was much impressed by these, and my father even more so. I liked the animal engravings even better than the paintings because I had sharp eyes and was often first to decipher them when they were hard to see, being very often superimposed one on another. Then there was the museum, which at that time was in the care of M. Elie Peyrony, father of Denis – both famous French prehistorians. Between them they almost personified the archaeology of the Les Eyzies region and the Périgord, at least until the end of the Second World War. We made friends with M. Peyrony, my mother as usual interpreting for my father. I suppose it was in his museum that I first became aware of the finely shaped flint tools and the beautiful decorated bone points and harpoons that came from the rock shelters, though rarely from the cave sites that in their inner depths contained mural paintings. Peyrony was excavating at Laugerie Haute during our stay, and naturally we went to see. Now, I shudder at the crudeness of his methods. I can't remember ever seeing him sieve the buckets of spoil that his workmen so rapidly dug out and brought to him; he simply picked out those pieces that could easily be seen and tipped the rest down the bank towards the Vezère, for the river to dispose of in due course. Horrifying now, but then powerfully and magically exciting because my father and I could, with M. Peyrony's apparent acceptance, search through his spoil heaps and find rich treasure; treasure we could take home and keep. My father started it, with his love of objects, but I was only a short distance behind and soon became the chief collector. There were, of course, old spoil heaps at almost every site, and the sites themselves were there in profusion. We found all sorts of good things of Upper Palaeolithic age, including fine Magdalenian tools, burins and endscrapers, made on the typically large and elegant flint blades of the period; we even found some of the pressure-flaked Late Solutrean pieces that collectors prized so greatly. For me it was the sheer instinctive joy of collecting, or indeed one could say treasure hunting: it seemed that this whole area abounded in objects of beauty and great intrinsic interest that could be taken from the ground. My father loved it too, but my mother took less interest. I did make some rudimentary classification of my collection for purposes of sorting, and I remember wondering about the ages of the pieces, and the world of their makers.

It was Les Eyzies, then, that first made me aware of Palaeolithic archaeology, though not so crucially that I determined then to make it my life's
work. It was a delightful place in which to spend time, as many people
have found before and since. In the first year my parents and I were
virtually alone at the hotel, but in the second year we had company, both
welcome and unwelcome.

The unwelcome element took the ominous shape of a governess. I can
recall, while we were back in London after the first visit to Les Eyzies,
overhearing a parental conversation that was not intended for my ears:
something really had to be done about Mary's patchy education. Should
they or should they not engage a governess? What would it cost? The
decision went the wrong way from my point of view, and in due course
one of the least attractive girls I have ever met arrived, charged with the
task of teaching me things like history and Latin. I could have told her
from the start it would be no good. She was comprehensively ugly and
gawky and for some reason her hands had a permanent bright red blush,
which fascinated but disgusted me. She was a recent and rampant
Catholic convert and perhaps even had a dose of real religious mania,
heightened by her oppressive earnestness. How could they do this to me?

This governess accompanied us on our return to Les Eyzies and did her
best for me, with predictable results. However, before long an American
family, the Mallorys, arrived for a long stay in the village. The father was
a professor at Ann Arbor University in the States, and he was on a sabbat-
ical year or semester, in which he was indulging a long-standing interest
in prehistoric archaeology with a tour of famous sites. There were also his
wife and daughter, and a small son, who, in spite of knowing no French,
forthwith made friends with the local carters and wagon drivers and spent
his days happily with them. The daughter, Cynthia, was about my own
age and at once became my close friend and ally. In this capacity she
shared my views of the appalling governess, whom she christened 'the
Uncooked Dumpling'. I fear that the combination of Cynthia and myself
gave that girl a taste on earth of the hell from which her prodigious virtue
would certainly protect her in the hereafter. But they make these gover-
nesses of stern stuff. When my father finished his work at Les Eyzies we
moved on to Cabrerets, and then for a while went to Rocamadour, a
nearby village. This was a place of pilgrimage; the home of a black
wooden madonna of great antiquity. For whatever reason, it was here that
the governess gave up.

I really think that Cabrerets is my favourite of all the French childhood
places, even though it was the scene of my first real tragedy. I went back
there in 1982, and such changes as there have been in and around the
village are small and all for the best, like the fine new museum at the
Pêch Merle Cave, a memorial to the Abbé Lemozi, who was the parish

priest at the time we lived there. The tiny village is still the same today: it clusters around the foot of the cliff where the Sagne River flows out of its valley to join the Célé, and the church crowns a hill on the edge of the village. I saw again the *place*, which in my memories will always be associated with a smell of roasting coffee. We used to stay at the small Hotel des Touristes, which has now become a private house. It was the best of all our hotels, not least for its marvellous food, which *madame* prepared on a huge open fire above which was a real iron spit. Who could forget her *gigots*, or above all the whole kid, roasted in her special way with sprigs of rosemary tucked in here and there to flavour the meat?

At Cabrerets I owned my first real fully grown cat, and kept him during our time in the village over almost two years. He was a big brindled tom, almost wholly wild, who attached himself to me, and later, when he broke his paw, decided that I was the person to mend it. It did indeed get better, though never again quite straight, but I think nature rather than I did the healing. However, he trusted me totally, and I alone in all the village was allowed to handle him. I gave him the name Judah Levy, taken from some book I had read. I could do anything with that cat: I even dressed him in a bonnet sometimes and he would sleep peacefully stretched out on his back with his head on my pillow. The village was amazed, but no one else wanted to touch him anyhow: '*Voici le chat de Mlle Nicol – méfiez-vous!*' was the usual attitude.

The most remarkable and distinguished person in the village was the Abbé Lemozi, who became our close friend. The son of a peasant family, he identified closely with his people and really cared for them, travelling vast distances on his old bicycle to provide what help might be needed and to say Mass in the outlying hamlets within his care. He was the best kind of parish priest, tireless in his quest for ideas to improve life in the village. He was highly intelligent, and learned far beyond his family background, and I am sure that the company of his old mother of 80, who kept house for him, merely increased his need for intellectual companionship, which is exactly what my father and mother could supply. My father, with my mother to translate, would hold immensely long evening conversations with the Abbé on theological topics and the practicalities of human religions.

But for me and for my father one of the best things of all was that the Abbé was a highly competent amateur archaeologist, who knew his area and local sites in intimate detail. Several worthwhile papers of his survive in the Palaeolithic literature of southwest France, the best-known being an account of the cave art of Pêch Merle, which had been discovered a couple of years previously but was not yet open to the public. The Abbé took my mother and me there himself and showed us everything; an experience that made a really profound impression on me, far more than the cave art of the Les Eyzies sites had done. We had to crawl with lamps for a very long way through low and narrow passages, quite unlike the modern entrance, and I remember my mother cut her head, which bled freely, but we pressed on. The cave itself was large and highly impressive by lamplight, and the paintings, seen hitherto by so few eyes, were magnificent. I cannot remember why my father did not accompany us, but perhaps with his big frame he was reluctant to squeeze through the very narrow passages.

The Abbé was a marvellous man and a wonderful friend. On Sundays I saw him in his professional capacity, since I attended his little church regularly, and I also went to catechism classes with the village children, though I cannot remember joining the children in the Easter rite of First Communion, a touching event in small French villages when the children walk in procession to the church, all dressed in white, the little girls with veils held in place by circlets of spring flowers. On weekdays the Abbé would often take me, with one or both parents, for long walks into the surrounding countryside, or up on the *causse*. The latter was the limestone plateau between the deep river valleys, where small oak trees, juniper bushes and aromatic plants grew. We would walk several miles and then get a lift home in a farm cart. I saw the Abbé again many years later, when Louis and I visited that part of France in 1950 with the children, and he delightedly made me very welcome and arranged for us to stay in an empty house in the village.

I could write more about the time at Cabrerets than space will allow me, and most of the memories are of great happiness, especially those from our first visit in 1925. The expeditions on foot were best, as they so often are, and among the most memorable were the two occasions when my mother and I joined the village women for their annual expedition to gather bunches of wild lilies-of-the-valley, which grew in great scented drifts in certain places nearby: it was a carefully planned and eagerly awaited traditional act of rejoicing in the spring, though not tied to any particular date or Christian festival. The women just went when the flowers were ready, according to the season of each particular year.

Nothing that is so near perfection can last forever, and often the best things last for far too short a time. In 1925 my father was in the best of health and painting as productively as ever. During the spring of 1926 he suddenly became ill, and in a very short space of time we knew that nothing could be done. My mother told me later that it was almost certainly cancer. His illness was short but painful; my mother nursed him alone and he was quickly too ill to want me much at his bedside. The Abbé, who had been a medical orderly in the First World War, came every day to administer morphine as a pain-killer and to sit by his bedside with my mother. For myself, I took to long solitary walks, mostly up on the *causse*, where I learned to watch animals without disturbing them. Sometimes I went at dawn, and not even the burden of knowledge of my father's illness could destroy the thrill of seeing foxes at play and occasionally seeing the rare wild boar. I could not have guessed how large the watching of more spectacular game was to loom in my life in Africa later on, but even then the sight of the animals at peace in their natural setting brought me some happiness and calm. So it still does.

Then, inevitably, all was over and my father, only 58, was dead. Uncle Percy had come out to join us a few days before the end, but no one could comfort me. I was too shattered to retain any clear memories of the funeral, but I know the whole village turned out and that our dear friend the Abbé took the service. I was barely thirteen, and I had just lost forever the best person in the world.

3
Growing up

ON OUR RETURN TO LONDON my mother and I went to stay at my grand-mother's house. There, we were faced with the immediate practical crisis of lack of money, our usual annual cycle having been cut short at a critical point. In the normal course of events it would have been several weeks or even a few months before my father returned to London to sell his pictures. Uncle Percy gave us a great deal of support and practical help during those very difficult days. One of the first things that had to be done was to raise some cash by the only possible means at our disposal; the sale of all the paintings my father had left. My mother and Uncle Percy organized this, and I recall that it took place at the Chapman Galleries in the King's Road in Chelsea. Fortunately it was a great success; partly through the kindness of my father's friends in promoting the sale, but mainly through the paintings' own considerable merit. Most of them sold, and sold well. Before long, my mother and I were staying at a board-ing house off Kensington Church Street, and there was talk of buying our own house shortly. Also there was talk of sending me to school.

This is the period of my mother's greatest influence on my life, though I doubt whether she ever substantially influenced it in exactly the direc-tion she intended or wished. If she and I never got on as well together as some mothers and daughters do, the fault was not hers, for she was never anything but kindness and devotion itself towards me. On the contrary, it is more likely that the major share of the blame is mine. Perhaps the whole thing can be attributed to the inevitable clash between our very different personalities, while the closeness between my father and me sprang from our many similarities and our strong community of inter-ests. My mother was in every sense a lady, retaining all the sophistication of her wealthy background in Italy during her own childhood. Like her three sisters, she was not really practical about housework, which they all hated; on the other hand, she was a really excellent and gifted cook. In appearance she was small, neat and beautiful, with hazel eyes and brown hair that changed to a delicate silver in her later life; she was immensely feminine always, with a taste for elegance that she was rarely able to indulge. Yet her warm and friendly nature endeared her to people of all kinds and she was equally at ease with, say, the wealthier of those who bought my father's paintings in London and the village women of

Cabrerets. The latter, I recall, regarded her as the kind of faithful friend to whom problems could be brought and family troubles told.

I think in fact that my mother's life was a rather hard one, with too many difficult times and too much unhappiness. There was the dramatic change of circumstances in her own childhood for a start, and if one has been brought up to expensive tastes, to be short of money for the rest of one's life must come very hard. Then there was the sudden and wholly unexpected loss of my father, after a relatively short marriage. Theirs had been a partnership of great happiness, brought about by mutual trust as well as shared love. Their tastes were by no means identical, however. My mother loved social gatherings of all kinds; my father loved good and serious conversations, but not really socializing for its own sake. If she was more sophisticated, he was more intelligent and had seen more of the world and gathered more experience. She absolutely worshipped him, and he was for her the best person in the world, as he had been for me. I cannot recall that they ever had any quarrels or rows except on a single subject: money. For there lay the only blind spot that I could detect in my father: he was mean over small matters. I remember for example his refusal to tip taxi-drivers adequately – acutely embarrassing to me, as I am sure it would have been to most children. On the other hand he would occasionally and without a second thought give relatively large sums away to people he knew to be suffering hardship. For whatever reason, however, he undoubtedly kept my mother needlessly short of money, and fought fiercely against each of the little hoped-for extravagances which would have pleased her so much and would also have done much for her morale. But, that one thing aside, theirs was an exceptionally happy marriage. If my father's death was a shattering blow to me, for my mother it was an even greater disaster, a tragedy and sorrow of inconceivable magnitude. And although she rode out the crisis and made the best of her remaining twenty years of life, it can hardly be denied that I myself later brought her much anxiety and did many things that caused her great anguish, none more so than marrying Louis, whom she disliked until the end of her life.

After the sale of my father's pictures my mother set her mind on making a new home for the two of us, and on getting me some education. The latter project was certainly fraught with many difficulties, as the episode of the earnest governess should surely have convinced her. But good Catholic children go to good Catholic convents for their good Catholic education, and, disastrously, there was such an institution more or less round the corner in Kensington Square, the Assumption Convent, or was it the Convent of the Blessed Assumption? I was hardly there long enough to find out. This Convent's school was large, and the classwork seemed to me wholly unconnected with the realities of life, while the girls of my own age, and even many of the older ones, seemed utterly juvenile compared to the company I was used to keeping. I could not find a single kindred spirit among either the pupils or the nuns who taught us. Even my fluent French did not avail me in the unwilling quest for academic distinction, since the nun who taught French was appalled by my provincial *midi* accent. To be fair, her own Parisian accent was as pure as the cut glass of a Louis XV chandelier, and it was assumed that that was better suited to young ladies. There were too many such assumptions among the nuns for my taste. I had been there less than a year when it was ruled that my tactic of hiding in the boiler-room to avoid a poetry class, at which I would have had to read aloud, was out of order. The punishment decreed was that I should recite poetry before the entire assembled school. I refused, whereupon the Mother Superior requested my mother to remove me from the school forthwith. I, of course, was delighted. My mother did not lecture me on the subject, but she was naturally distressed and it must have been a considerable blow to her.

About this time my mother concluded the purchase of a small suburban house in Wimbledon, and we moved there. Sadly, Wimbledon too was blessed – if that is the appropriate term – with a Catholic convent school, this time run by Ursuline nuns. I think that I lasted out here a little longer than I had at the Assumption Convent, but my criticisms of the establishment would be generally similar. No doubt for the right kind of pupils both places were absolutely admirable, so please regard my views as purely personal. Besides, some of the nuns were quite pleasant. But I cannot recall learning anything useful at the Ursuline convent, so I may as well pass straight to the manner of my departure, which involved the customary interview between the Mother Superior and my own mother. I expect there was some thin-lipped stuff about 'Dear Mary is such a high-spirited girl', but at the heart of that discussion will have lain the well-documented charge that Dear Mary had not merely simulated a fit in the classroom, using soap to produce the symptom of frothing at the mouth, but that she had further deliberately caused an explosion in the chemistry lesson. Such behaviour clearly did not accord with the precepts of the blessed St. Ursula, or anyone else who mattered in these circles, and Dear Mary was therefore out on her ear with immediate effect. I don't suppose she put it quite like that, because that is hardly how you get to be a Mother Superior. I would like to record in her favour that in an earlier interview with me on the same subject I distinctly perceived a twinkle in her eye. But I hereby plead guilty on both counts as charged. As for the explosion, it was quite loud and quite a lot of nuns came running, which will have been good for some of them. My colleagues will I hope tell you that my reputation is for sober and scientific reporting, and this has prevented me from painting an exaggerated picture of the event, in which the whole convent is destroyed by my efforts and I step from the smoking ruins as the sole survivor. Alas, it was not so. The only ruins were those of my career as a schoolgirl, and probably the only real surprise is that I had paid enough attention in earlier chemistry classes to achieve what I did. After this second expulsion, even my mother gave up on convents. At least I ended my school career with a bit of a bang.

I think we must have lived at the house in Wimbledon for something like two years. When we moved there, my mother got out of store furniture that had belonged to my father and herself and had last been used, I believe, when we were living at Hemingford Grey nine or ten years earlier. Though there was easily enough for the house, she then let fling in a way that my father would never have allowed and bought several more pieces of fine quality, some of them antique, which we certainly didn't need. That I am sure was the way she would always have acted if she had had the chance, and at this moment there was a little money in hand from the picture sale, even after the house had been paid for. Our new home had a small garden: it was the first time I had ever lived in a house where we owned any garden at all and I was delighted because I could try my hand at gardening, which I loved at once. I grew all sort of flowers, quite successfully, and made myself a rockery which incorporated a fish pond.

But even better, I could have a dog of my own – in fact, as it turned out, two dogs. The first was an Alsatian called Drago, every bit as fierce as his name suggests. A friend of my aunts bought him for me even before the house in Wimbledon was ready for us, and until we could move in he lived in kennels in Earls Court Road. At the kennels was an ownerless young black Cocker Spaniel called Fussy, with whom I made friends when visiting Drago, and surprisingly I was allowed to have him too. I loved them both, but Drago unfortunately was not a success; he was too possessive of me and inclined to be somewhat aggressive. In particular, he would not allow my mother to come into my room. It just would not do, and after a while my aunts agreed to take him over themselves. I was very sad indeed at his departure and as a consolation for my loss, Jorrocks arrived fairly soon to join Fussy. Jorrocks was a Dalmatian, my very first. That was about 55 years ago, and with hardly a break I have had one or more Dalmatians ever since.

Two trips that we made from our Wimbledon house can be regarded as being of some significance. The first was a short excursion made specifically at my request, when Uncle Percy drove my mother and me down to see Stonehenge. This reflects the fact that my archaeological interests had very much survived the death of my father and were becoming broader than any mere passion for collecting objects. I had never seen Stonehenge, although it was certainly one of the most famous and important sites in England. Nor was I disappointed on arrival, for Stonehenge is profoundly impressive and I don't know many people who can claim to be quite unaffected by the first distant view of it as one comes over the brow of the hill on the road from Amesbury and sees the great stones huddled together against the gentle rolling background of greens and blues and perhaps harvest gold that is Salisbury Plain. All around stand great grassy barrow mounds: a few are close by, but most are at a respectful distance, seeming to look inwards to the circle of the great sarsen stones, their backs turned to their surroundings as if in perpetual conference. Something momentous seems to be happening, and it must be happening at the very centre of the circle. As a visitor, one feels an intruder on a very ancient landscape. The view from close at hand is quite different, and no less impressive, but now the wonder is all about the size of the huge sarsen uprights, and how the great lintels could ever have been placed in position.

From Stonehenge we returned via Avebury, a huge stone circle with high earth banks and a deep ditch, almost as big in area as the pretty Wiltshire village that lies partly within it and partly outside. There are various settings of huge sarsen stones within the circle, and an avenue approaching one entrance. It could hardly be more different from Stonehenge, though in its own way it is at least as impressive. How sad that in recent years the great elms that lined the road through the circle have fallen victim to the elm disease that has ravaged Britain and so many other countries.

Avebury had, and still has, one thing that Stonehenge does not and never should: an English pub of the nicest kind. In the late 1920s it was a simple place that offered cheap accommodation, and it at once caught the eye of myself and my mother. So it was that we returned the next summer to stay there for a short holiday, in which we enjoyed ourselves walking in the beautiful chalk downland of Wiltshire. But the main thing was that at Avebury there were excavations in progress. These were not at the great henge monument itself, but up at Windmill Hill, an important Neolithic site beyond the village. My mother found out that a Mr Alexander Keiller was in charge of the work and sent a polite note to him introducing us and asking if we might visit. So it was that I met Keiller and his second wife, and Dorothy Liddell, his sister-in-law, who was actually directing the digging. These were major names at the time in the study of the English Neolithic and indeed of other periods.

Keiller – a member of the famous marmalade-making family from Scotland – was perhaps the last of the rich gentleman landowners who indulged their serious interest in British archaeology by running major excavation programmes, which they financed themselves. The previous century was their heyday, but Keiller was a latter-day member of their race. He achieved much that has lasted, but my own impression was that he did it rather gracelessly and that his wealth and the power it brought had made him rather opinionated. Dorothy Liddell, on the other hand, I found charming and kind: as it happened, I was to meet her again before long. She was a sound scientific worker, especially by the standards of the late 1920s, and had her own original ideas in what proved to be quite an important formative period for Neolithic studies in Britain.

Perhaps when I met Miss Liddell this first time I absorbed there and then the notion that a career in archaeology was certainly open to a woman. Whether or not that was so, the forces were now beginning to operate that impelled me in that direction, and as I now look back there is a very clear chain of events, at the time only loosely linked, that decided what I should become.

Following my explosive departure from the second convent school and my mother's reluctant acceptance that schools and I were an impossible combination, the two of us discussed what I should do next. At first she still harboured dreams of some kind of formal education, and a couple of private tutors were hired for a while. There was a young English school-teacher to coach me in maths, and Bertha Hitchcock, an Australian, to teach me Latin. It did not work of course; but I cannot recall doing anything particularly awful to either of them, and in fact, until her death last year, Bertha Hitchcock and I still exchanged letters at Christmas. With their departure, my mother really did abandon hope and the talk began to be of career training rather than of classroom subjects. As I had kept up my hobby of drawing since the early visits to France, and was clearly becoming proficient, there was serious consideration of whether I should follow my father into an artistic career. The alternative seemed to be to take up archaeology seriously. In my own mind there was never much question that the latter was the right choice. I do not recall that my mother offered serious opposition, but the whole record of our relationship suggests that if she had I would in any case have gone my own way. This decision was one reason why, about a year after I left the Ursuline convent, my mother sold the Wimbledon house and rented a flat for us at 54 Fulham Road, in Kensington. It was over a cleaners' shop; very noisy and altogether a less suitable home for the two dogs. The merits were its large, spacious rooms and its location. From my point of view there was easy access to Central London, where one could attend lectures in archaeology and related subjects, which I would certainly need to do if I were to pursue my intended career seriously. That would be a very different matter from going to school, and promised to be of great interest.

I had never passed a single school exam, and clearly never would, and there was accordingly no way in which I could become a candidate for entrance to any university to study archaeology or anything else. Initially that did not deter my mother, who went to Oxford to interview none other than Professor W. J. Sollas on my behalf. He was Professor of Geology there, having also a strong interest in Palaeolithic archaeology, and certainly counts as a distinguished name in the history of both disciplines. I have no idea how my mother made contact with him, but she was never afraid to approach anyone on any subject, and doubtless used all her charm in obtaining an audience. But Sollas soon made her face realities: certainly Oxford would not accept me, and no, it was *not* even worth trying. He was, of course, quite right. Curiously, my next direct contact with Oxford University, as opposed to individuals working there, was when they gave me an Honorary Doctorate in 1981. I also became an Honorary Fellow of St. Anne's College: but all that lay over 50 years ahead.

For my mother, the new home in Fulham Road was within easy walking distance of her mother and sisters in Lincoln Street. Their company and cheerful family gossip were a great pleasure to her. I am not sure exactly how we managed for money: there was the sale of the Wimbledon house, of course, and for a while my mother made hats to sell, as her sisters had once done, but since she always chose expensive materials because they were nicer, worked hard on them, and then soft-heartedly sold her creations cheaply, I cannot believe she made much of an income if indeed she avoided making a loss. As for the dogs, I took them every day for walks to Kensington Gardens, where they had plenty of space to run. My route up Exhibition Road took me past the big museums, including the Natural History Museum, to which my father had taken me when I was quite small, and where I liked the giant sloth best. It is still there. In those days, he and I had sometimes travelled on the open-top double-decker buses that were at that time an ordinary part of the public transport system of London.

It was after we moved to Fulham Road that horses came into my life for the first time, though oddly enough the stables, run by an ex-Boer War Sergeant-Major, were back in Wimbledon, beside Wimbledon Common. I used to go out there on the No. 14 bus, across Putney Bridge, and he took me riding on the Common itself and also from time to time in Richmond Park. I greatly enjoyed this new activity and it was something to which I returned much later when my own children were growing up in Nairobi.

Rather more remarkable perhaps, when one thinks back to the early 1930s, is the fact that I should also have adopted gliding as a hobby. Somewhere I read about the London Gliding Club, whose headquarters were, as they still are, near Dunstable in Bedfordshire. Joining the club required no great formalities, although I was one of the youngest members and, I think, the only unmarried female. Now, the sport is expensive but expanding, but in those days it was in its infancy, and the gliders and supporting equipment were somewhat rudimentary. The gliders were launched from the edge of the chalk escarpment by a catapult arrangement consisting of a heavy rubber rope known as a 'bungey', which everyone would help pull back to the point of maximum tension to launch each glider. One then simply stayed aloft as long as possible and landed somewhere convenient, when hopefully a car would arrive to tow the glider back to base. There were various certificates of proficiency and I did manage to pass the first two of these, but in my attempt on the third one I crashed – not very badly, but I didn't get the certificate.

But life was far from just a matter of hobbies at this time. On the home front I had a tragedy of my own when Jorrocks, my Dalmatian, suddenly became ill and died. He was very young still and this was the first time I had lost a pet with the finality of death rather than by having to leave one behind in one of our moves. To console me came a second Dalmatian, called Bungey after the name of the glider catapult. Bungey had the unfortunate feature for a Dalmatian of a ridiculous curly tail, but he was a most entertaining dog and I kept him for several years.

By the end of the summer of 1930 I had begun to attend lectures in London, which I continued to do for several sessions over two or three years in all. I had also taken part in my first real excavations. As regards the lectures, I went for geology to various courses at University College, a part of London University, and for archaeology I went to the London Museum, which at that time was in Lancaster House, not far from St. James's Palace and Clarence House. Of all these, the archaeology lectures given by R. E. M. Wheeler, better known under his later title of Sir Mortimer Wheeler, remain clearest in my memory. Wheeler was a striking, somewhat larger-than-life character and he certainly lectured well. Later he was to become a popular television personality, among other things. I listened and learned from his lectures, but privately I thought him a distinctly unattractive character and I never revised this view. Indeed, I can't help wondering whether many of the achievements in archaeological discovery and methodology that are so often attributed to him did not rightly belong to his charming and extremely able first wife, Tessa. Still, Wheeler is only of passing interest in this story. I was determined not to restrict my self-imposed training in archaeology to mere attendance at lectures. If I were to become an archaeologist it was also absolutely essential to gather field experience, for my heart was set on field archaeology far more than on the theoretical and interpretive side. I had none of my mother's ability to approach people directly, in person, nor the particular kinds of personal charm that enabled her to be so successful. Instead I used to write letters offering my services to anyone I heard of who was conducting excavations that sounded even slightly interesting. Most sent polite refusals, but Wheeler was the first person actually to offer me a place, on his dig at St. Albans, the Roman site of Verulamium, and there in due course I presented myself. In the event, I left after a week. There were far too many people, most of them immensely earnest, but no one seemed to know what they were actually doing, or why, and I decided I should not learn there any of the things I so desperately wanted to know. So far as Verulamium is concerned, I think in fact that posterity will associate the name of my cousin Sheppard Frere with excavations there during the present century rather than the name of Wheeler, for he was later to work there for many years. Fortunately a second acceptance was to hand – from none other than Miss Dorothy Liddell, whom I had met and seen in action at Windmill Hill when we stayed at Avebury. In the summer of 1930, therefore, I went off for the first of several seasons at Hembury in Devon, as one of her assistants.

The Hembury dig was started by the Devon Archaeological Exploration Society. Some of their members had found pottery there which obviously resembled that found at Windmill Hill, an excavation which British archaeologists were following with close attention. So the Society wrote to Keiller for advice and the upshot was that he sent down Miss Liddell to conduct a trial excavation. In fact it grew to a much bigger operation and we had summer seasons there in 1930, 1931 and 1932, with a spring season in 1934. The site proved to be a causewayed camp and is still one of the earliest major Neolithic sites of southern Britain. Dorothy Liddell had two main assistants for the first season, of whom I was one. The other was Aileen Henderson, later the wife of Sir Cyril Fox, himself an important figure in British archaeology. Also present was Thurstan Shaw, then a schoolboy at Blundell's, one of the leading English Public Schools of the southwest. Thurstan was the son of a Devonshire vicar, and had first become interested in archaeology by reading Breasted's *Ancient Times* and an article on surface collecting by Moysey, in the Devon Archaeological Exploration Society's journal. Summer excavations are great places for beginning friendships, and Thurstan Shaw and I have kept in touch ever since our first Hembury season. We remained close friends and met frequently on excavations in Britain over the next several years, and Thurstan was an undergraduate at Cambridge while Louis was a Research Fellow there. I usually visit him and his wife Ione at Cambridge, where he has retired, whenever I pass through England.

My fellow assistant, Aileen Henderson, I did not find nearly so sympathetic. Dorothy Liddell, as I indicated in describing our first meeting, was a very well brought-up lady with a strict sense of decorum, and she decided that she as Director would wear a coloured overall – green, I think it was – and that we assistants of lesser rank should wear brown or tan; and with a garage hand's khaki overall I duly equipped myself. Not so Miss Henderson: she turned up in kingfisher (or was it royal?) blue. Need

I say more? We did not become firm friends and I'm sure she thought me thoroughly disagreeable.

We stayed at a small and very pleasant boarding house in Honiton, called the Queen's House; or at least the female members of the team did, while the men lodged in the local pub. In this first season, Miss Liddell's sense of what was proper decided her to take her meals alone downstairs while Aileen and I took ours in our rooms, though in later years we all had cheerful meals together. Transport to and from the site was in Miss Liddell's bull-nosed Morris car, officially a two-seater. There were various other people on the dig and of course there was the site foreman, W. E. V. Young. William Young was an excellent foreman and a good archaeologist, and an ideal person for me to learn from. He was the son of a village blacksmith in Wiltshire, who found himself unemployed at the end of the First World War until Keiller took him into regular employment as his site foreman: thus he had already worked under Dorothy Liddell at Windmill Hill. She persuaded Keiller to let her borrow him for Hembury. Young always remained outwardly respectful to Keiller, but he clearly 'had his number', as the saying goes, and privately regarded him in much the same light as I did. Keiller had founded for his work in Wiltshire what he rather grandly called the Morvern Institute of Archaeological Research, but for William Young the initial letters signified Marmalade Institute of Awful Rot.

Hembury was a beautiful place, especially when one arrived on site first thing on a lovely summer morning, the dew still on the grass and the wild flowers. The work, too, was always interesting, and had its moments of excitement – like the time I was working on the entrance, and its cobbled causeway came to light. Over the several seasons we became a good working team and I grew greatly to like and admire Dorothy Liddell. Between the field seasons, at her request, I drew some of the finds, including the flints, and this was the first time I actually drew stone tools for publication, an activity that was to prove of far-reaching importance as my career developed. That I can still look at those early published drawings without shame suggests that they turned out reasonably well.

It was my first flint drawings that at about this time, late 1932 or early 1933, brought me to the notice of Dr Gertrude Caton-Thompson, who asked me to draw the stone tools from her famous excavations at Fayoum in Egypt for her book *The Desert Fayoum*. Gertrude was the epitome of that remarkable breed of English ladies who for archaeology's sake would go out alone into harsh desert environments and by determination, skill, expertise and endurance achieve discoveries of major and permanent importance. I immediately liked Gertrude, who had a strong presence but a kind nature and seemed to treat me from the outset as an equal whose professional assistance she was asking as a favour, though as I saw it she was really offering me an extraordinarily attractive opportunity and at the same time showing me an ideal towards which I might aim my career. I will say more of Gertrude Caton-Thompson later, for she unwittingly played quite another part in the story not long afterwards, but I cannot resist saying at once that at the age now of 95 she is one of my oldest and dearest friends.

We dug at Hembury for three glorious seasons and then there was a pause while many of the same team, including Thurstan and myself, dug for a single season with Dorothy Liddell at Meon Hill, near Stockbridge, Hampshire, an Iron Age site which also proved to contain a Saxon cemetery. Here I recall dowsing for metal objects as diviners do for water, something I had learned at Cabrerets from the French prehistorian Armand Viré, whom I once met there. Unfortunately, at Meon Hill my only substantial find was an iron drain pipe – all too modern, but at least it did demonstrate that I was on the right track, and that my dowser's twig reacted to metal! Here also William Young, that most meticulous excavator, fell down into a large pit containing our carefully excavated Saxon skeletons, on his way home from the pub one night. The skeletons were never quite the same again. As I recollect, Miss Liddell said, on her arrival early next morning, 'Goodness me! What can have happened?' It was a fair question and very mildly phrased; but she never found out.

We all went back to Hembury for a final season in 1934, this time in the spring. The site and the people and the landscape were much the same as they had always been. But for me it might have been some completely new and different world because by then I had got to know Louis Leakey, and we were deeply in love.

4
The beginning of a partnership

IT WAS GERTRUDE CATON-THOMPSON who introduced me to Louis. She was pleased with the drawings I had produced for her Fayoum book and was anxious to further my career in any way she could. I am not sure whether she knew that Louis was specifically looking for a draughtsman to produce illustrations for the popular book *Adam's Ancestors* that he had recently started writing, or whether she thought perhaps he could use my services in due course. In any case she thought it would be good for me to meet him and a few other leading figures of the archaeological world on the occasion when Louis was to give a lecture at the Royal Anthropological Institute in Bedford Square. Plenty of interesting people would be there, for Leakey had caused quite a stir with the expeditions he had already made to East Africa, and with his discoveries of early Palaeolithic material and even of remains of early Man himself. One of the most notable finds was the Kanam jaw, which had received wide publicity and about which there had been only very recently a special meeting of the Institute's human biology section in Cambridge. This lecture was to be about his work in Africa and would probably even mention that remote place Olduvai Gorge, which he had succeeded in reaching. So Gertrude invited me to the lecture as her guest and of course I gladly accepted. Further, being herself a leading member of the Institute by virtue of her own achievements, she arranged that we should both attend the dinner that followed the lecture, with the speaker as the chief guest, and she even arranged that I sat next to him.

It would have been appropriately romantic to think that I fell dramatically in love, there and then, at first sight; but it simply was not so. I liked Louis and talked a lot to him, and it did seem a little odd that he was directing so much of his conversation to me when there were more senior and important people there. But I thought little of it. He did indeed ask me to help him with the *Adam's Ancestors* drawings, and of course I delightedly agreed and we made some arrangement for me to collect the specimens, but again I cannot recall what it was. And that was really all there was to it at that stage.

In that can be seen my complete naïvety and preoccupation with pre-historic archaeology at the time; I was just 20 years old. My mother was certainly beginning to get restive about finding me someone suitable to marry. She had occasionally sent me to a dance, partnered by one or another young man who in her view fell into the 'suitable' class. I cannot recall the name of a single one, and I classified them all as spotty youths. I had nothing against men in general, and got on splendidly with people like Thurstan, but my mother's attempts to start me on boyfriends as such were if anything counter-productive. Louis was ten years older than I, fully mature and an established and experienced archaeologist. More-over he had a taste for wild places, working in the field, and being alone among wild animals about which he knew a great deal: all things that appealed to me. Above all he seemed from the very start, like Gertrude herself, to treat me as an equal and a colleague to be consulted. How could I fail to like him? My naïvety concealed from me two things that were relevant, and which were known to many others. Firstly, Louis had throughout his life that powerful if indefinable quality of attractiveness to women that is perhaps ultimately a matter of chemistry. Secondly, he was certainly on the lookout at this moment for the solace of a new girlfriend in whom he could confide, because his marriage to his first wife, Frida, was proving to be from his point of view a complete failure, notwithstanding the birth of their daughter Priscilla in 1931, or their recent move to a larger house in Cambridge, or even the fact that Frida was in the earliest stages of expecting a second child. In fact I knew later that Louis had several girlfriends at about this time, though they all melted away over the next few months. My commitment to the *Adam's Ancestors* drawings would certainly have assured Louis that he could count on seeing me regularly for some while to come, if his first im-pressions were indeed as favourable as they seemed, but the drawings were a quite separate issue and he would undoubtedly have commis-sioned me to do them for him whatever he had thought of me. Soon afterwards I went with Miss Liddell to the Meon Hill excavation, with my innocence intact and also with some African hand axes to draw in my spare time in the evenings. They presented a pleasing challenge because they were made of volcanic rocks, not flint, and their different surface texture demanded quite a change of technique.

The Meon Hill dig was a summer one, and in Britain the end of the summer is a time when various annual meetings and conferences occur. One body that has a large gathering at this time is the British Association for the Advancement of Science. It selects some suitable centre, usually a city or town that has a university and a surrounding region of varied interest, and there a conference is held for a week or a fortnight with many sections, including geology and archaeology. There are excursions, scientific sessions and the usual social events: quite an occasion, and more so in the 1930s perhaps than now, rising costs having somewhat changed the nature of the event. In 1933 the British Association had its meeting at Leicester, and there Louis and I met again.

Because of my work on the drawings we had corresponded throughout the summer, but we had not actually met. Were his letters perhaps just a little more frequent that was strictly necessary? I always replied at once, and the correspondence was certainly friendly, with minor exchanges of news as well as details concerned with the drawings, but if it had a pleasant warmth it had nothing further. It was, in fact, quite independently that I decided to go to the meeting at Leicester. No doubt Louis had mentioned that he would be there, but I had no preconceived plans concerning him when I set out. Yet from the time we met up soon after our arrivals we became inseparable companions, and it was here that I first felt and instinctively recognized something that was new to me: the mental stimulus and physical thrill of having Louis with me. Yet no proprieties were breached. Louis lived in one set of conference accommodation and I in another: to these we returned separately each evening, and our final farewell was entirely proper. But it was clearly understood between us that we would meet again, soon and frequently.

As summer drew on into autumn. Louis found more and more material for me to draw, some of which was to appear in later books, since *Adam's Ancestors* was nearly complete. The relevant material was at the British Museum in Bloomsbury, and there we used to go so that I could work on it, in a room that was also occupied by Sir Thomas Kendrick and Christopher Hawkes, both members of the Department of British and Mediaeval Antiquities ('British' having the archaic special meaning of 'belonging to the Ancient Britons'). There I worked, and Louis would look in from time to time so that inevitably the nature of our relationship became clear to the other two occupants of the room, both of whom were to become major names in British Archaeology. Christopher Hawkes chose to turn a blind eye, or at least not to interfere, but Tom Kendrick, who was the senior of the two, felt it incumbent upon himself to do something. He was clearly worried for me, assuming that I was simply dazzled by Louis and that I might well be hurt, which was kind of him. So one day he invited me to lunch as his guest at the old Holborn Restaurant, which has long since disappeared, and he set himself to open my eyes and warn me. The one sentence of his that sticks in my mind referred to Louis: 'Genius is akin to madness, Mary: you must be careful.' Those were his words, and there was much more along the same lines; but he might as well have saved his breath for all the notice I took.

Inevitably it was not long before my mother found out what was afoot, and naturally it shook her to the core and upset her beyond measure. It is one thing to hope that your daughter will attach herself by a bond of fondness to a suitable young man and end up married to a charming, distinguished and possibly wealthy husband, but quite another matter when she takes the whole thing into her own hands and forms an attachment to a married man ten years older than herself. In fact the ten years difference would not have mattered in the least to my mother, since my father had been just that much older than her. But she simply could not stand Louis and mistrusted his stability, even when she had met him. That event was not long delayed, for during that autumn he began to come to Fulham Road to take me away for weekends. So my mother remained in a state of total dismay and set herself to change my mind, right up to the time Louis and I got married; and even after that she never really reconciled herself to the situation. My aunts too, so often my allies in the past, were quite against the whole thing from the moment they got to hear about it. My grandmother never heard the news at all. She was getting very old, and they rightly decided to keep it from her.

One of the visits that Louis and I made together during that autumn was to Cambridge, and he took me to meet his wife. That may sound like the most foolhardy undertaking, especially when I add that I was taken actually to stay at their house, The Close, at Girton just outside Cambridge. I stayed there for something like a week. Officially, I was going with Louis to see the remainder of his African collection, and to learn about certain aspects of palaeontology in connection with my assistance to him in preparing his various publications. What was more natural than that the young colleague, who could hardly afford hotel accommodation, should be invited to stay at the host's own home? In any case, Frida Leakey had become used to erratic behaviour by her husband, who was working extremely hard, as he always did, and kept unconventional hours. Louis was at this time a Research Fellow at St. John's College, and in that capacity had rooms there in New Court, just across the famous Bridge of Sighs. He would often work late and decide to sleep there instead of going home, and apart from that he made frequent trips to the Royal College of Surgeons in London, to work on material relevant to his studies of human evolution. This he had been accustomed to do for some while before he met me, and there, too, work and perhaps other attractions would sometimes detain him. I recall that during this week he quite suddenly disappeared for a couple of days. It seems to me that even then he and Frida were almost living separate lives. Yet I might have been any casual visitor in the home of an unremarkable Cambridge academic family. In the evenings Louis used to teach me string figures ('cat's-cradles'), which remained a hobby of his and later on to a lesser extent became one of mine: at one time I could do sixty or seventy different ones, mainly of African or Eskimo origin.

Thus would the scene at Girton have appeared to any onlooker. But when Louis and I were alone in his rooms in College we might have been two quite different people. Tension mounted until on a day when the atmosphere was almost electric he told me, quite suddenly, that he now knew the one thing he wanted was to end his marriage to Frida and marry me. I cannot remember exactly what I replied, if indeed I heard myself speak. Such a thing had simply not entered my head and I felt more a sense of shock than of exhilaration. Eventually I managed to gasp out something that I intended as acquiescence and he clearly understood it as such. After that for some moments neither of us was really in a position to speak at all.

With this understanding between us, the course of events became inevitable, though not particularly rapid as it turned out. Immediately, during the late autumn and the winter, we began to spend weekends together regularly, in spite of my mother's protestations. And from his point of view, if, in the 1930s, one had decided to get oneself divorced, adultery was the only practical means to achieve one's end.

There can be no doubt that Louis felt bad over the way he was treating Frida, and it would be quite wrong to suppose that he had no thought at all for her feelings. Things were complicated by the fact that she was expecting their second child. I think that even before the baby, his son Colin, was born on 13 December 1933, Louis had made the act of separation by moving completely from The Close to his rooms in College, and Frida perhaps knew that he had no intention of returning. But of me he still said nothing, and he waited until the new baby had settled in before he confessed the true situation. Frida was every bit as furious as any wife would be, and indeed she was fully entitled to be. She summoned us both to The Close and told us with admirable clarity exactly what she thought of each of us. I do not remember her words clearly enough to quote them, but the upshot was that Louis was a cad and a traitor to her and to his own children, while I was a worthless hussy, utterly lacking any moral sense, who had seduced him. She then walked out of the room. Louis and I heard her out – I was not, thank goodness, required to undergo the ordeal alone – but the only conclusion we ultimately drew was that she did not wish to see either of us again and that we could therefore proceed along our chosen path and take the consequences.

Frida's friends in Cambridge were soon informed. The whole story quickly became widely known there, and no one, without exception, had a good word to say for either of us. This was naturally a far more serious matter for Louis than for me, for I had little connection with the world of Cambridge. But there was one very saddening consequence for myself, which was that I lost the regard and friendship of Gertrude Caton-Thompson, and indeed I really only fully regained them towards the end of Louis's life and after his death. This was a heavy blow. Gertrude, who had a Fellowship at Newnham College and lived in Cambridge, knew Frida at least as well as she knew Louis, and Frida told her the story directly. Gertrude, for all that she was entirely blameless, was absolutely appalled at the terrible consequences of her act of kindness in introducing me to Louis, and she felt, understandably, that I had betrayed her. She now did her level best to get me to turn back, urging among other arguments the effect that it was all likely to have on Louis's parents out in Kenya. They were missionaries; Canon Harry Leakey and his wife Mary, the gentlest and finest of people, and in 1933 just retired from active service and about to come to England to visit Louis and his family. Yet even Gertrude's appeal to me fell on deaf ears. I had no intention of turning back for anyone, and nor had Louis.

I have never before told this whole story in such detail, and I hope and believe that my account is as accurate as I can make it. In its origins and also in its development, both up to this point and later, the whole affair was intimately mixed up with the progress of my incipient career as an archaeologist. Without the latter, none of it could or would have happened. I can now, not without relief, let the archaeology for a while become the dominant theme of the story. For 1934, after this somewhat torrid start, was to see a good deal of progress under that heading. For much of the time Louis was with me and he also gave me a good deal of useful advice and practical help. That, of course, was as between archaeologists. When his parents arrived in England later in the year, Louis had inevitably to tell them that he and Frida had separated; but somehow he managed to conceal my existence from them entirely. The news of the broken marriage was a heavy enough blow to them by itself.

My fieldwork in 1934 was at Hembury in the spring, at Swanscombe in midsummer and at Jaywick near Clacton in the early autumn, where I directed my own dig for the first time. Because the finds at Olduvai over the past 25 years have been so exciting, many people seem to think of me as entirely a Palaeolithic archaeologist. In fact I have worked on sites ranging in time from the Miocene fossil beds of West Kenya, something like 18 million years old, to those belonging to the African Iron Age of just a few centuries ago, and I have become deeply involved at one time or another with problems that interested me in virtually every period. It has always been the existence of a fascinating problem or an interesting body of material, regardless of age, that has provided my motivation – not dedication to any single period.

I was conscious that the 1934 season at Hembury was my last training excavation, for the work at Jaywick was already firmly planned, so I gathered all the experience I could. Thurstan was there again, being by now an undergraduate at Cambridge, and he knew Louis too; he recalls visiting him at St. John's and Louis showing him something he had never seen before; hand axes of the same types as the flint ones in Britain and France, but made from African volcanic rocks. This greatly impressed Thurstan, whose own thoughts had already turned in the direction of Africa: Louis was able to open his eyes to the enormous possibilities that African archaeology held. Louis and I each separately confided in Thurstan, telling him what had happened to us and what our intentions were for the future. Notwithstanding his upbringing at the Devonshire vicarage, Thurstan says that he was far more intrigued than shocked, and this is worth mentioning because we were so used to universal condemnation as each new person came to hear the story. Louis would come down to Hembury and spirit me away for weekends. Dorothy Liddell liked him, and watched with approval and deep interest when on one visit he gave a demonstration of flint-knapping. Thurstan has a vivid memory of Louis standing on top of one of the Hembury ramparts, with a great block of flint at his feet. Knapping had early become a special skill of Louis's and throughout his life he loved to demonstrate it: he was an eagerly anticipated sideshow at many an international conference, and sometimes the demonstration included butchery of some animal with stone tools he had just made. Now that it was spring our weekends were no longer spent at pretty country pubs or little boarding houses, but camping with our own small tent, just big enough for two, here and there in the beautiful unspoilt places of southwest England. Louis did the cooking (another special enthusiasm and real skill of his) and we would walk to look at hill-forts, or find foxes or other animals to watch, which reminded me of the *causse* at Cabrerets. Could that really be only eight years ago?

In 1934 too, we both worked at Swanscombe. It was really Louis's dig in which I joined, not only to help him and be with him, but also to gain experience and information directly relevant to my own dig, which was soon to begin at Jaywick. The main work was done by undergraduates from Cambridge, chosen by Louis, and they camped at the site. Louis and I made frequent visits, together or independently, and many other people came to see the work, including some who were already, or soon afterwards became, well known in British Palaeolithic studies. One blazing hot day Tom Kendrick came down from the British Museum, with Christopher Hawkes and his wife Jacquetta. Another visitor was the amateur archaeologist A. T. Marston, who the following year found the first fragments of the famous Swanscombe hominid skull. The skull itself was found at Barnfield Pit, which we visited briefly in 1934, but our own work was at another gravel pit nearby. Louis was hoping to solve certain problems concerning the nature of the so-called 'Clactonian' industries of the British Lower Palaeolithic, but the operation was no more than a moderate success and Louis never got round to publishing the results as they were more or less superseded by those from my own dig at Jaywick.

I had become interested in the Clactonian myself through Louis, and it was in the cause of solving some of the same problems that my own project had been planned. Jaywick is adjacent to Clacton, in Essex, where Clactonian material had first been discovered. Because Clacton was a favourite English holiday resort, certain areas of land that could be expected to yield good archaeological and geological information were rapidly being built over, as estates of seaside bungalows and chalets spread, so the dig had an element of urgency about it.

The work at Jaywick was to be mine and Kenneth Oakley's, whom I had first met during my brief stay at Wheeler's dig at St. Albans. At this time he held a post in the Geological Survey, though he was afterwards to spend most of his working life at the British Museum of Natural History. At the time of which I am writing, one of his special projects concerned the Pleistocene geology of the Lower Thames Valley, and hence arose his particular interest in Clacton. Kenneth himself had little training in archaeological excavation while I had little specialist knowledge of Pleistocene geology, so our roles at Jaywick were complementary to one another.

During the reconnaissance stages, Kenneth and I went down a number of times to discuss the site over picnic lunches with S. Hazzledine Warren and his wife. Hazzledine Warren, usually called 'Hazzy' by his friends, was a charming man and a most gifted amateur archaeologist, well respected far beyond his home county of Essex. He had studied the Clacton site since as long ago as 1910 and had made most of the important finds himself. These picnics were delightful, but I still shudder at the memory of Mrs Warren's 'Camp' coffee. Most of Warren's best Clactonian sites lay on the foreshore and could only be examined at low tide, so no conventional form of archaeological excavation was possible. We, however, were to dig a little way inland, where we knew that an extension of the deposits lay. It was not a large operation, but it was a successful one. We had about four labourers, I think, and a few undergraduate assistants, of whom Thurstan gladly agreed to be one. My mother came down and kept house for me and some of the others in a seaside bungalow, and clearly enjoyed doing so, and the arrangement had the additional bonus that I need not be parted from my dogs. Louis came for weekends, and so did Kenneth Oakley.

As the dig progressed we found some good faunal remains. In particular, I remember the uncovering of the largest elephant tooth yet discovered in Britain; a fine and complete specimen. I had never before seen an elephant tooth, and although it was so obviously something very particular I was quite unable to identify it – rather a loss of face for the young Director! Fortunately Louis turned up while we were considering

Aged about four, and holding my beloved Pimpy – much more a companion and social equal than a mere toy.

LEFT: With my mother at a very early age.
RIGHT: A photograph of my father taken during his travels in Egypt as a young man.
BELOW: Playing with my father in the garden of our cottage in Hemingford Grey. Even at that age it seems I was none too keen on having my photograph taken.

LEFT: A photograph Louis took of me at the London Zoo in 1935, shortly before he left for East Africa.

BELOW: Steen Cottage in Hertfordshire, where Louis and I spent some of the happiest days of our lives during 1936. Bungey the Dalmatian is looking out of the window to the right of the front door.

TOP RIGHT: At Olduvai in 1935. Peter Kent, Louis and myself pose beside fossil elephant bones encased in protective plaster of Paris.

BELOW RIGHT: The *Miocene Lady*, our home during many working holidays at Rusinga.

ABOVE: An expedition to Olduvai in the 1950s. Louis is beside the Land-Rover and I am resting on the running board of the Dodge pick-up I drove, accompanied by my dogs.
BELOW: Jonathan and Richard enjoying a bathe in a pool during a safari to Kariandusi.

ABOVE: Working on rock paintings at Kolo, just north of Kondoa, in 1951. Many of the paintings were high above ground level, and tracing them was often extremely awkward.
BELOW: A particularly realistic painting of ostriches and a pair of white rhinos at Kisese.

Louis and I with Jonathan and Richard at the Tower of London during our leave in 1950. Richard, then five, looks a little doubtful, but his older brother is clearly impressed.

the problem and not only identified it but also helped us to lift it undamaged by encasing it in a plaster-of-Paris jacket.

The Clacton dig was a very happy occasion, and the technical report on it was published, in the *Proceedings of the Prehistoric Society* for 1937, jointly by Kenneth Oakley and myself. It was my first publication. Had I remained in England, I am sure we would have had other seasons there. The finds were good and we lived well in our simple way, thanks largely to my mother's cooking. I remember with particular pleasure a special kind of mushroom that grew in early autumn among the tufts of grass not far from the sea. We loved them, all except one member of the team – Kenneth Oakley, who sometimes could be extremely fussy. It seemed that this was not the kind of mushroom that grew where he lived, and nothing would make him try them. This was the only time I ever worked directly in the field with Kenneth, but I always kept in touch with him and visited him when in England during his later years. He made many outstanding contributions to archaeology and was one of those responsible for unmasking the Piltdown fraud.

With the end of the season at Jaywick came a turning point in both my life and career. Louis had succeeded in raising money for his next East African expedition, his fourth, and he was to leave by boat in October, taking with him three young assistants, Peter Kent (later Sir Peter Kent) as geologist, Sam White as surveyor and Peter Bell as ornithologist. One of the main reasons why Louis had received generous financial support for this trip was his previous spectacular success in discovering hominid fossils at Kanjera and Kanam in 1932. But certain doubts had since arisen over the age and status claimed by Louis for the famous Kanam mandible in particular, and among the other aims of the expedition, Louis was to conduct Professor Percy Boswell to the Kanjera and Kanam findspots in January 1935 to check the relevant evidence. In fact it all turned out disastrously for Louis, who was shown in Boswell's subsequent report to have made unfortunate and avoidable errors, through inexperience, during his 1932 fieldwork, although some of the errors of which he was accused were due to circumstances beyond his control.

So Louis left in October 1934, but before he did so we made an arrangement that I should join him in April 1935 in Tanzania. By then Louis would have finished the first part of the expedition, and would be ready to go again to Olduvai Gorge. On the basis of his previous visit, Olduvai clearly seemed to offer the greatest potential for exciting early Palaeolithic discoveries anywhere in East Africa, and therefore perhaps anywhere in the world. He wanted me with him, and from the descriptions he had given me I could hardly wait to see Olduvai. Meanwhile, I was not to be left kicking my heels for five or six months in the Fulham Road. My mother had not been won over by Louis, not even in the happy atmosphere of the Jaywick dig, and she still had aspirations of getting him out of my mind and indeed out of my life. It was therefore arranged that she and I should go in January for a visit to South Africa and Zimbabwe (then Southern Rhodesia), where we would see prehistoric sites and also some of the other tourist attractions. No doubt my mother hoped that with Louis out of sight and out of reach I would find other attractions and come to my senses, and that when April came she would bring me safely home with her. From my point of view it would be an easy enough journey in April from Zimbabwe to Tanzania, and much quicker than going from London. Louis gave us various introductions for use on our arrival in Cape Town, and I looked forward to the trip with excitement and a light heart. My mother ended our rental of the Fulham Road flat, and she and I moved with the dogs for a short stay in a flat in Hamilton House, near Hyde Park Corner, for the final period of preparation. January 1935 came at last, and while Louis was having a difficult time at Kanjera and Kanam, my mother and I, having left the two dogs in safe hands, joined a Union Castle liner at Tilbury and set out via St. Helena for Cape Town and, more importantly, for Africa.

5
Africa for the first time

SOUTH AFRICA is an immensely beautiful country. The famous view of Table Mountain as our boat first entered the harbour at Cape Town was an impressive start. The mountains of the Cape Fold Belt are spectacular, running for hundreds of miles across the southern tip of the continent, an area that looks so compact on a map or globe but when you get there is huge. The coast is one of the most fiercely beautiful I know, where even in calm weather huge waves crash onto sandy beaches or hurl themselves against jagged cliffs creating plumes and columns of brilliant white spray which may rise in the same places but are somehow never the same shape twice. Since for me, if not for my mother, South Africa was a staging post on my way to Louis and to Olduvai, I will not dwell too long on our stay there but will write just of what impressed me most and what had more than passing importance.

Upon arrival in Cape Town we established ourselves in a small boarding house and lost little time in using the first of Louis's introductions by making ourselves known to A. J. H. Goodwin. John Goodwin will always remain one of the great names and influences in the development of Stone Age studies in South Africa, and quite apart from that he was as hospitable as so many people in that country were in those colonial days, and indeed still are: they really enjoy visitors from overseas. John Goodwin was delighted with the chance to take us to see everything that was worth seeing, including many of the famous archaeological sites. Even more pleasing to me, he suggested that we should go with him to his current excavations at Oakhurst Shelter, and that I should dig with him there. This was agreed; we all stayed with the owners of the cave, Mr and Mrs Dumbleton, and I became part of the digging team for a few weeks. Although I had seen many rock shelters in France, this was my first experience of the proper scientific excavation of one (this choice of words enables me to discount the efforts of M. Peyrony which I had watched as a child at Les Eyzies). If I had thought Dorothy Liddell a scientific excavator, I now found John Goodwin to be way ahead of his time, and I was deeply impressed by his care and minute attention to detail in everything. Modern techniques have, of course, developed in all manner of directions since then, but even in retrospect I retain a very high opinion indeed of the standards he maintained. The levels in which we were working mainly belonged to the Late Stone Age and are now known to be somewhat less than 20,000 years old. Although there are local differences, the artefacts we were finding were not so very dissimilar in character from their equivalents in Kenya, and my experience at Oakhurst proved directly useful to me before very long when, in 1939, I found myself in charge of important rock shelter excavations in Kenya, near Naivasha.

From South Africa we went by train to Zimbabwe, crossing the vast expanse of the Karroo. I had never before seen anything like this huge semi-arid landscape which, as the miles passed, gave way to fully arid conditions. The Karroo is perhaps most beautiful when patches of it bloom with brightly coloured flowers after rain, but we travelled across it in the dry season. We arrived at Bulawayo in due course and introduced ourselves to another of Louis's friends, the Rev. Neville Jones, who lived with his wife on a mission near Bulawayo, where we were at once invited to stay for as long as we wished.

For me a particular highlight of the visit to Zimbabwe was being taken to see some of the famous rock paintings of southern Africa. These are certainly very different from the cave paintings of Pêch Merle, Font de Gaume or La Mouthe, which had been one of the childhood influences turning my mind towards archaeology, and many of them are undoubtedly much younger. Some are a few centuries old and many a few millennia, though how much further back in time the earliest ones go is still not known. In the Kalahari region many of the paintings are connected with the culture of the present-day Bushmen and their predecessors. As well as paintings, which occur on open cliff faces or in rock shelters or even on free-standing rocks, there are also engravings, of which we saw some fine and famous examples at Koffiefontein in the Orange Free State. The southern African rock art has a distinctive style, with lively and characteristic representations of both human and animal figures, and it pleased me greatly. I was also very glad to be seeing it then, not just for the sake of my early visits to the French cave paintings and engravings, but also because before we parted in England Louis had made me a promise that later that year we would go together to see rock paintings at Kondoa in Tanzania.

While in Zimbabwe my mother and I also did some other sightseeing. We went to the capital Harare, then Salisbury, and also to Livingstone, which was just across the border in Zambia – at that time Northern Rhodesia. Here, of course, the great attraction was the Victoria Falls. Quite often one can feel disappointment when finally coming face to face with some natural or man-made wonder as famous as this, but the Victoria Falls, far from disappointing me, exceeded my wildest dreams. It was not the time of year when the greatest volume of water comes down – indeed, the river was said to be low – but surely, even in the dry season, this must be the greatest waterfall in the world. No one who has not stood near the Falls can imagine the thunderous sound and the sheer majesty of the sight as that huge curtain of water pours over the rock wall and falls – so slowly, it seems – into the narrow space far below, where one can look down and see rainbows. Above the Falls the Zambezi is a wide, smooth river with hardly a ripple on its surface: below, it becomes a raging torrent in a narrow, twisting gorge struggling to contain all that water.

We also took a boat trip on the upper Zambezi, which we both enjoyed. Anyone who goes to Africa for a first visit sees new things, or has new experiences every day, and for me that boat ride brought the first sight of a hippopotamus in its natural environment, and also of a crocodile. In general, however, there is much less wild game to be seen in southern Africa than there is in the wild areas of Tanzania for which I was bound. In the southern Cape, in the Republic of South Africa, for example, there are many huge farms and cattle ranches where the game animals have been ruthlessly slaughtered.

But I had not yet seen wild Tanzania, and the time was fast approaching when I should do so. I do not suppose my mother by now retained any hopes of deflecting me from my chosen path. On 17 April she returned to Cape Town by train and in tears, to catch a boat back to England, while I boarded a plane to fly to Moshi in Tanzania, excited and secure in the knowledge that Louis would be at the airport to meet me. In fact he was not there when my plane touched down that evening. I was very disappointed, and rather cross, but it did not occur to me to suppose that he had met with some serious or fatal accident. I soon learned that in this part of Africa the rains were in progress, and that the roads in certain places were in a bad state. I was advised to go to a hotel for the night and to expect Louis in the morning. So I ended up in a German-run hotel in Moshi, which I thought rather sleazy. In the morning I had my first glimpse of Kilimanjaro; an unforgettable sight. When the mountain casts aside its veil of cloud, as it often does in the early morning hours, you are faced with a soaring snow-capped dome, quite unimaginable while the cloud remains in place and quite incongruous in the setting of tropical vegetation.

While I was eating my breakfast, Louis appeared. As predicted, he had been delayed by the road conditions, and I soon learned what every traveller in East Africa discovers; namely that no journey, however simple, can be counted on to run to schedule. By the same token, one should never expect one's guests or visitors until one sees them arrive. This is a wild country, and what we humans are pleased to regard as 'our' roads and lines of communications are there entirely at the mercy of nature's forces. The weather and changes of season are far more potent than man

53

with all his technological aids. During my years in Tanzania and Kenya I have had more journeys than I can count that in one way or another have gone dramatically wrong. And so have most of my colleagues. Yet among all my journeys, that first epic trip from Moshi to Olduvai stands out. It was just as well that I was with Louis: he was thoroughly experienced in such things, but even he regarded it as out of the ordinary.

At the time, Louis had a rather ramshackle lorry which went ahead with the supplies and the African staff for our work at Olduvai, as well as the stock of petrol, which was unobtainable where we were going. In those days petrol was supplied in four-gallon tins, packed for transport in stout wooden boxes. These were an invaluable adjunct to camp life. After removing the tins, the boxes could be piled one on another, some sideways and some end-on, to make cupboards in the tents, rather in the manner of modern Scandinavian bookcases. The four-gallon tins were also in great demand for carrying and heating water, and for many other purposes. When camp was closed down the tins were avidly sought by the Masai and we would pack our fossils in the wooden boxes, padded with dry grass.

From Moshi, Louis and I got reasonably easily to Arusha, where we collected Sam Howard, a friend of Louis's who was joining the expedition on leave from the Shell company. We were to travel more comfortably in a reasonably tough Rugby car, with enough food for one day's journey. The lorry got through without difficulty to a camp at the top of Ngorongoro, where Peter Kent, Sam White and Peter Bell were already waiting, having travelled down beforehand from Nairobi. Ngorongoro is a great steep-sided caldera, a collapsed volcano, and it constituted a formidable obstacle on the road from Arusha to the Serengeti Plains. The route by which the lorry and we ascended had only just been made. It was a track, through forested country, which clawed its way to the top in a series of hairpin bends before running along the narrow rim of the huge crater itself to reach the District Officer's headquarters (and precious little else). This is now my regular route to Olduvai: the spectacular road has been graded and surfaced, though in the rains it still suffers badly and its state of repair still leaves much to be desired. In 1935 its surface was fine when dry but turned with even moderate rain to sticky black mud; and we arrived after a prolonged heavy downpour. It took us two and a half days to manhandle the car some sixteen miles up that impossible slope, mostly in pouring rain, and of course we ran out of food and dry clothing in the process. When we finally reached the top, black with mud from head to foot, we could look down into the caldera itself, the Ngorongoro Crater, two thousand feet below. The great circular area is some twelve miles across and always densely populated with game, while the shallow soda lake that occupies one small part of it is often pink-fringed with flamingo. If any game can be made out with the naked eye from above, it is elephant, rhino or possibly buffalo if they are near, but with field-glasses one can see animals by the thousand.

We rattled and slid on towards a much-needed visit to the District Officer's camp to clean and revive ourselves for a couple of days before starting the descent from Ngorongoro to the Serengeti. In a few more miles I was looking spellbound for the first time at a view that has since come to mean more to me than any other in the world. As one comes over the shoulder of the volcanic highlands to start the steep descent, so suddenly one sees the Serengeti, the plains stretching away to the horizon like the sea, a green vastness in the rains, golden at other times of the year, fading to blue and grey. Away to the right are the Precambrian outcrops and an almost moon-like landscape. To the left, the great slopes of the extinct volcano Lemagrut dominate the scene, and in the fore-ground is a broken, rugged country of volcanic rocks and flat-topped acacias, falling steeply to the plains. If it is the rainy season, as when I first came in April 1935, the grass beside the road will be green and fresh and growing, and there will be many wild flowers. Some of the acacias, too, will have their sweet-smelling white blooms. Here and there, dark rain-storms gather as the day proceeds, but everywhere else shimmers in the hot, bright sunshine. Out on the plains can be seen small hills – like Naibor Soit, Engelosen or Kelogi near Olduvai: the scale is so vast that one cannot tell that the biggest is several hundred feet high. Olduvai Gorge itself can also be seen. Two narrow converging dark lines, softened by distance and heat haze, pick out the Main Gorge and Side Gorge, each of which is in reality many miles long and in places half a mile across. I shall never tire of that view, whether in the rains or the dry season, in the heat of the day or in the evening when one is driving down straight towards the sunset. It is always the same; and always different. Now, nearly half a century later, that view means to me that I am nearly home.

I shall leave a proper account of Olduvai Gorge itself until later in the story, when I describe my work there and my own camp as it now is. In 1935 it was just a place that was incredibly beautiful and where nearly every exposure produced some archaeological or geological excitement. It was also the best time of the year to make a first visit, in the rainy season when animal life abounds, notably the huge herds of grazing animals congregated on the plains for the fresh new grass, and with them the predators. This was the time of the game migration, and even today the animals come in the same hundreds of thousands whenever the rains begin. In those days some species were still plentiful that have since been hunted or poached to virtual extinction, such as rhino and leopard.

When we reached Olduvai we camped half-way down a gently sloping area within the Gorge. Louis would never pitch tents under the trees because their roots had usually broken up the calcrete, a form of lime-stone, and brought hard blocks of it up to the surface, so we looked for somewhere where there was at least a little soil where tent pegs could be hammered in. Oddly, it was only years later that we hit on the idea of attaching the guy ropes to blocks of the calcrete. Louis and I also had a lot of trouble with our air-mattress, which Louis had to inflate by blowing into a tube since the pump never seemed to work. The typical vegetation of a semi-arid zone like Olduvai abounds in thorns of all kinds, and only too often we would wake in the small hours to find we had subsided onto hard fragments of calcrete or consolidated volcanic ash, our air-bed having been punctured during the night.

By day we explored the Gorge minutely and slowly, mainly concentrat-ing on the Side Gorge and areas which we now know to be among the most important and prolific anywhere at Olduvai. Almost everything was new, because Louis's 1931 expedition had hardly touched the exposures where we now were. Louis liked to name areas after their discoverers, and soon everyone's initials had been given to at least one or another site or locality which they had first identified. Each was a *korongo*, which means 'gully' in Swahili, or a cliff, designated respectively by K or C. Thus there were SHK and SC for Sam Howard, SWK for Sam White, BK for Peter Bell, and PEK for Peter Kent. Mine was MNK (Mary Nicol Korongo), where, on an eroded surface of Lower Bed IV, I found two fragments of a hominid skull. Hand axes lay near but we could find no other pieces of the skull. Needless to say, we were both very excited. These fragments became O.H.2. (Olduvai Hominid 2) and in modern terminology belong to *Homo erectus*. It was twenty-two years since O.H.1, a human skeleton, had been found by Hans Reck, and its age had long been controversial; we now know it to be of very late Pleistocene age, presumably a representative of the Late Stone Age population and about 17,000 years old. From his first sight of the Gorge Louis had felt, or one might say known instinctively, that it was the kind of place that would sooner or later yield early hominid remains *in situ*, and here at MNK was confirmation. As it happened another twenty years were to pass before the next find, two teeth, and in fact the main body of the now numerous Olduvai hominid remains has accumulated since 1959.

This first visit to Olduvai was full of other excitements and incidents, such as meeting a rhino head-on while walking up the narrow, steep-sided stream bed of the Olduvai River, and our driver being pursued on foot by an infuriated lioness who was protecting her cubs. I recall ex-cavating, at SHK, the remains of what must have been a small herd of gazelle-sized antelope, the extinct form *Phenocotragus recki*. We dug here again in the 1950s and 1960s and found an important Developed Oldowan occupation site in the upper part of Middle Bed II. At another site I found and worked on a pig skull which was in a very fragile condition, successfully encasing it in plaster so that it could be lifted safely, much in the way Louis had taught me at Clacton. My success in this interested a very important member of the African staff, Heslon Mukiri, who was a member of the Kikuyu age group into which Louis had been initiated during his upbringing in Kenya, long before he first came to England. Heslon had become deeply interested in Louis's archaeological work and by this time had already helped him on several field expeditions, as he was to do many times afterwards: he and Louis were lifelong friends and virtually scientific colleagues. Heslon had been somewhat suspicious of me up to this point, but he now accepted me as a worthwhile member of the team and as someone who might even be worthy of Louis.

Our camp life was to some extent dependent on maintaining supplies of food and water. Though we had come down from Ngorongoro to Olduvai in the rains, they were nearly at an end, and we had a lot of trouble over our water supply once the rapid drying out of the landscape had taken place. The river in the Gorge sank to a series of stagnant and evil-smelling pools, which eventually became muddy patches in which the liquid element consisted as much of rhino urine as of drinkable water. One day there was a late storm with marvellous rain to refresh our supplies: pools of water lying in hollows in our tent canvases delighted us, and we rushed to capture it in our containers. No one thought of the insecticide with which the canvas had been so thoroughly impregnated, and we all became very ill. Fortunately it was not a lethal poison. As for food, we had the stores we had brought, and they were supplemented with game shot by Louis. He loved all animals but was always prepared to hunt at need, while I would have preferred to go without meat. When camp was established for our stay at Olduvai, our meat regularly included Grant's gazelle; I genuinely disliked it, as well as disapproving, but was not prepared to be thought 'soft', so I made myself eat it without complaining.

At our camp we ran a medical clinic for the local Masai people, who came in large numbers. This was something Louis had done when he first came to Olduvai, and many were old friends of his. Indeed, there was much to cure, from malaria to spear-wounds, and some came out of sheer curiosity. It was one of the latter whose arrival led to my first visit to another place that was to be immensely important to me in later years: Laetoli. The casual visitor in question was an African, Sanimu, half Masai and half Kikuyu, who viewed our finds with great interest and told Louis of another place away to the south, towards Lake Eyasi, where there were more 'bones like stone', to which he would take us if we wished. He even went on foot to fetch us some samples, and when we saw that they included genuine fossil bones and teeth we agreed to go, and set off a few days later in Louis's car, taking the lorry with supplies. Nowadays I can drive from my camp at Olduvai to Laetoli by a direct track which we ourselves have made, and the journey takes about an hour. In 1935 we followed an adventurous route which took us in a wide arc across the Serengeti as far as Lake Ndutu (then called El Garja) and thence across to Laetoli, passing near the Naibadad inselberg, a prominent landmark in the plains. Because of its shape it is now sometimes called Twin Peaks, or, much more frequently, Kilima Titty, which is partly Swahili. There were no tracks and it took us over two days, since on the plains the grass was still exceptionally high after the rains, so much so that the vehicles kept overheating when their radiators became choked with grass seed. At Ndutu the level of the shallow soda lake had already fallen enough for us to drive across the depression on dry sediments, passing, incidentally, quite near the place where in 1974 a hominid skull was excavated at an Acheulian site which in the wetter part of the year is under water. Game of all kinds abounded on the plains, and in the maze of wild thorn-bush country gently rising from Ndutu to Laetoli, which few vehicles cross even today. But our guide, slightly to Louis's surprise, took us with little trouble to our destination, where we made camp under the fever trees beside a river of good sweet water.

Laetoli proved to be not quite so beautiful or colourful as Olduvai, but it was clearly a place of considerable potential for fossils. A German survey party had reached the area before the First World War, and had made maps, naming a nearby river the *Vögelfluss* or Bird River in honour of the rich variety and enormous numbers of birds in the valley. In the green undulating landscape we found large areas of exposed greyish sediments which had been cut through by the river itself and by numerous erosion gullies. These deposits clearly contained much volcanic ash, among which consolidated layers could also be seen. Fossil bones and teeth in excellent condition were abundant in many of the exposures, just as Sanimu had said. We found no stone tools other than a surface scatter of Middle Stone Age material, clearly much younger than the grey sediments. We collected samples of the bones but did not see any hominid remains. I choose my words carefully here, because in fact there was a hominid canine tooth among the bones we brought back from Laetoli – a collection which Louis in due course gave to the British Museum. There it was catalogued as 'monkey', and lay unrecognized in a box of odds and ends until it was rediscovered only a few years ago.

At Laetoli our arrival and activities were regarded with some amazement by the local Masai people; I remember that they were never quite sure of my sex, because I wore trousers. There were many game animals near where we camped. One morning as we explored, I suddenly met a lioness, face to face, not far from what we now know as 'Locality 10', where fossil termitaries were excavated in 1980. Louis, who had seen fresh lion tracks and was sure that one was not far away, had warned me not to stray too far by myself, but, being still new to Africa, I felt entitled to walk where I wished. I almost trod on the sleeping lioness before I saw her. She and I were mutually horrified and fled in opposite directions. 'I told you so,' said Louis, with more accuracy than tact. In fact, meeting a lioness on foot is not as disastrous as it may sound, unless she has her cubs with her. Lions were very common at Laetoli, and we often saw them at Olduvai too. There are still several prides at both places today at times when the game is abundant.

We returned to Olduvai, well satisfied with the time spent at Laetoli, though we were unable to draw many conclusions about the relative ages of the two sites. The Laetoli faunal remains were clearly of greater age than Olduvai, however. As it transpired, I did not go there again for another 24 years, and it was 40 years before my major excavation campaigns at Laetoli began.

By the time we got back to Olduvai, the local water supply had dwindled almost to nothing and all supplies were running low, notably petrol: we could not even spare enough to fetch fresh water from the springs across the Balbal depression eighteen miles away. Some members of the party were now due to go back to Nairobi, *en route* for England, and they set off in the lorry, which was to go via Loliondo, where petrol could be obtained. It was to return to us with stores from Nairobi as soon as possible; but this it failed to do. Eventually, having waited a fortnight and feeling that we had subsisted for long enough on the rice, sardines and apricot jam to which our diet had been reduced and, far worse, having long since run out of cigarettes, Louis and I set out by car on the route towards Loliondo, hoping to meet or if necessary rescue the lorry, which by now was nearly a week overdue. This proved to be another epic journey, but our adventures have been recorded elsewhere in some detail so I will only mention the highlights briefly.

We got to the Kenya border at Pussumuru without much difficulty, but there we found the Indian trading community terrified by the news that Masai at Narok had murdered District Commissioner Grant in retaliation for his making some of their warriors work on the roads, which they saw as something worse than an insult. The Indians were clearly in fear of a Masai revolt. Not much farther on, Louis accidentally drove the car off the road and into a deep gully, where it stuck fast, in the middle of nowhere, with nightfall near. There was nothing to do but sleep beside the car overnight. We then spent all next day trying to dig a shallow ramp through the side of the ditch, up which we could try and push the car onto the road. The only really odd thing about this operation was that our digging equipment consisted of table knives and two enamel dinner plates. The inevitable crowd of young Masai warriors gathered to watch, with great amusement, and one can see that our efforts did indeed have considerable entertainment value. It was beneath the warriors' dignity to help, of course, and with the news that we had gathered at Pussumuru Louis did not seek to persuade them, though in fact they showed no signs of hostility. By dusk we had actually successfully completed the digging, though daylight would be needed before we attempted to move the car itself, and so we prepared for a second night. But at that point our own lorry turned up, loaded with useful items like shovels and tow ropes, and in no time the car was safely back on the road and we were hearing the history of mechanical troubles that had caused the lorry's delay. Next day we all returned safely to Olduvai.

We did not stay many more days at the Gorge, since other commitments were waiting. Louis had promised the Tanzania Government that he would make a visit to, and report on, a large site with ruined stone buildings which had been reported by various travellers. It was at Engaruka in the Rift Valley, some few miles south of the still-active volcano of Oldonyo Lengai, and so that was where he and I were bound next. We were to go back up the long climb to Ngorongoro and on towards Arusha as far as the descent into the rift at Mto wa Mbu near Lake Manyara, where we would turn off along a hazardous and indistinct track following the base of the rift escarpment. But as it turned out we first spent a day at Ngorongoro down in the crater, a detour made when a sudden opportunity arose for Louis to test a recently developed theory of his. We heard that lions had killed a hippopotamus somewhere on the crater floor. Louis believed that in the Ngorongoro crater there might be a hippo population that had survived an immensely long time in this isolated situation and could, therefore, show evidence of descent from *Hippopotamus gorgops*, the Pleistocene form found at Olduvai. So we made the 2,000-foot descent on foot, starting early in the morning, and found the skull. Alas, it was an ordinary *H. amphibius*, and we climbed back up the same day and spent the night in an extraordinarily draughty log cabin which stood where one of the spacious tourist lodges has since been built. That episode was typical of the way Louis liked to work: he was always full of ideas and never lost any opportunity to put one of them to the test. More often than not his hunch would prove correct.

Engaruka came next, and there we made a three-week stay. Archaeologically, the results were in some ways disappointing, for expectation had been that the 'ruined city', as travellers had called it, would prove to be of considerable age. We excavated one of the huts, of which there appeared to be two or three thousand, but we found only a few beads, some sherds of not very distinctive pottery, and iron fragments:

vague evidence, for what it was worth, of a rather recent date for that particular building. What we had hoped would prove to be burial mounds turned out on excavation to be empty cairns or heaps of rubble. But there was much clear evidence to show that the site's inhabitants had used a remarkable and quite sophisticated system of irrigation for their agriculture, damming the local river and diverting its water into a complicated system of channels to produce fertile plots of land. It was a system not unlike that used by the Wasonjo of Peninj in recent times to sustain their agriculture in an otherwise arid area. Without such irrigation, Engaruka could never have supported a permanent agricultural settlement, let alone as large a one as we could see around us.

As a place for working and camping, Engaruka was superb. We lived in the huts of a government rest camp and our own tents were under the fig trees, beside a river of the clearest water one could wish for. The river could be seen cascading down the wall of the rift a mile or so away, removing as it fell all memory of the stagnant slime on which we had depended at Olduvai after the rains were over. There was superb bathing, marred only by rather numerous leeches, which would attach themselves to one's person and require rapid removal. Yet even in this beautiful place we suffered one horrifying reminder of the continual clash of interests between man and nature which has destroyed so much of the Africa that once was. Henry Fosbrooke, a former student of Louis's, was at that time the local District Officer, and some of the Masai who had their *manyattas*, or homesteads, near Engaruka had recently complained to him about lions which were attacking their cattle: the trouble must have been quite serious, for normally Masai warriors welcomed the chance to hunt lions themselves. While we were at Engaruka, Henry drove down in a lorry and shot the entire offending pride. He and his wife stayed with us at the camp and Henry proudly exhibited the dead lions, slung into the back of his truck. It was one of the most appalling sights I have ever seen. How many destroyed lions has it taken to bring about today's attitude towards them, in which Henry would not have been allowed to do such a thing at all, let alone to do it like an exterminator of vermin?

From Engaruka we went on to Kondoa and the redemption of the promise that Louis had made to me back in England a year earlier, that he would take me to see the Tanzanian rock paintings when I came out to join him. We travelled by the so-called Great North Road to Babati and on to Kisese, where one of the main groups of paintings was, and where we were to camp. The existence of the rock art had been first reported only in 1908, and Louis's own previous brief visit had been made in 1929. We now had just three weeks to spare, since it was already August when we arrived at Kisese: I particularly remember that, because Louis's birthday was on 7 August and on that day I was able to give him a birthday present of a wrist-watch. This was a minor triumph on my part, because he had lost his own watch in Lake Victoria while at Kanam in the early part of this expedition, before I joined him. On learning of this I had written to my mother in England and begged her to find a suitable watch for Louis and send it to me as soon as possible. It seemed unlikely that it would reach me at all, at Olduvai, let alone in time for Louis's birthday. But by a miracle the small package arrived in the Olduvai mail and I was able to give it to Louis at Kisese on the very day. He was deeply touched and more delighted with that gift than with any other I ever gave him.

At Kisese we had a beautiful camp site not far from the principal painted rock shelter, known to us as Kisese I. Water was abundant not far away and fruit and local honey were in season; we had almost limitless quantities of bananas, huge juicy tomatoes, and fresh green vegetables too. It seemed like a luxurious holiday after the rigours of the past few months. Even hot baths could be taken in a canvas camp bath filled by hand, something that had been beyond the limits of imagining while we were at Olduvai. One evening my languorous enjoyment of this particular pleasure was shattered by the sight of a small garter snake circling the canvas tub and clearly anxious to reach the water. I could either rush naked to safety through the men's quarters just next to the bath tent, or I could shout loudly for Louis. I chose the second alternative and he came running, and quickly killed the snake.

The rock paintings I found absolutely entrancing: beautiful animal and human figures were represented in a number of entirely naturalistic styles, with many superimpositions suggesting that they had been painted over a long period of time. The shallow caves and rock shelters in which many of them occurred were in the fault scarp above the flat, bare country known as the Masai Steppe. We studied in particular the Kisese I and II sites, and a large shelter near Cheke. The steep rocky slopes where the sites were located were clad in beautiful *Brachystegia* woodland, with huge baobabs dotted among the smaller trees. The paintings were often difficult to find or reach, though we were helped by local Masai, not least because Sanimu, our guide on the Laetoli trip, was with us again and could speak to them in their own language. Thus we were shown many paintings we might otherwise have missed. We were anxious to record everything we could in the limited time available, but had brought no special equipment to help us. I used greaseproof paper to make what tracings I could, and we had watercolour paints with which to copy the colours. The paintings were still in good condition in 1935, though they have been damaged since the area became settled after a programme to eradicate the tsetse fly. At first the local people, the Warangi, used to chip away fragments, especially those with red paint, for use in magic. More recently there has been some outright vandalism. Before we left Kisese I had made up my mind that I would return one day to make a proper study of this beautiful rock art, and perhaps excavate some of the sites. And so eventually I did, but I had to wait sixteen years before the chance came.

Meanwhile it was time to make our way to Kenya, to Nairobi, as a first stage on the long road home. For Louis, Kenya in many senses *was* home and as we neared Nairobi he praised the country's beauty, though to me the landscape seemed rather dull after the parts of Tanzania we had visited. So, in late August of 1935, I came to Nairobi for the first time and was installed at the Salisbury Hotel, which is now the Safari Hotel. Louis naturally went to visit his parents at Limuru, but I was not produced for their inspection or even mentioned. They had known for some while that Louis and Frida had separated, but they still cherished hopes of a reconciliation; to people like them, in those days, divorce was something extreme, almost as unmentionable as adultery.

After a very brief stay in Nairobi, where I knew no one but Louis, we made our way to Mombasa, laden with archaeological material that was to accompany us to England on a French *Messageries Maritimes* passenger and cargo boat sailing via the Red Sea and the Mediterranean. To while away the three weeks of the voyage, Louis wrote most of a book, which I typed for him: it was his *Kenya: Contrasts and Problems*, and he completed it soon after we reached England. It was controversial enough to attract several hostile reviews and create a minor political storm when it was published during the following year.

We were back in England before the end of September: I had been away less than nine months. So short a time had wrought little change in England, but Mary Nicol would never be the same again now that Africa had cast its spell on her.

6

Marriage to Louis

I DID NOT INTEND to stay long in Kensington, where my mother had taken a flat within easy reach of my grandmother and aunts, but before I could rejoin Louis he had to find somewhere for us to live. It needed to be somewhere convenient for his work in England, which would centre on London and Cambridge, and it needed to be cheap. His Fellowship at St. John's College was at an end: the repercussions of his break-up with Frida had removed any possibility that the College would consider renewed tenure of his research fellowship, even less election to something more permanent, which would otherwise have been a distinct possibility. So not only did Louis have no base in Cambridge, and no salary either, but there were numerous books and belongings which the College was eager for him to remove from his old rooms. Fortunately there were plenty of little villages in the country between London and Cambridge where accommodation could be rented very cheaply indeed by those prepared to tolerate rather rudimentary facilities. After a short search Louis took a lease of Steen Cottage at a village in rural Hertfordshire with the rather charming name of Nasty, whose derivation I never discovered. Some people, however, preferred to call it by the alternative name of Great Munden. The autumn of 1935 was still young when the dogs and I moved in, by which time Louis had filled several rooms with books, papers and archaeological objects, not to mention a few clothes. He had also secured the use of a rather battered but still willing Model A Ford car, which Vivian ('Bunny') Fuchs had used in Kenya during Louis's 1931–32 expedition and had afterwards driven back to England across the Sahara. Louis actually gave me driving lessons in this vehicle, but he proved to be a nervous instructor and virtually refused to take me into anything that resembled busy traffic. Not surprisingly, therefore, I failed my test. Perhaps I would have done so anyhow, as I have failed every kind of examination I have ever taken, except the first two parts of the gliding proficiency test. Model A Fords and gliders are rather different creatures. I learned my driving and got my licence later on in East Africa.

Steen Cottage was a delightful place; its oldest parts were sixteenth century and the building had once been a row of three tiny cottages, each of one room upstairs and one down, before being converted to form a single six-roomed dwelling. There was a huge old fireplace with a brick-built bread oven, such as so many English cottages possessed down to the nineteenth century. A neighbour, Mrs. Wallace, came in to clean for us occasionally, and for the rest we looked after ourselves. There was no electricity of course, so we used oil lamps; there was no heating either, but I doubt whether we could ever have afforded to run it, even if it had been there. Baths were taken in a tin tub in front of our real old-fashioned kitchen range, on which the water, fetched from our own well, was heated. We had a chemical toilet in an outhouse in the back garden. The garden itself was my pride and joy. The cottage was built almost directly onto a roadside in the village, so at the front we had only minimal space for narrow flower beds, while there was a plot of reasonable but manageable size at the back, blessed with all the fertility to be expected when a cottage has had an earth closet for some centuries. The back of the cottage also boasted a built-on verandah, where it was nice to sit. I hadn't gardened since my mother and I lived at Wimbledon, but I soon set myself to grow vegetables and flowers. My sweet peas were a great triumph, and many of the surplus vegetables found their way to my mother and my aunts, for Louis and I made frequent working visits to London. One of my experiments with flowers at Steen Cottage even gained me a small reputation as a gardening expert in the village: the blacksmith had assured me that something or other would never grow successfully where I had planted it, but it did.

I was blissfully happy at Steen Cottage and it is hard to believe that we were there for little more than a year. The village was a real rural community, quite unspoilt; I do not know what changes the half-century that has passed may have wrought there, and perhaps it would be better not to find out. The village people naturally assumed that Louis and I were husband and wife, and we certainly gave them no cause to think otherwise, at least until the story broke of Frida's successful divorce proceedings against Louis, which took place in 1936. But even then they did not regard it as a matter of great importance: such high-mindedness was for bigger places than a Hertfordshire village – places like Ware, one of the local towns, where Louis was thrown out of the tennis club when the news became known.

Those of our relatives and friends who knew of our living together at Steen Cottage either accepted the situation or, more often, left us strictly alone in deep disapproval. My mother remained very sad and upset by the whole business, and my aunts also disapproved strongly. Their principal and practical concern, however, was to keep the news from my grandmother, who was now getting very old and frail: they judged that the shock would be too much for her health. She was given to understand that I had gone off to live in the country to be near my work as an archaeologist, and that of course was quite true. The gifts of vegetables from my garden gave support to the story, and my grandmother never did get to know the truth. Uncle Percy, who had taken a slightly more charitable view, was brave enough to come and visit us at Steen Cottage, which he rather liked. I showed him round the garden, where he made the only critical comment I can remember: 'Mary,' he said disapprovingly, 'you haven't tied up your dahlias properly.' He was a keen gardener himself. About Louis and I he made no comment.

Thurstan Shaw also stayed with us at Steen Cottage, I think more than once. We had much to show him that we had brought back, and he wanted to hear every detail of our archaeological work in Tanzania. Thurstan did not at all disapprove of our relationship, and if he was embarrassed by the fact that we were obviously sharing a bedroom he did not show it. He says that he found it rather exciting to be staying in the house of two people who were, in the dramatic phrase of the day, 'living in sin'.

We were not only extremely happy at Steen Cottage, but we were also remarkably busy. It was necessary both to support present life and to make what future plans we could. Louis was writing again – an autobiographical book this time, *White African*, which would bring in urgently needed money in the form of an advance payment from the publisher, plus some royalties eventually. He was also preparing the Munro Lectures, to be given at Edinburgh University in 1936. Not only was the series a prestigious one, and Louis among the youngest scholars ever asked to do it, but there was a useful honorarium payment and the lectures were published in the same year as another book, *Stone Age Africa*, for which I provided the drawings.

But though these things kept us busy and though it was a productive year in terms of work and publications, there seemed to be no sign of a permanent salaried post for Louis, though he did make a few unsuccessful applications. He needed a position that would enable him to build his career and make firm plans for all the urgent fieldwork in East Africa to which he was longing to return. Meanwhile the divorce proceedings, begun by Frida in January 1936, were grinding on and we were determined to marry as soon as their completion left us free to do so. Something needed to turn up, and at more or less the right moment something did.

While preparing his Munro Lectures, Louis had spent some time in Oxford and had talked to anthropologists there about his Kikuyu upbringing and his special knowledge of the language, tribal structure and customs of the Kikuyu people. Some of them had said how useful it would be if he could one day undertake a formal study of the Kikuyu. Suddenly and quite unexpectedly during the summer of 1936, Louis received an offer from the Rhodes Trust of funding for two years, both salary and expenses, to undertake a major study of the Kikuyu, for publication. He could start early in 1937 if he were willing to undertake the task.

It did not take us too long to decide that he should accept, though there were various factors to be considered, long term and short term, and life at Steen Cottage was too good to give up just on the spur of the moment. Who would look after Bungey and Fussy for two years? What would our prospects be when the two years were up? Would Louis miss some better opportunity if he now vanished to Kenya for that length of time? How could I usefully employ my own time on archaeology in Kenya while he was at work with the Kikuyu? Would the Kikuyu elders take kindly to the idea of such a study, and let Louis reveal what amounted to intimate tribal secrets?

People who think everything out in minute detail before agreeing to a project often end by concluding that it is too risky or too difficult to undertake. Louis and I had already developed a relationship of mutual trust in which our philosophy was not to fret over difficulties but to accept opportunities and overcome obstacles as they presented themselves, using whatever resources were to hand at the time.

Things now took on a momentum of their own, as not infrequently happens, though only hindsight may reveal it. The final divorce was granted to Frida in mid-October, along with possession of the house at Girton, which was hers anyhow, and full custody of the children, as was only right and proper. Louis's precarious financial situation ruled out his being called upon to provide more than maintenance for his children. We were therefore free to get married and to go where we pleased, and since our departure for Kenya was set for early in January 1937, with much to be done in preparation for it, there was little enough time to fit in the small matter of a wedding.

Some girls get married in cathedrals or fashionable churches, in a blaze of silk, flowers, summer sunlight and elegant social rejoicing. My mother had long given up any hopes in that direction that she might once have cherished for me, but even so she must have felt that the event that took place at the registry office in Ware on 24 December 1936 went too far towards the opposite end of the scale. She and one of my aunts, Mollie, came as reluctant witnesses of what they both regarded as a major disaster for me. Louis had no member of his family present, but he pressed into service as his best man a visitor from Kenya who happened to be staying with us at Steen Cottage. This was Peter Mbiyu Koinange, son of the Kikuyu senior chief Koinange, whom Louis had known from his boyhood days in Kenya. Peter Mbiyu Koinange was on his way to spend a year at St. John's College, Louis having made the contacts there for him. He was amazed to discover that there was to be a wedding, since at Steen Cottage he had assumed that we were married already. These were the only three guests, and there was nothing that could be described as a wedding reception afterwards, though before the ceremony I made lunch for us, including a rather successful apple tart. It was a cold day that Christmas Eve, and we had to wrap up warmly for the ride to Ware, Louis wearing what we may call his best overcoat, though I am quite sure it was his only one. As the moment to depart arrived we discovered that Bungey had chewed a large ragged hole in the hem of it.

From small and unlikely beginnings, great things may grow. This unspectacular wedding marked the official beginning of what was to prove a marvellously happy and successful personal and professional partnership which for some thirty years was everything one could wish for in a marriage. On that particular day I had no sense of a great new step taken or a turning point reached in my life, or whatever a girl is supposed to feel on her wedding day, and there was no time to stop and search for such feelings in the days that followed, even if I had felt so inclined. We arranged to sub-let Steen Cottage, furnished, during our absence. My mother agreed to take over the care of Fussy, the spaniel, while Bungey was found an excellent home with an actress who wanted a dog and liked the idea of a Dalmatian. Though I had no inkling of it at the time of parting, as things turned out I was never to see either of the dogs again. Hurriedly, luggage was assembled and about three weeks after our marriage we were on our way to Kenya and whatever might await. Under that heading, something that loomed upon the immediate horizon was my introduction to Louis's father and mother, for by now Canon and Mrs Leakey knew not only that Louis was divorced from Frida but that he was on his way to Kenya bringing as his second wife a girl ten years younger than himself, whose existence he had previously concealed from them. How was I to approach our first meeting?

7

The war years in Kenya

WHEN WE REACHED KENYA, Louis made straight for the home of Chief Koinange. He needed urgently to discuss with him the project of studying the Kikuyu and to ask for his assistance and permission to proceed: he also needed advice on how to set about the task in a way that the Kikuyu themselves would find acceptable. Chief Koinange lived at Kiambaa, a few miles outside Nairobi, and he at once offered us the hospitality of his own guest house while a council of elders was called to consider Louis's request. Since his first marriage, Louis's own rank as a member of the Kikuyu had been that of an elder, and indeed he would have made no progress at all with the project if he had not had that status. As it was, an agreement was reached.

As soon as we were settled in, the question came to the fore of how I should best occupy my own time while Louis was at work. I could hardly help him study the Kikuyu, of whom I knew virtually nothing, and in any case such a notion would have been completely unacceptable to them. There was no drawing for me to do this time, and what I most wanted was a site to excavate – it did not much matter what period, because I was interested in everything prehistoric. Louis therefore put me onto some trial digging at a cave he knew at Kiambaa itself called Waterfall Cave, where there was believed to be some Middle Stone Age material known as Stillbay. I had not been long engaged on this, however, when I began to feel distinctly unwell and in a very short time I was down with a very serious bout of pneumonia, which in those days could easily be fatal. I was rushed to the old Maia Carberry nursing home in Nairobi. The nurses were immensely kind and also extremely skilled, but I was dangerously ill, and my mother was actually sent for from England and flew out on an Imperial Airways flight that took four days. It must have been a harrowing journey for her because, as I was told afterwards, nobody expected me to survive and she must have been aware of this. The fact that I did was undoubtedly due to the devoted nursing and to Louis's determination that I should not give up: somehow he managed to convey this to me.

Finally I did recover, and out of all the worry that I inadvertently caused to so many people some good did come. One thing was that while my first encounter with Louis's parents, who came to visit us at Kiambaa, had not overcome the awkwardness they felt, when I became ill all their natural compassion and kindness overcame any hesitancy they may still have felt in accepting me and they did everything they possibly could to help. My desperate need, and doubtless Louis's acute anxiety about me, quite won them over, and from that time we were firm friends. I was especially fond of Louis's mother, who was also called Mary, and her sister Sibella, Louis's aunt Sibbie. Even Canon Burns, Sibella's husband, who had reacted very strongly against Louis's separation, divorce and remarriage, allowed himself to take kindly to me. It was also through my illness that my mother came to meet Louis's parents, and to my pleasure they got along splendidly together.

My convalescence was rapid, and after we had returned to Kiambaa Louis was able to resume full-time working on his Kikuyu study, though we did not remain there long. He had by then already reached the stage of writing a draft text and he had two chosen elders of the Kikuyu assigned to him to assist with the research and supply him with information. There was therefore no need for him to stay at Kiambaa, nor could we occupy Chief Koinange's guest house indefinitely, and it was decided that it would be better from every point of view if we moved out to Nakuru in the Rift Valley north of Nairobi: Louis had worked some years earlier on various archaeological sites in that region and could easily find me some fieldwork of genuine importance, following up the results his own expeditions had obtained. The two elders would accompany us so that Louis could work there as easily as anywhere and might even be able to assist me during spare moments. I was delighted with this plan because the country around Kiambaa did not greatly appeal to me and I could not match Louis's enthusiasm for the Kikuyu study. The archaeology of the Nakuru region would certainly offer me the kind of opportunities for which I was longing.

The main site Louis commended to my attention was a rocky ridge called Hyrax Hill, a couple of miles south of Nakuru township and overlooking the famous lake which occupies a depression in the floor of the Rift Valley. Louis had worked in this area some ten years earlier on various caves and shelters containing burials, including the well-known Gamble's Cave near Elmenteita and the Nakuru burial site only a quarter of a mile away from Hyrax Hill. This little hill, so called because of the colonies of hyraxes that live in the crevices in its rock faces, rises out of the grassy plains bordering the lake. In the late prehistoric past, the level of the lake had been much higher, and our excavations revealed an old shoreline at the foot of the hill with which the earliest of the sites I was excavating seemed to be associated. This was a most likely place to find domestic sites belonging to the people who had left the burials, and these would tell us how they had lived and help us to date their culture. Quite apart from its exciting archaeological potential, Hyrax Hill was a very

attractive place in a beautiful setting. The broad view extended west-
wards across the lake to the Mau escarpment with the lake itself a few
miles away, its famous flocks of flamingoes – well over two million of
them at certain times of the year – fringing the shallow soda lake with a
broad irregular band of pink, paler when the sun was high and deepening
to a rose colour in the rich evening light when the grassland turned
golden.

When we went to Hyrax Hill in April 1937 the grass around the hill had
recently been burned, and traces of stone structures could clearly be seen.
I needed no persuading to take on the project, and we decided to move
there as soon as we could and obtained permission from the landowner to
excavate. We should have to live as simply and as cheaply as we could;
the Rhodes Trust funding to Louis was certainly not intended to cover
projects of mine like this. In July we moved to Nakuru and set up camp at
the site with tents for ourselves, our small African excavation staff, and
Louis's two Kikuyu elders. We built ourselves a grass hut to serve as a
living and working room. It was a very pleasant grass hut, but we had
some trouble for a while with a cobra that liked it enough to take up
residence in the roof.

The excavations at Hyrax Hill gave me wonderful value. Near the base
of the hill I found a Neolithic (Late Stone Age) settlement, with its own
cemetery of nineteen burials, contained in low stony mounds. This part
of the site had also been occupied in Iron Age times by people who built
stone-walled enclosures and buried their dead in pits. On the opposite
side of the hill there were groups of pit dwellings, one group identifiable
as a small village, whose date appeared to be intermediate between our
Neolithic and Iron Age occupations. Among the Neolithic finds were
various stone implements, almost all of them made of obsidian, a shiny
natural glass of volcanic origin which can be flaked like flint or chert:
there were two varieties, one dark grey in colour and the other bottle
green. At the time we guessed that the grey obsidian had come from the
Njorowa Gorge near Lake Naivasha, where prehistoric mines of similar
obsidian were known, and the green variety from Mount Eburu on the
west side of Lake Naivasha, where a green obsidian also occurred naturally. Now, thanks to the work of Dr Frank Brown of the University of
Utah, these sources have been positively identified by chemical analysis
and it is interesting that the obsidians were transported as far south as
Olduvai Gorge during late prehistoric times. There was also much pottery, including characteristic beaker-shaped vessels, while many of the
burials had stone bowls or platters with them. The Iron Age levels yielded
pottery of a different kind, bones of domestic cattle, a few iron objects and
some glass beads and other items traded from the coast. I prepared a full
report on our work at Hyrax Hill, and Louis contributed a detailed study

of the human skeletons we had found, but it all had to wait until 1945 for publication because of the outbreak of war.

My work at the site proved of great interest to people living nearby and we had many visitors. They even contributed money, over £100 in all, for which we were extremely grateful, and this enabled me to continue work in 1938. Commander Couldrey, then editor of the *Kenya Weekly News*, went so far as to inaugurate a fund for the dig and subscriptions to it totalled twelve pounds and eight shillings, a far larger sum than it seems today. A local resident, Mrs Mary Selfe, who lived right by Hyrax Hill, was so impressed by my work that she afterwards bought the land and gave it to the Government to make into a national archaeological monument. It still survives as such today. Part of the Neolithic cemetery has been roofed over as a display site, and the custodians now live in the house that Mr and Mrs Selfe had owned.

Some of our visitors came to offer practical help. Among them were Molly Paine and Mary Catherine Davidson, teachers at the local school in Nakuru, who wanted to dig for me. Their coming marked the beginning of long-lasting friendships. Mary Davidson not long afterwards married Bernard Fagg, and the two of them played a major part in African archaeology for the next thirty years or more, largely in Nigeria. I have kept in close touch with them, and always stay at their home in Oxford on my visits to England. Mary, who in England seems more often to be called by her second name, Catherine, reminds me that I started her and Molly Paine off at the bottom of the archaeological ladder when they arrived, by putting them to work on sieving to see if their enthusiasm would stand the test. It certainly did, and they worked with me throughout the time at Hyrax Hill and afterwards at other sites in the area. Mary's first impressions of me were that I was very serious and methodical about the work, and said very little. She and I also remember vividly the clouds of grass mosquitoes at Hyrax Hill, from which we suffered greatly. Cigarette smoke helped to keep them away, and we also had an anti-mosquito preparation called oil of citronella, but nothing prevailed for long against such numbers.

Apart from the excavations I also made a complete survey of Hyrax Hill, recording many other traces of settlements. An interesting discovery in the course of this was the presence of many sets of cup-marks made in the rocks at the base of the hill for the well-known African 'bau' game, which is played with counters and has numerous local variants. There was no way of dating these particular occurrences, but the game, which is still played today and even has souvenir versions specially made for tourists, very probably goes well back into the prehistoric past.

Another visitor at this time who became a firm friend was that remarkable lady the Hon. Mrs Nellie Grant, mother of the writer Elspeth

Huxley. She was running, virtually single-handed for most of the time, a thousand-acre farm at Njoro, on the high ground overlooking the Nakuru basin. The story of Nellie Grant has been told by her daughter in various books, of which *The Flame Trees of Thika* is the best known, with its sequel *The Mottled Lizard*. In these, Nellie appears as the narrator's mother Tilly, while her husband, Col. Joscelyn Grant, is the Robin of the books. These two immensely popular works are in fact evocations of a period, based on events in Elspeth's childhood; for a straightforward factual record one needs to read another book of Elspeth's: *Nellie, Letters from Africa*, published in 1980. In all three books, full justice is done in different ways to Nellie Grant's ingenuity, her unfailing desire to achieve self-sufficiency wherever she happened to find herself, her strong interest in almost anything that seemed worth finding out about, and her love of people and of animals. It was natural that she should come to visit us at Hyrax Hill as soon as she heard about the excavation, and that not long afterwards she should tell us that she had found a place that she thought looked interesting, in the forested part of her own land. With typical hospitality she invited Louis and me to stay with her and see the new site and material, and we gladly went as soon as an opportunity arose.

Nellie's site, known as Njoro River Cave, was indeed interesting. Within a few minutes of our arriving there Louis picked up a flat disc bead made from chalcedony, a totally unexpected find. When she saw our enthusiasm, Nellie pressed us to come and excavate the site. This we did before long, but first I should conclude my account of the visitors to Hyrax Hill. One evening we had three who were a great deal less welcome than Mrs Grant: local men from the Lumbwa tribe, who stole everything from our tent – bedding, clothing and such few other possessions as we owned, though fortunately not the archaeological finds or Louis's Kikuyu text. We saw them running away in the dark and gave chase, causing them to drop most of their booty, which we recovered. But it was an unpleasant incident and we decided immediately that what we needed was a dog. So it came about that I welcomed Janet, the first Dalmatian I ever had in Africa, and since that day I have never been without one or more. We had no more burglars at Hyrax Hill.

Over the Christmas holiday at the end of 1937, Louis and I were able to take up Nellie Grant's invitation to go to the Njoro River Cave and do a trial dig there. In her resourceful way, Nellie built us a grass *banda*, or thatched hut, as a headquarters near the edge of the forest in which the cave was situated. We were able to spend a second and longer period at the cave in 1938, completing our digging there. On that occasion the Grants went off to the Serengeti for a camping holiday and we willingly agreed to look after their dogs and sundry other animals while they were away. What Dalmatians are to me, Dachshunds were to Nellie, and she had them in large numbers. I believe there were seven when we were there: Nellie herself seemed sometimes to have lost track of the total and once when she had informed a visitor that there were six, another head popped up through a hole in the floorboards. Our own four Dalmatians accompanied us, and got on splendidly with the Dachshunds.

Njoro River Cave turned out to be a very important Late Stone Age burial place, where the dead were accompanied by a variety of interesting objects, some of them fragile but remarkably well preserved. The cave consisted of a large rock shelter with a narrow cave at one end. It was a burial place with unique cremated burials, quite unprecedented in the Late Stone Age archaeology of Kenya. The cremation process had led to the survival of the fragile objects, which had become carbonized and were wholly or fragmentarily preserved in the shallow graves instead of crumbling away as they would have done otherwise. About 80 individuals had been buried in the area we excavated, and we found that prior to cremation the bodies had been bound into tightly contracted positions with plaited cords, fragments of which had been preserved. They had been wrapped in skins and were often wearing ornaments such as pendants and bead necklaces, many of the beads being of semi-precious stones spaced by hard sedge seeds. We were able to reconstruct the patterns and lengths of the necklaces by sticking matchsticks in the ground to mark the position of each stone bead and counting the numbers of intervening sedge seeds. Each burial seemed to have been accompanied by a stone bowl with a pestle and grindstone, and there were remains of basketwork and of handwoven fabrics which we decided included simple forms of string-bag and part of a belt. The most unusual object was a wooden vessel, probably a drinking cup, elaborately carved over its entire surface with close geometric patterns: it remains a unique find. There were also remains of gourds of the kinds still used in Africa today to carry water, and we found sherds of simply decorated hand-made pottery and stone tools made of the greenish-black obsidian from Mount Eburu. We estimated an age for the burials of about 850BC. Some years later a radiocarbon date was obtained from the charcoal, which indicated that we had not been far out: the actual date was a little older at 970BC±80 years.

The excavating team at Njoro River Cave was small: Mollie Paine and Mary Davidson assisted Louis and myself and our African diggers. Louis studied the human remains and reached the interesting conclusion that the population had been quite different from all the recent negroid inhabitants of Kenya. For me, the excavation and coping with the fragile finds was immensely valuable experience – and very exciting. We had no funding to enable us to use elaborate equipment, and we preserved the delicate materials by dripping diluted Durofix onto them as a hardener when they were uncovered: it worked well, and they afterwards travelled successfully to the Coryndon Museum in Nairobi. We worked hard at Njoro but felt well rewarded. Nellie Grant showed us every kindness and was delighted with our finds. Elspeth Huxley quotes a letter of hers, written at the time:

'... The poor Leakeys are held up for wages money and only have two months' work in sight on the skeletons, and need two years. They live on the smell of an oil-rag themselves, work all day on the site and up to eight or nine o'clock at night, sorting and labelling the day's finds.'

Nellie, Letters from Africa

It was while we were at Njoro that I had two memorable experiences. The first was that I gave my first public lecture, if one can call it that. Nellie Grant persuaded me to give a talk at the Njoro Country Club about Hyrax Hill, and it really amounted to no more than speaking informally to a roomful of settlers and friends about what we had been finding at Hyrax Hill. Although I said right at the beginning that the idea of public lecturing terrified me for many years, that really came with formal lectures later, and I did not look on this as a daunting occasion or get into a nervous state about it. Oddly enough, Louis did: he seemed to be terrified on my behalf, and could hardly bring himself to listen.

The second experience was while we were digging. I was uncovering a rather fine skull, clearly of an important personage in view of the number of ornaments with which it was associated. Without warning I felt a hard thump on my left shoulder as though someone had given me a hearty slap on the back. I remember being annoyed that anyone should do this to me when I was engaged in the delicate operation of uncovering the fragile skull, and saying crossly, without looking up, 'Go away, for God's sake'; but nobody was anywhere near me and everyone confirmed that they had not moved from their allotted positions on the dig. The Kikuyu workmen considered this to be a warning from the spirits not to disturb the skull and urged me to cover it over immediately and leave it alone. I cannot explain this happening, but a similarly inexplicable event occurred many years later, at Langata, which I will relate in due course.

The beginning of 1939 brought the end of Louis's grant from the Rhodes Trust for the Kikuyu study project, and it therefore brought us a financial crisis. For Louis to complete the production of the final text, and for me to work on my excavated material for the site reports, we had moved back from Nakuru to Nairobi, renting a small house near a golf course and afterwards one just outside Nairobi, our primary concern being to find somewhere to exercise the dogs. When Louis's text was finished it was at least 700,000 words long and, not surprisingly, the Rhodes Trust withdrew their offer to finance its publication: few people would have wanted to purchase such a massive work at what would necessarily have been an extremely expensive price. They requested Louis to cut and edit the work drastically, and he firmly refused. No commercial publisher would take it on so, in the end, it just got put aside. In fact, after Louis's death I was able to rescue the manuscript. Louis's sister, Gladys Beecher, carried out some major editing, and it was published in 1977 by the Academic Press, with the assistance of a generous grant from the L.S.B. Leakey Foundation, California. It pleased me greatly that all Louis's work was not wasted, and the volumes stand as a memorial and tribute to his remarkable association with the Kikuyu people, his love for them, and his unique understanding of their culture.

Meanwhile, what were we to do next, as the year 1939 progressed sombrely towards the outbreak of the Second World War? In the deteriorating international situation there could be no question of our returning to England. Louis managed to earn a little money in two ways. Officially the government gave him a salary to undertake some civil intelligence work, using his knowledge of Kenya and of the Kikuyu in particular. Anti-British propaganda was beginning to create a problem among the Kikuyu and it had reached almost fifth-column proportions in 1939. Louis's principal task was to trace the sources of the propaganda, to counteract it in any way he could, and to identify the ringleaders among those who were spreading it. Quite unofficially, he supplemented his pay by some trading of goods to the Kikuyu in outlying villages as he travelled among them. Louis simply bought items wholesale in Nairobi and sold retail, making a small profit. I remember that patent medicines were his main stock-in-trade, there being a considerable demand for them. We could pay our rent for a while, but there was almost no money at all to spend on anything but strict necessities.

When war finally broke out at the end of August, there was little direct effect on our part of Kenya at first. Things had been different when the First World War began in 1914. In those days neighbouring Tanzania had been German East Africa; substantial enemy forces were actually present in East Africa and there was considerable fighting. In 1939 the nearest enemies were the Italians in Ethiopia and Somalia, who certainly constituted a threat to Kenya's northern border, but around Nairobi and in Tanzania it was a question of rounding up and detaining the individual German settlers, all civilians. Louis's work in intelligence, under the Special Branch, now became more regular and intense, and he travelled a great deal in connection with it. This he greatly enjoyed, and he rather fostered the 'cloak and dagger' aura that he acquired. He also made a further personal contribution to the military effort by running guns to the Ethiopian border for local guerrilla groups who were operating against the Italians. The authorities supplied him with all the weapons he could take. Needless to say, Louis also used the opportunities provided by all his travelling to visit any archaeological sites where he happened to be, and to keep an eye open for promising new localities; some of these discoveries were followed up after the war. He also had occasional brief periods of leave during which we could make archaeological field trips almost as if things were normal, though later on these were restricted by petrol rationing.

As the war progressed, Italian prisoners of war and detailed civilians began to be brought into Kenya, and some of them were charming and highly intelligent men, like the della Giustina brothers and Ferucio Menengetti, who were employed at archaeological sites or given work in the Coryndon Museum. Other people arrived too, because of the war. Bernard Fagg, for example, who had studied archaeology at Cambridge, came with the troops sent to strengthen the defences of Kenya. He soon introduced himself to Louis and I remember them arriving together at our house in an ancient motorcycle and sidecar that had belonged to Louis's father and mother. It was through us that Bernard first met Mary David-son, whom he married in 1942. Her parents lived in Nairobi. Jack Trevor also came to Nairobi as a soldier: he was a physical anthropologist who taught at Cambridge University, and he arrived as Louis's opposite number in Military Intelligence. I was not called up for any kind of war work, and in fact we were able to get quite a lot of archaeology of one sort or another done during the war years, which might in other circum-stances have been a total blank. In 1940, Louis officially took over the curatorship of the Coryndon Museum in Nairobi from Dr Vernon van Someren, albeit in a spare-time and more or less honorary capacity. Van Someren's relationships with the other members of the staff, notably the botanist Peter Bally, had deteriorated to crisis level, but I doubt whether he had expected the Trustees, of whom Louis was one, to accept the resignation threat he made in 1940. He was a brilliant man and was responsible for executing with great skill some of the earliest habitat groups ever made. I remember particularly the leopard on a rocky ledge and the bongo in thick forest. Regrettably, he became totally embittered after leaving the Museum, retiring to a house at Ngong which he never left until his death 30 years later. When his son Cunningham van Som-eren joined the Museum staff at the age of 72 his father, then 90 years old, cut him out of his Will. Louis's offer to cease being a Trustee and act as Curator was mainly a move to keep the Museum going and open to the public during the war. Louis devoted enormous energy to his work for the Museum in the evenings and such other time as he could manage amidst everything else that was going on, while I worked in the Museum daily to help him. The other practical effect of his taking the curatorship was that van Someren left the official Curator's house and we moved into it. The house, an extensive bungalow made of wooden boards and corrugated iron, had certainly been elegant when the Colonial Administration built it many years earlier for John Ainsworth, Provincial Commissioner of Nairobi at the time, but it was now in poor condition. Still, it was conveniently located next to the Museum: by early 1941 we were quite happily established there.

While all this was taking place I had continued my own archaeological work. Much of my time had been taken up with studying in detail the material excavated at Hyrax Hill and Njoro River Cave, and preparing the drawings and text for the reports. But I had also had another unexpected opportunity to excavate a prolific site during late 1939 and early 1940. The site was the Naivasha Railway Rock Shelter. Naivasha is about halfway between Nairobi and Nakuru and like the latter place is a small town by a lake in the Rift Valley. The railway needed to be realigned for some reason, and making the new track would destroy most of the deposit below a promising-looking shelter which was already known to contain abundant Late Stone Age material, though it had never been excavated. Hundreds of small obsidian tools and flakes could be picked up from the surface of the area to be destroyed. This was therefore an exercise in what is now called 'rescue archaeology', and I had the assistance of two keen volunteers, Madeleine Worthington and Millicent Ellis; Louis visited at weekends. The railway authorities allowed us to dig a single long trench. The finds were certainly prolific, but not quite as interesting as our Neolithic finds from Hyrax Hill and Njoro. There were simply too many stone artefacts – our one trench produced over 75,000 finished tools and something like two million waste chips. Most of the finished pieces were microliths, that is to say, small flakes or blades chipped to geometric shapes, and they were very repetitive. We recovered enough other material, of various ages, to make the operation worthwhile, but before the material had been analysed for publication, termites destroyed all the cardboard containers in which the specimens were stored so that all 75,000 of them became inextricably mixed. To this day I have never had the courage to sort them out again, and the site remains unpublished.

While I was directing the Naivasha Railway Rock Shelter work, I stayed down by the lake in a very pleasing small house kindly lent to us by its owner, Allen Turner, a member of the technical staff of the Coryndon Museum. There were many hippos in the lake, and at night we could hear the sounds of them all around, grunting and splashing in the water and thoroughly enjoying themselves.

Another pleasure was that the dogs were able to come and live with us: they stayed at the house by day, and in the evening were brought up to the site for their walk. This always caused a minor panic because they had to cross the railway line and we had to listen carefully for approaching trains. The road past the site was carrying more traffic than it usually did, because frequent long military convoys passed that way *en route* for the border with Ethiopia, where there was fighting with the Italians. Allen Turner, our host, had caused something of a sensation in Nairobi by marrying an African girl and producing half-caste children, which everyone seemed to find shocking, none more so than Leonard Beecher, Louis's brother-in-law, who was later to become Archbishop of East Africa. We only thought it rather awful that people were shocked, and wondered about the children's future.

Another member of the Coryndon Museum's staff was Peter Bally, who came from Switzerland and was the expert in botany. It was he who van Someren had so disliked, though Louis and I thought highly of him and his work. He had recently married an Austrian girl, Joy, who became a brilliant painter of botanical and other natural history subjects and afterwards of people of the local tribes. Joy Bally was, however, much better known by her surname of a later marriage, when she became Joy Adamson and wrote several famous and popular books about the lioness Elsa: *Born Free*, and other titles. When we were living in Nairobi before moving into the Curator's official residence, Peter and Joy lived in the guest quarters that belonged to our house. Joy was still a recent arrival in Kenya and Louis, professionally on the lookout for Germans, infiltrators and general subversive influences, was at first deeply suspicious of Joy because she was an Austrian, but he soon found plenty for her to do at the Museum, employing her artistic talents to the full. Joy was not a sympathetic personality, nor particularly easy to get on with, but her love of animals was wholly genuine and all the funds she accumulated from her books and film rights were unstintingly made over for the benefit of wildlife, in one way or another. For this one had to admire her.

In 1940, Canon Harry Leakey, Louis's father, died, much mourned by the people of his missionary parish. I am very glad that I knew him if only for such a short time. I remember that he died just after the Germans had entered Paris and we were all at great pains to keep the news from him because of his love of France. But this same year was to see a birth as well as a death in the Leakey family. Even before the end of the Naivasha excavation I had known that I was expecting a child. Fortunately I did not turn out to be one of those for whom pregnancy brings sickness and fragility and I was able to carry on with my work almost without noticing. My doctor was Hope Trant, who had come out to Kenya as a member of the A.T.S. On 4 November our son Jonathan was born. As he arrived two or three weeks earlier than expected, Louis was actually away at the time, and did not get back until several days later. We were both delighted and gave Jonathan his two grandfathers' names, Harry and Erskine.

I quite liked having a baby – I think I won't put it more strongly than that – but I had no intention of allowing motherhood to disrupt my work as an archaeologist. Jonathan in fact caused very little trouble, though there was rather a scene at the hospital a few days after his birth when my Dalmatian Janet was brought to visit me. 'No dogs in hospitals', was the matron's view, and I did not subscribe to it. The worst thing that happened in Jonathan's early childhood took place soon after we had moved into the Curator's house at the Museum. Its walls were full of holes, and through the holes ants could get in: not just occasional relatively harmless ants, but *siafu*, army ants, in thousands. One night this happened and they attacked Jonathan in his cot, climbing up the legs of it, and getting under his mosquito net and all over his body before they started biting him all at once. In this way they very rapidly kill small animals and they would undoubtedly have killed Jonathan if we had not heard his screams immediately and rescued him, badly frightened and still covered with swarms of biting ants that had to be got off him quickly. He survived, and we saw to it that in future the legs of the cot stood in shallow pans of water and paraffin. On another occasion the ants broke into our bedroom and fought a two-day battle to the death with two colonies of bees that were resident in the hollow walls. Presumably the ants were after the honey and possibly the grubs in the bees' nests. The bees eventually won, and we were left to sweep up unbelievable quantities of ants that had been stung to death, and many bees that the ants had killed.

The next major event for me came when Jonathan was only a few months old. Peter and Joy Bally had for some time been planning a short trip to Ngorongoro to carry out certain botanical work in the forested area there. They urged me to join them, since the trip would enable me to examine some stone-built burial mounds that were known to exist on the crater floor and to have produced human remains and stone bowls which sounded as if they resembled those from our excavations in the Nakuru area. When Tanzania had been part of German East Africa, two brothers, Adolph and Friedrich Siedentopf, had had farms down on the crater floor, and Adolph had taken stone from the cairns covering the burials for his buildings: this was when the first finds had been made, and subsequently a certain amount of excavation had been carried out by other Germans, including the geologist Hans Reck. The farms were abandoned when the First World War broke out, and various burial mounds still existed, some of them undisturbed. Louis encouraged me to go, and to take Jack Trevor, who had some leave due, to study any skeletal material we might find. I needed little persuading, since four months of breast-feeding seemed quite enough for someone who, while loving her small son very much, regarded herself first and foremost as an archaeologist. Provided Jonathan could be properly looked after, I would gladly go, so I set about weaning him onto solid food and finding a reliable nurse who could help Louis care for him while I was away. Louis was quite happy with such an arrangement: I think he rather regretted having missed the very early days of his children by his first marriage, through being engaged on one of his African trips in the case of Priscilla and through having separated from Frida at about the time of Colin's birth. Jonathan co-operated over the weaning, and the fact that I was still producing abundant but unwanted milk was nothing worse than a minor inconvenience, as Jack and I set off with the Ballys in April 1941.

It had to be a short trip, and the amount of excavation we could achieve in a fortnight was very limited. That we could dig at all was largely due to Jack Trevor's having persuaded Cambridge University to give a grant of £50 for the work. One of the two stone mounds we chose turned out on excavation to be of recent origin, but the other proved to contain eight or nine burials with an interesting assemblage of stone bowls, pestles, grinding stones, obsidian tools and ornamental items, including beads made of various materials. There were strong general similarities to our finds at the Njoro River Cave, though the Ngorongoro mound produced some ornamental objects not previously found: ivory lip plugs, like those still worn in parts of Africa.

Our safari to Ngorongoro had its share of East African local colour and incidents. There was no road by which a car could get down to the crater floor, so we had to leave ours at the top and walk down with a line of Wambulu porters carrying our stores and equipment. On the crater floor we met a rhinoceros, which the Ballys' small Cairn Terrier decided to take on in single combat, uttering what may have been Scottish war-cries which annoyed the rhino intensely. The standard and excellent advice to travellers on foot who encounter an angry rhino is to climb a tree, but we happened to be in an open grassy part of the crater, entirely treeless, an eventuality on which the manuals of advice are silent. After some rather fraught moments the rhino decided to move off. It was a long walk across to the ruined farm of Adolph Siedentopf and we were exhausted when we got there. Bearing this in mind, when the end of our stay came, Jack Trevor and I decided to ride back on donkeys, which we sent a member of our staff to borrow for us from a German farmer, Herr Rohde, who lived at the foot of the Crater and was the only German in East Africa not detained at the outbreak of war, being completely trusted by the British. On our ride back we encountered a lioness, and the donkeys bolted. I was thrown almost at once and Jack was borne off headlong into the middle distance. Fortunately the lioness was also startled into flight and eventually we pulled ourselves together, caught my donkey and made our way to where the Ballys were at work in the forest.

Another important archaeological site that was discovered during a brief wartime excursion was Olorgesailie, and this time it was Mary Fagg, with Ferucio Menengetti, who accompanied Louis and me during what was just an Easter leave weekend. Olorgesailie is in the Kenya Rift Valley about 30 miles southwest of Nairobi by road – at that time no more than a rough track which led up onto the shoulder of the Ngong Hills and then descended spectacularly to the Rift floor in a series of steps, the temperature rising with each mile. This road now has a tarmac surface, and it eventually runs on past Mount Olorgesailie to Lake Magadi, where the Magadi Soda Company pursues its trade in conditions of scorching heat and aridity. Lake Magadi contains a higher concentration of soda than any of the other East African soda lakes, and the soda is extracted, carried to Nairobi by a special railway constructed by the company, and shipped overseas. The view from the Ngong Hills overlooking the Rift Valley is justly famous: there are days when one can clearly see the whole of Kilimanjaro, with every detail of the snow-cap distinct, a hundred and twenty miles away. Mount Olorgesailie, down in the Rift, looks deceptively close and sometimes it is possible to make out the thin horizontal white line at its base which marks the diatomaceous sediments of a former lake, of Pleistocene age, now completely dry. Around half a million years ago it was a substantial body of water on whose shores Lower Palaeolithic hunters camped in a grassy landscape rich in game. The geologist J. W. Gregory (who gave his name to the Gregory Rift) had surveyed this area long before and had reported finding a bank of diatomaceous white sediment on which stone tools lay; he even thought they had been used to dig the sediments. Louis and I had recently been looking for the place he had described, but had so far found no more than the occasional isolated hand axe. But on this weekend in 1942 our luck was in. The party was spread out over a few hundred yards of the bushy country that fringes the white sediments when Louis and I, quite independently but at the same moment, each came upon a great spread of typical hand axes and cleavers. We were within shouting distance and Louis hurried over to see my find first. It was an extraordinary sight: the implements ran into hundreds and lay in close concentration on an eroded sloping surface of lake sediments, looking as if they had only just been abandoned by their makers. The place that Louis himself had found was not quite so rich, but was also most impressive. Before long Mary and Menengetti had also found sites near by.

We agreed there and then among ourselves that the particular concentration of implements that I had come upon ought, if possible, to be left permanently in place, and so it was. Today, Olorgesailie is a tourist attraction, and a raised wooden walkway, known as the cat-walk, has been built around that spread of implements. This became the very first open-air museum in East Africa, and it was the Italian prisoners of war, directed by the della Giustina brothers, who did the manual work of setting it up and built the group of *bandas* where visitors can rest from the heat or stay a night. Both of the della Giustinas decided to return and live in Kenya after their repatriation to Italy at the end of the war, and one of them was for many years the custodian at Olorgesailie.

That, however, is looking a little way ahead. The first task was to make a basic survey and assessment of the site, and to excavate. This task fell to me. I was quite willing to undertake it and in any case was the only person available with sufficient experience. Accordingly, taking with me only Jonathan and a small team of Africans directed by Heslon Mukiri, I went and camped down at Olorgesailie for several months in 1943 to tackle the numerous geological and archaeological problems the place offered. The dogs came, of course, but I did not have even a car at my disposal at the site. The people from the Magadi Soda Company were very helpful, stopping whenever they passed to see if I was all right. Lions came frequently around the camp at night, but we had no real problems except that it was extremely difficult to extract any useful archaeological information from the sites, which had seemed so promising when we first found them. The geology was very complicated and key layers often did not extend from one of my trenches to the next, making correlations almost impossible. I was to dig on several occasions at Olorgesailie over the next ten years and I never did make much real progress: I fear the best moments there were probably the very first ones, when we discovered the dramatic spreads of hand axes. I also remember the journeys home from the site, because one particularly steep section of the ascent out of the Rift always proved too much for our car. Louis would take a run at the hill and get as far as he could and then everyone, adults, children, dogs, would have to jump out and those of us who could would push, ramming stones under the rear wheels to maintain each yard of ground gradually won. That stretch could take us three-quarters of an hour, easily.

Olorgesailie and Ngorongoro were by no means the only archaeological sites that occupied us in the period 1940–44. Among other things, in 1942 I made my first visit to Rusinga Island in Lake Victoria, at the mouth of the Kavirondo Gulf as it was then called. This was one of a number of places with deposits of Miocene age, on which Louis had been working from time to time since before I met him. The deposits in question were very rich in fossils, including extinct species of apes. The Miocene is much older than the Pleistocene, and the ape fossils at Rusinga were about 18 million years old – far earlier than the first true humans and the beginnings of the Old Stone Age, but of the greatest interest with regard to the descent of man from our remote primate ancestors, and the separation of the groups of primates that led on the one hand to the *Hominidae* (early and modern man) and on the other to the *Pongidae* (the modern great apes and their predecessors). Louis had already found several ape fossils of great importance and he went whenever he could to look

for more, either on Rusinga Island or at sites of similar age on the mainland of West Kenya, like Songhor and Koru. Rusinga was in later years to
be such a frequent destination of ours that it became like a holiday home,
and it was also, as it happened, the scene of some of our most exciting
discoveries.

The 1942 visit was a quick one during a short period of leave for Louis.
Jonathan came, and we took with us Mary Fagg, who was a welcome
member of so many of our expeditions in those days, and also Heslon
Mukiri. We did not attempt or achieve much on the island that time, but
the journey there was memorable. To get to Rusinga we had a long overland drive on rough roads to Kisumu on the Kavirondo Gulf, and then a
journey by boat of several hours. Louis had previously hitched a lift on a
motor launch belonging to the Fisheries Service, but this time none was
available, so we arranged a passage overnight on a locally owned dhow,
sleeping as best we could on top of the cargo of sacks of maize. Unfortunately we got completely becalmed half-way and were still stationary late
the next morning. The boat was crawling with cockroaches, the biggest I
have ever seen, and there was no proper lavatory: just a seat projecting
over the side. Use of this arrangement in public seemed normal enough to
the crew, but we passengers were coy enough to improvise a screen by
holding up a blanket when one of our number felt the need. We were all
extremely glad when a favourable wind finally got up again and we could
get to Rusinga.

Mary Fagg remembers that voyage as well as I do, and we were recalling
some of its highlights only recently when I was staying with her and
Bernard in Oxford. Our reminiscences also included an epic visit we all
made on another occasion to Kisii, to the District Commissioner Storrs
Fox, who had known Louis at Cambridge: 'D.C. Kisii', we always called
him. During the war years, alcoholic drinks were often in extremely short
supply, and many people including ourselves experimented with home
brewing or distilling of various kinds, using whatever was available. It
would be kind though perhaps somewhat flattering to describe our pro-
duct as a form of mead. D.C. Kisii was far more successful; his beverage
achieved an enviable potency which ours lacked, and this presumably
accounts for the vagueness of my own memory of where we were bound
for when we left him one evening. I do know, however, that we ended up
driving very cheerfully down the jetty at Kendu Bay – and that Louis
came to his senses only just in time to stop, inches from the end.

It was lucky that Jonathan was such an easy and accommodating child
to travel with, even in his earliest years: he came with me on much of my
wartime fieldwork and in East Africa one never quite knows what is
going to happen next. It was about this time, probably also in 1942, that I
made a short visit to assess a large surface scatter of Lower Palaeolithic

hand axes that had been reported at Lewa, in the farming country that lies on the northern side of Mount Kenya. I was with the geologist Robert Shackleton, who was then engaged on a long survey of the geology of northern Kenya. Jonathan was with me, and Janet, my senior Dalmatian. One day, Bobbie Shackleton was bitten by a puff adder. Such a bite can be fatal if rapid action is not taken, and the patient must be kept absolutely still to prevent the poison from circulating, while serum is brought. We had serum with us, but it was in the car two miles away. I had to abandon Jonathan and Janet, tying her to a tree and telling him to stay with her, and then run as fast as I could to get the serum. Everyone survived this potentially disastrous episode quite cheerfully. Jonathan grew up to become an expert on snakes, and in his time he has survived several snake bites, including those of both green and black mambas, either of which could have proved fatal.

There was one other project of the wartime years which I must mention, because it was of great fascination to me at the time, and very different from the other kinds of archaeology with which I was involved. It took Louis and me again to West Kenya, to Kavirondo, because that was where our friend Archdeacon Owen lived – a remarkable man who was in charge of the northern region of the Mombasa Protestant diocese from 1918 until he retired in 1944. He had a striking presence, was immensely energetic, and was also an indefatigable if sometimes rather unscrupulous collector of archaeological objects and fossils – amassing them with little regard to their position or what they were associated with. He was deeply interested in the Miocene sites in the Kavirondo area, but this time, in 1944, he wanted Louis and me to look at some unusual pottery he had discovered, and we gladly went, again in a brief leave period. The pottery certainly *was* unusual, in several respects: the variety and shapes of the vessels, the elegant styles of decoration, and especially the presence in the base of nearly every pot of a curious deliberately made small hollow or dimple. From this last feature I named the pottery 'Dimple-based' ware, and at that time it was something quite new. We visited some of Owen's sites, notably Urewe, and satisfied ourselves that they all belonged to one period: the Iron Age. He pressed me to undertake a descriptive study of the pottery for publication, and I was delighted to do so as it was certainly an important find: the material was probably connected with the southward spread of the Bantu people. At that time the only possible parallels we could discover lay to the north in Uganda and the Sudan, but since then finds of Dimple-based pottery have been made over a wide area of East and Central Africa. Various dates have been obtained, mainly early within the first millennium AD, though a few from west of Lake Victoria are some six or seven hundred years older. Owen died before the report could be published, but at least he read the completed typescript. He would have been glad to know that the report was fruitful in that it led to many further discoveries of similar pottery in East and Central Africa.

With the death of Archdeacon Owen we lost a close friend who was one of the liveliest and most colourful characters I ever met in East Africa. He must also have had an iron constitution, for I myself can testify that when thirsty he would drink from any puddle he happened to encounter in the road and that he never took any harm from it. I also remember he had a most voracious appetite for pork pies. His son John, incidentally, later became Director of the Tanzania National Parks and was often at Seronera when I moved to Olduvai in the late 1960s. The Archdeacon was a tall and handsome man, a born fighter who provided himself with causes to champion throughout his life – the rights of native Africans in Kenya, the need to stamp out the practice of female circumcision, and many more. He was also the kind of person around whom stories or legends grow: how, for example, if he was not finding many fossils he would get down on his knees and pray for better luck. It was also said that many years ago he had found a skull of *Proconsul* in one of the Miocene deposits and, thinking that it would conflict with the Old Testament version of the Creation, on which his congregation was strictly brought up, had it buried again. One version said he had dropped it down the earth closet at his house. He was deeply opposed to Louis's divorce and re-marriage and when I came out to Kenya in 1937 he wrote to Louis asking him not to bring me with him on a visit he wanted Louis to make to see some new finds. Louis complied, but talked to him about me to such good effect that when we did meet, not long after, Archdeacon Owen was very friendly to me and we became the best of friends for the rest of his life.

We were undoubtedly lucky during these years over the slight effect the war had on us in Nairobi, but our life was not without its tragedies. A cousin of Louis's, Nigel Leakey, was killed in action while serving with the King's African Rifles in the Ethiopian campaign, winning a posthum-ous V.C. for the brave action that cost him his life. An altogether more immediate tragedy was the death in early infancy of our second child, a daughter whom we had named Deborah: she was about three months old when she succumbed to an attack of dysentery. I suppose it would have been much worse if it had happened when she was older, for when she died I felt that she had hardly begun to be a real person. In a very short space of time we also lost our four adult Dalmatians, Janet and her pup-pies, to an outbreak of infectious jaundice which we were powerless to treat. Only one young puppy, Minnie, survived. To keep her company we acquired Sally, a Dalmatian with long silky hair and an elegantly feath-ered tail. She must have been a throwback to early eighteenth-century Dalmatians, of which some prints still survive. At that time they were used for hunting, often as harriers, and it was only when the breed was converted to coach dogs, to run behind carriages, that the short coats of present-day Dalmatians became established. Sally had one descendant long haired like herself, but all our attempts to re-establish the strain were unsuccessful.

In the later years of the war we had a constant stream of visitors staying with us in Nairobi, mostly officers on leave or on their way to join their regiments. I remember that Desmond Clark, now the doyen of African prehistory, came several times. We also had visits from Tony Arkell, then Provincial Commissioner in the Sudan and later Commissioner for Archaeology there, and Kenneth Kirkwood, now Rhodes Professor of Race Relations at Oxford, who was then a young.soldier with a South African contingent. One of our visitors during this period inadvertently imported bedbugs, doubtless from Ethiopia, which eventually infested the house and made us rather glad when the Museum Trustees decided it was falling to pieces and should be demolished and a new bungalow built. It was certainly no place to live with two small children; Richard, born in 1944, was still a baby and we therefore moved out for a while to Karen, an outlying suburb of Nairobi named after the writer Karen Blixen, who had lived there. We rented a house on the edge of the forest, but I remember very little about it except that its ceilings for some odd reason had been painted black. The dogs loved the nearby forest, and spent much of their time hunting in it. Long-haired Sally hunted hares, with great success. She would eat as much of the meat as she could and then regurgitate it for her puppies when she got home. On one occasion the three Dalmatians completely routed a visiting leopard in our garden and sent it off in headlong flight. Another time, Minnie got herself bitten in the mouth by a puff adder: remarkably, she survived, though she was eventually killed by a snake when we were at Kariandusi a couple of years later. As ever, the Dalmatians were one of the most important parts of our lives. In 1944 for the first time we entered Minnie and her puppies at dog shows organized by the East Africa Kennel Club, and they had various successes.

We were at Karen when the war ended, Jonathan being then five and Richard one. I had a succession of *ayahs*, or African nannies, to help me look after the boys, and having two children was therefore no more of an obstruction to my work than having only one. Louis and I had made vague plans that we would go on leave to England as soon as the end of the war made it possible: after all, when we left Steen Cottage we had thought it would be for no more than two years. There were things we needed to attend to, quite apart from being due for a holiday. But by the autumn of 1945 it had become clear that my mother's health was very poor and rapidly getting worse, and it was decided that I should set off for England just as soon as I could book a passage, taking the two boys with me. Louis would follow as soon as he was free to do so. It was December of 1945 when we left. We were to meet up in London, which we had not seen for nine years, and where it would soon be the coldest part of the European winter. No doubt we would find it a very different place from the city we remembered.

8
After the war

THE JOURNEY TO ENGLAND by boat through the Red Sea was about as uncomfortable as it could be. The boys and I, with two other mothers whom I did not know, with one child each, were all crammed into one of the inside cabins. It was all that was available, and of course did not have a porthole to offer air or light. It might be deep winter in England, but the first part of our journey, up the east coast of Africa from Mombasa and through the Red Sea, was baking hot. Richard developed a painful earache, and sometimes to comfort him and avoid his crying keeping the other inmates of the cabin awake, I had to walk up and down the corridor with him in my arms for the whole night. For the last half of the journey at least, there was very genuine danger from wartime mines, which were still very common: the risk was such that once the children were in bed we three mothers took turns so that one was always in the cabin, ready to scoop up the children and rush them on deck when the explosion came. But we got there in the end, and made our way to boarding house accommodation in the Cromwell Road, South Kensington, which my mother had booked for us.

My mother was indeed failing fast, and she died just a fortnight after our arrival. The funeral service took place at the Assumption Convent in Kensington, which had been the scene of the first of my unsuccessful attempts to be a schoolgirl, and she was buried at Ware, where my aunt Mollie was buried and where Louis and I had been married.

London was full of signs of the war, particularly the massive amount of bomb-damage: there seemed to be unfilled craters and uncleared rubble everywhere. Later in the year we saw some of the devastated areas in the city become pink with flowering spikes of willow-herb, which had colonized the open spaces and was by now well established and thriving there. In the cold beginning of our visit, the children wore woolly sweaters and scarves which I had knitted for them in the last few months in Nairobi, about the only time I ever did any serious knitting, a pastime which I find most irritating, even to watch. I had also managed to get overcoats made for them out of blankets, this sort of warm clothing being more or less unknown for children in Kenya, where it never gets very cold. Jonathan took a great interest in his strange surroundings in London, but I think what he liked best were the escalators in some of the bigger shops and most of the tube stations. He would ride happily up and down these for as long as I would let him. The shops themselves also had an air of wartime: rationing of food and clothes was still in force and indeed some things, like sugar and sweets, continued to be rationed as late as 1950. At the boarding house where we stayed, boiled cod seemed to be the principal item of food.

But we did not remain in London for the whole of our stay. One of the best parts of the entire trip was a stay in Cornwall on the farm of Catherine Garnett. She was a girlhood friend of mine, her maiden name being Catherine Martin, and she had been on the Hembury dig while I was there. We had kept in touch ever since, and when she heard we were coming to England she invited us all down to stay with her. Catherine, incidentally, was one of the very few people who actually gave me support and encouragement in the early days of my relationship with Louis, for which I was very grateful. She had gone into farming, and when Louis left for East Africa in 1934 I had visited her on a pig farm near Winchester, about which I can remember little except that she seemed to spend much of her time castrating pigs. Down in Cornwall she now ran her own mixed farm near Wadebridge, with the help of a land-girl. Catherine's farm included a few pigs, which were a great source of entertainment to Jonathan, who used to chase them at every possible opportunity. The farm also had ponies, and he was therefore able to have his first experience of riding. To my delight, he loved it. It was a very happy holiday for us all.

While in England we also arranged for Steen Cottage to be taken over permanently by the people then renting it. It had had a history of different occupants during our absence, arranged by correspondence. Eventually a tenant to whom Louis had let the cottage had arranged to buy it, and was living there as owner though continuing to pay Louis rent! At some stage all our belongings had been turned out into the barn of a neighbouring farm, where many of the books had got damp and grown mould, though our other possessions were safe. It was by now clear to Louis and me that our own future lay entirely in East Africa, and it was therefore necessary to cut this particular link with our past, happy as we had been there. The time was in fact at hand to end our visit to England and get back to Nairobi, where much was waiting to be done.

Our return was not to the house on the edge of the forest at Karen, but to the newly completed Curator's house, standing back from Museum Hill behind the Museum itself. We lived there in fact for the next seven or eight years. The new house was a bungalow: it may have been structurally more sound and more up-to-date than its tumbledown predecessor, but we felt cramped in it from the start. It had small rooms, and far too many of the demerits that attend suburban bungalows the world over. Even worse, the ventilation was very poor, and with no verandah as a protection against the sun it could get like an oven inside. The accommodation was inadequate, too. Our family filled all the bedrooms, leaving us without a guest room unless the children doubled up, and that led to problems. This was particularly awkward on one occasion when a young couple with two young children were forced to take refuge with us and all four sleep in one room. The reason for this seeking asylum now seems quite beyond comprehension but was symptomatic of the attitude then prevalent towards socializing between the different races and especially towards mixed marriages. The young couple whom we had to squeeze into one room with their two children were a case in point: a young Asian married to an English girl, both charming, highly intelligent and well-educated people who had been at university together in England. He belonged to a prominent Nairobi Asian family who were so outraged at his marriage that one or other of them had attempted to dispose of his English wife by arsenic poisoning. Admittedly, this was an extreme case of the racial prejudice that then existed, but it was generally prevalent to an extent hard to believe by the standards of 1983.

Our chief preoccupation on getting back to Nairobi in 1946 was with the organization of the First Pan-African Congress of Prehistory and Palaeontology. This was very much Louis's brainchild, although there was general agreement at the end of the war that African prehistoric archaeology had come of age and that a meeting of all those interested was highly desirable. Louis threw all his immense energy into getting official agreement and support for the holding of the Congress in Nairobi, and into obtaining promises from leading prehistorians to attend and give papers. This stage of the planning he achieved before and during our visit to England, by correspondence and by going to see people: in England he secured the participation of, among others, Wilfred Le Gros Clark, the leading expert in primatology and human palaeontology, and he went to Paris to enlist Abbé Henri Breuil, generally regarded as the world's foremost prehistorian, not merely as a participant at the Congress but as its official President. Numerous other distinguished prehistorians and palaeontologists gladly agreed to come: Raymond Dart, Robert Broom, Alex du Toit, John Robinson, John Goodwin and Peter van Riet Lowe among the South Africans; Frederick Zeuner, Kenneth Oakley, John Waechter and Dorothea Bate among those from England; Camille Arambourg from France, Wendell Phillips from the United States, and many others. Desmond Clark would be there of course, and Bernard Fagg.

With all this enthusiasm, and with financial aid promised by the governments of several of the countries sending delegates, and with the official support of the Governor of Kenya, Sir Philip Mitchell, and his Chief Secretary, Sir Gilbert Rennie, there was no doubt that the Congress would take place. What we had to do in the remainder of 1946 was to make all the practical arrangements – a huge task, for which little enough time remained since the Congress was to be held in January of 1947. There were to be excursions to many of our chief sites, with some preparation required at several to make them fit to be visited, and accommodation, meals and transport to be arranged for these trips into remote country. Somewhere suitable had to be found for the main Congress sessions to be held, and the whole programme of contributions had to be planned. There was to be the official opening of the Olorgesailie Site Museum: special exhibitions were also to be arranged in the Coryndon Museum. Apart from that, the arrivals, departures, Nairobi accommodation and special requirements of over 80 delegates had to be efficiently organized. I was deeply involved in all of this. Inspired and driven on by Louis, a small voluntary staff achieved everything in time. I remember we only had a single secretary, Margaret Tait, working in a small office in the Museum and using a portable typewriter that had seen considerably better days. Among our other helpers was Sonia Cole, whom we had come to know because her mother-in-law, Lady Eleanor Cole, owned the land near Elmenteita on which the Kariandusi Acheulian site lay. Louis had first dug there in 1929, and the quantity of artefacts, which included many hand axes of obsidian, was visually spectacular. It was decided to open a new and larger trench at the site specially for the Congress members to visit, so that was something else that had to be fitted in. The trench was so successful in fact that it was later made into another open-air museum and can still be visited today.

The Congress opened on 14 January 1947, by which time, fortunately, everything was ready. All our hard work was well rewarded because it was voted a tremendous success. The official sessions took place in the Nairobi Town Hall. The delegates stayed in hotels, or in the private houses of people who had volunteered to have them as guests and Louis and I invited them to dinner in relays during the week, in the Curator's house at the Museum. For this we had to buy a new and proper dinner service, because in eleven years of marriage this was the first time I had ever had to undertake anything like official entertaining. At the end of the conference I received a special mention in the official speeches of thanks to Louis for organizing it, but what meant even more to me was when Raymond Dart went out of his way to thank me and said that I had 'an exceptional gift for making people feel at home'. This made me very happy; the dinner parties had certainly not been in vain.

At conferences like these it is often the excursions that people remember most vividly, rather than the sessions, and certainly they tend to produce the treasured stories that go the rounds and get handed down. We had various excursions, the first one being the day at Olorgesailie for the official opening there. The outdoor museum impressed everyone, for the Italians who had built it had done an excellent job. The Masai had agreed to cede the few acres of land that contained the Olorgesailie sites in return for a borehole to provide water for their cattle a little distance away: Louis had negotiated this, so that the site museum could be built and opened to the public. On the opening day, Sir Gilbert Rennie performed the ceremony and Breuil almost lost his trousers when his braces broke as he rose to make a Presidential reply. In spite of his formidable reputation, I had marked him down mentally as pompous and self-opinionated, especially on this occasion. My opinion was evidently shared by others because he was known to many of his colleagues as 'the Pope of Prehistory'.

There was another excursion, involving one night away, that went north up the Rift Valley as far as Nakuru, where I was able to show the Congress Hyrax Hill. It included visits to several other places, including Louis's favourite site of Gamble's Cave and our new Kariandusi trench. But the long trip to Ngorongoro, Olduvai and the rock paintings at Kisese was more memorable, and more adventurous, because it involved several days and nights. This was a genuine safari, and Louis had given the organization of it to Mr and Mrs Howard Williams, who had experience as tour operators. Olduvai was a highlight of the entire Congress for everyone who came: accommodation overnight was at Ngorongoro, and the vehicles went down to the Gorge next morning with a picnic lunch for everyone. It was hot enough, after visits to the main exposures, for many of the delegates to think a bathe would be nice, for there were reasonable pools of not-too-stagnant water in the seasonal river. 'Men's' and 'Ladies'' pools were hastily designated, discreetly out of sight of each other since nobody had a swimming costume. Sonia Cole, Kay Attwood (another of our team of volunteer helpers) and I availed ourselves of the ladies' pool and were amused if slightly embarrassed to find that part of the French delegation preferred to watch us, unobserved as they thought, rather than to bathe themselves. Those who were new to African safaris had a chance to experience the atmosphere when some rhinos wandered into the expedition's food store at Ngorongoro and ate all the pineapples and most of the vegetables.

Kisese and the rock paintings were the next stop, and there the supplies of vegetables could be partly replenished, but it turned out that insufficient meat had been brought. Numbers of chickens were slaughtered for us by the local people, who had prepared a camp for the visitors and also cut paths to the sites. Those chickens were the scrawniest and toughest of their kind I have ever tried to eat, and there were even a few complaints. However, everyone was fascinated and deeply impressed by the rock paintings; Breuil, predictably, to the point of great pontification. The camp at Kisese was a great success, apart from the chickens and the fact that those who put up the camp thought one earth closet (or *choo* in the local language) would be sufficient for the entire party: I think there were well over 50 of us!

The return journey to Nairobi was enlivened by a flash flood, which was sweeping across the road. Almost everyone had to get out of the vehicles and wade through, led by Robert Broom. He was over 80 and held in great esteem and affection by everyone at the Congress. Throughout the excursion he insisted on wearing a formal suit, and a stiff-collared shirt with a bow tie. He got to all the sites with ease and it was characteristic that he should be first into the water on this occasion, pausing merely to roll his tidy trousers up above the knee.

While we were away on the excursion, Mary Fagg's baby was born in Nairobi; a daughter, Monica. This was very much a Congress event, and at Bernard's particular request and to general delight Abbé Breuil was prevailed upon to christen her and Mary asked me to be a godmother.

A few delegates stayed on for a while after the end of the Congress to make further visits, privately arranged. Louis and I took a small party to Rusinga to see something of the Miocene fossil sites, a trip on which Kenneth Oakley, Dorothea Bate and John Waechter came. It would have been an arduous undertaking even under ordinary circumstances for the elderly Miss Bate, who had been born well back in the reign of Queen Victoria and whose high moral principles were appropriate to that period. But the circumstances soon became far from ordinary. At least Miss Bate did not have to travel on a dhow such as we had in 1942, but that seemed less of an advantage when the motor launch lent by the Fisheries Authority to take us from the mainland to Rusinga was put gently but firmly onto a submerged rock just off the island by an inexperienced helmsman and stuck fast. Many of the islanders, who were Luo, swam or waded out to help us. Some were old friends of ours, but all were undeniably completely naked, and Miss Bate had to cover her eyes. Worse was to come, for the boat in its laden state could not be lifted off the rocks and we were faced with wading ashore or being carried on the shoulders of the cheerful and still naked Luo men. Miss Bate was not prepared to wade.... It was nightfall when we were all safely ashore, and there remained a walk of seven miles across first swampy and then rugged terrain to our camp. Kenneth Oakley, who had kept a reasonably stiff upper lip while being shipwrecked, was very perturbed by the idea of walking across a bit of wild Africa in the dark. He clearly regarded it as far more dangerous even than those local mushrooms on the dig at Jaywick in 1934, though we assured him that in the thickly populated Rusinga Island there were no particular perils. Miss Bate, freed from the embarrassment of the naked Luo, perked up and made light of the long walk. We had only one lantern, and it was carried next to her so that she could see her way. Somehow, Kenneth kept popping up between her and the light, where he felt a bit safer. We reached camp at last, and next day we showed our visitors the Miocene fossil beds. John Waechter, who always loved boats and water and swimming, probably thought the trip particularly enjoyable.

We had one other trip in 1947 which arose out of the Pan-African Congress, though it was not in any way part of it. One of the delegates at the Congress was a Belgian geologist, Dr J. Janmart, who worked with a diamond company based in Angola. The company had generously made a donation towards the Congress running expenses. He already knew enough about stone implements to have collected examples, and at the Congress he learned much more. Realizing that at different periods there were different types of stone implements, he recalled that some of the alluvial deposits in Angola which were dug for diamonds also contained tools of the kind we found in Kenya. He therefore approached Louis and me: would we not like to visit Angola, expenses paid, and make a study of them? We were quite ready for a brief interesting holiday after the hard work of the conference, so we agreed. Janmart had in mind for us to make one of the oddest uses of typology I have ever encountered. There were two series of deposits, one good for diamonds and one poor, though they looked superficially the same. Since they had originally been laid down at different periods, they contained stone tools of rather different types. He wanted us to find and classify them and thus identify for the mining company the good and bad places to open their quarries! In a general way, our efforts were quite successful, and the company was well satisfied. We also produced a report on the Pleistocene geology and Stone Age material of Northeast Angola, which was published in 1949. One other quite different thing came out of this visit: we found that there was in Angola a lively and unrecorded local tradition of string figures, something for which Louis was constantly on the lookout. We learned many new ones from the local people and taught them some of ours; it amazed them that we, as Europeans, should know about string figures and be interested in them. We published a joint paper in 1949 on the Angolan string figures as a result of our visit: it proved very popular and was recently reprinted by the L.S.B. Leakey Foundation.

There was something else of a more enduring nature that came out of the success of the first Pan-African Congress, and that was the setting up of the British-Kenya Miocene Expedition. I have mentioned twice the Miocene sites of West Kenya, of which Rusinga Island was one. By the time of the Congress, very large numbers of finely preserved fossils had been collected, pride of place going to the fossil ape material belonging to the various species of the genus *Proconsul*, but there were also fossil remains of mammals, reptiles, fish and molluscs of many kinds. A special exhibition had been arranged at the Museum, and various important papers given. The impact was tremendous and Professor Wilfred Le Gros Clark was as impressed as anyone. With Louis's enthusiasm and insistence, and Le Gros Clark's eminence and authority brought to bear upon them, the Royal Society in London agreed to provide the bulk of the funding to start an altogether more formal and properly organized project to continue the research. The British-Kenya Miocene Expedition accordingly came into being only a few months after the Congress had ended. Although the Royal Society's support only envisaged work in 1947–48, the whole project was able to thrive on its own success in the field and therefore to keep going for many years. Indeed, research that relates to it is still going on in West Kenya today.

Louis and I were directly involved with the Expedition from 1947 until the middle 1950s, and Louis continued his work on the Miocene material long after that. We always took the children with us when we went out to the sites, which was at least once a year and usually more often, so the whole thing was quite a family affair from our point of view; but since the Expedition had a budget of its own, various specialists in geology and palaeontology would join us in each field season. Throughout this period we were always short of money. Some people might say instead that we were always trying to do far too many things with the limited amount of money we had at our disposal. The great success of the Congress had brought Louis and me, and our various East African discoveries, to the attention of far more colleagues than ever before, and if this did not necessarily bring in money, it brought a useful degree of recognition. The invitation to Angola was a small example, and the birth of the British-Kenya Miocene Expedition a more important one. If one is trying to get important fieldwork done and money is short, recognition and practical success are the best foundations on which to build, and of that art Louis was always a supreme master.

The Pan-African Congress had been very important to us, and it was equally important that the work on the Miocene sites should be a success. I would never claim that the Miocene, then or now, was one of my major interests, but as it turned out I had more than a mere supporting role to play. As for the fossils themselves, many seemed to me merely boring and repetitive while others were among the most exciting things I have ever seen come out of the ground. They will therefore begin the next section of the story. Awaiting me in the Miocene deposits on Rusinga Island, where it had lain for about 18 million years, was one of the most spectacular discoveries of my entire life.

ABOVE: Resting at one of the rock shelters along the Bubu River in 1951.
BELOW: 'The bathers', one of the most lively and delightful of the rock paintings we found at Kolo, just north of Kondoa. The tallest figure, fifth from the left, is about 12 inches tall.

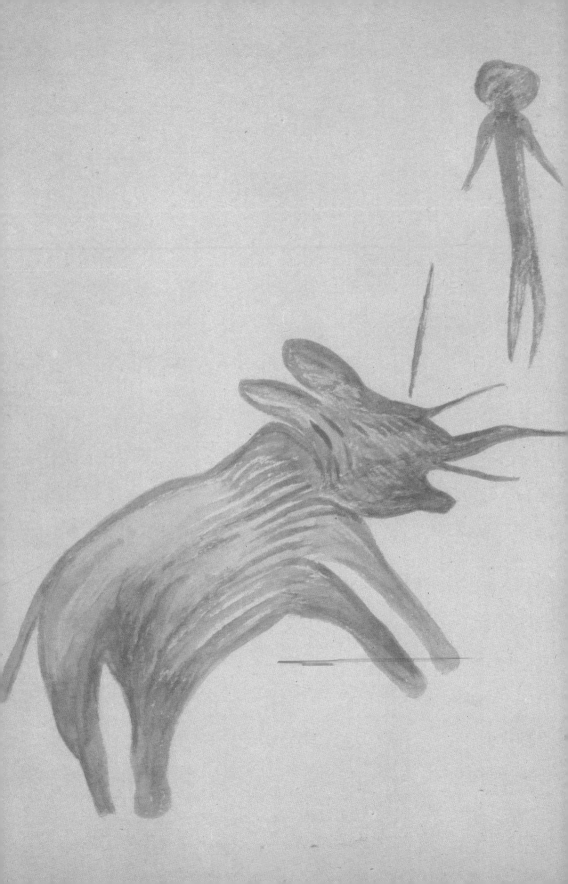

LEFT: 'Hunter spearing an elephant', a scene that vividly captures the animal's rage as it rears up, trumpeting at its attacker.
RIGHT: 'The pipe player.' This elegant, 34-inch-high figure is playing a musical instrument. The dashed lines issuing from the end of the pipe were often used to depict music.
BELOW: 'Hartebeest frieze', one of the most pleasing of all the rock paintings in the Kondoa area. The animals are shown grazing, feeding and ruminating.

ABOVE: Looking across the rim of Olduvai Gorge to the distant backdrop of Lemagrut.

LEFT: Heslon Mukiri, our companion on countless digs, excavating a *Deinotherium* tooth at Olduvai.

RIGHT: Louis and me showing a group of visiting scientists round Olduvai Gorge in 1961. We are gathered round the partly excavated remains of a *Deinotherium* – an extinct relative of the elephants.

LEFT: My assistant, Mike Tippett, tending a Masai woman and her child during the daily clinic at Olduvai camp.

BELOW: Evenings were usually spent hard at work on documenting, cleaning and piecing together fossil finds. Here, Mike Tippett works on the lower jaw of a fossil rhino, while Margaret Cropper and I work on other fossils.

RIGHT: A convivial meal at Olduvai in the 1960s. On my right is Dr Melville Grosvenor, President of the National Geographic Society; his wife Ann is sitting on my left.

BELOW RIGHT: A plinth and marble slab now mark the spot where 'Zinj' was found. This photograph shows me at the site holding a cast of the skull.

Louis and me at work on the *Homo habilis* site in Olduvai Gorge. Working down through the strata required hours of meticulous work, and sunshades were frequently used to reduce glare.

9
From *Proconsul* to 'Zinj'

WHAT WITH THE TALE of the becalmed dhow in 1942, followed by the launch aground on the rocks in 1947, I have probably given the impression that getting from the mainland to Rusinga Island was always fraught with hazards. In fact most of our crossings were relatively uneventful. Once we had reasonable financial support we could make better arrangements, and for the 1947 season we hired our own launch, the *Maji Moto* (Swahili for 'hot water'), and we had money to employ a labour force. After that, things got even better, thanks to the magnificent generosity of Charles Boise. He was a businessman living in England, though of American birth, and he had a particular interest in prehistory and palaeontology. He also loved Africa, where he had once worked, and had personally experienced the kind of expeditions in remote places with which Louis and I were concerned. The 1947 season produced some good finds: several more jaw fragments from fossil apes and an almost complete skeleton of a new species of rhinoceros, among other things. Louis, for whom publicity was always a means towards the end of pursuing further research, wrote a letter to the London *Times* describing the finds, and it was printed. Charles Boise, of whose existence we did not even know, saw it and, admiring this splendid example of British research in Africa, sent Louis a cheque for £1,000 towards the cost of further work. He later added a second gift of the same amount, when he heard via Louis that an American expedition with impressive financial resources and led by Wendell Phillips, was seeking to move in on the West Kenya Miocene deposits.

A thousand pounds, let alone two thousand, was a very large sum of money in the late 1940s, and Louis was able to spend Charles Boise's first gift, with the donor's approval, on a specially fitted Commer truck, equipped with two bunks, and cupboards, which we used for many years and later took on expeditions to Olduvai. Now we could get from Nairobi to Kisumu in comfort, and, using our new mobile home, we could visit other of the important Miocene fossil localities on the mainland, some of which, like Karungu, were some way along the southern side of the

Kavirondo Gulf. Although during the several years of the Miocene Expedition Rusinga produced our best finds, we worked at many other places, including two other islands, Maboko, just off the north shore of the Kavirondo Gulf, and Mfangano, some miles out into the Lake beyond Rusinga. If I remembered Karungu for no other reason, I should still remember it for the *choo* – the earth closet in its own hut, in the District Commissioner's camp which we sometimes used. It provided what zoologists would call a favourable microenvironment for a varied fauna. This included bats and many insects, but more remarkable were the large soliflugids, spider-like creatures with huge jaws who scuttle around at unbelievable speed, waving their long, hairy forelegs in a most aggressive manner. Sonia Cole, who was also impressed by them when she was with us at Karungu on one of our trips, records that they ran about the floor and that their waving forelegs were extremely ticklish. This, while true, tells only part of the story: they also lived *in* the closet itself, under the seat, and what they tickled was the only part of one's anatomy they could reach from there.

Though now, with the lorry, we were well equipped for the overland part of our journey, in 1948 we still had to rely on the Fisheries launch, which dropped us and our equipment on Rusinga Island when we went there in late September, with an arrangement to collect us again on a set date some weeks later. In that year we camped on the west side of the island, at Kathwanga, where we excavated some trenches and also explored exposures of the sediments. On the afternoon of 2 October, Louis had found a worthwhile specimen of some extinct form of crocodile and settled down to excavate it. I have never cared in the least for crocodiles, living or fossil – so I continued to explore the eroded surfaces not far away. New species of vertebrates were all very well, but the real prizes among all these Miocene creatures, so far as I could see, were the fossil apes, among which we might hope to find some evidence of man's own line of evolution.

I had not long left Louis when I saw some interesting-looking bone fragments lying on the sloping surface and, letting my eyes travel upwards, I saw a tooth in the section. It had a hominoid look. Could it be...? A few moments later I was shouting for Louis as loud as I could and he was coming, running. Very gently we brushed the sediments away from around the tooth. It was true: not only was it a *Proconsul* tooth, but it was in place in a jaw, and although the specimen was undoubtedly warped and in many fragments, it was clear that a considerable part of the facial area and rather more than half the skull were present. This was a wildly exciting find which would delight human palaeontologists all over the world, for the size and shape of a hominid skull of this age, so vital to evolutionary studies, could hitherto only be guessed at. Ours were the first eyes ever to see a *Proconsul* face, or, to be strictly accurate, the bony structure that had supported it.

It took several days of anxious excavation and minutely careful sieving to extract from the deposit every scrap of bone that belonged to our find, and we entrusted the task to Heslon Mukiri. Erosion had destroyed or removed some parts for ever: the whole of the occipital area seemed to be missing, for example; but on the other hand the upper and lower jaws were complete, and we had all the teeth. The find was remarkable in its own right, but it was to have an even more extraordinary sequel. More than 20 years later, Martin Pickford, an old school friend of Richard's and by then himself a palaeontologist, discovered a long-ignored museum collection labelled from the same Rusinga site but dated 1947. At first sight the collection seemed to consist entirely of fragments of tortoise scutes – the small bony plates beneath the shell. Pickford's keen eye recognized among them a number of hominoid skull fragments. Almost unbelievably they proved to be missing pieces of our 1948 *Proconsul* skull!

Back at the camp in 1948, working for long hours, I set myself to fit together the 30 or more separate pieces of the skull. Once I dropped a tiny piece into the dust on the tent floor – only a crumb of bone, but a vital link in joining two larger pieces. It took ages to find, but we got it. At last the task was done, but we had to wait for the return of the Fisheries launch before we could get the find back to where we could reveal it to the world. We decided there and then that it should go as soon as possible to England, to the laboratory in Oxford of Wilfred Le Gros Clark, at that time the leading authority on primate evolution and the person to whom we chiefly owed the setting up of the Miocene Research Expedition.

When the magnitude of our discovery had sunk in, back in our camp at Kathwanga, Louis and I wanted to celebrate. We were exhilarated and also utterly content with each other and we thought that quite the best celebration would be to have another baby. Jonathan was now exactly eight and Richard approaching four. Even if *Proconsul* is perhaps not a direct human ancestor, maybe our personal tribute was not wholly inappropriate. In any case, that night we cast aside care and that is how Philip Leakey, now a member of the Kenya parliament and an Assistant Minister in the Government, came to join our family the following 21 June. But the chain does not end there. Thirty years later, Philip was to donate one of his kidneys to save the life of his brother Richard. So, without being too fanciful, one can say that Philip owes his life, and Richard his 'second life', to *Proconsul*, human ancestor or not.

When we did eventually get back to Nairobi in mid-October, Louis cabled the news of our find to Le Gros Clark and set about arranging for me to fly to England, taking the *Proconsul* skull. He generously insisted that I should go since it had been my find, although I know he would dearly have liked to go himself. A way of minimizing the cost soon occurred to him. Through the good offices of Sir Malin Sorsbie, the East Africa manager of BOAC (which later became British Airways), the airline offered me a free flight to London and back in return for the very considerable publicity it could get out of carrying *Proconsul*. In due course I set off in an airliner that was a converted RAF York bomber, with the precious skull in a box on my knee. The flight in those days took a long time and involved many stops. When I had to disembark in Cairo the Captain locked the box with *Proconsul* into the cockpit. Otherwise I kept it with me the whole time. One of the landings, I forget which, probably Khartoum or Benghazi, was an extremely bumpy one – the Captain even came through to see if the skull and I had survived it. In the airport buildings at Heathrow I found large numbers of press photographers and interviewers with microphones waiting for me, something to which I was completely unaccustomed. Since everyone's attention was fixed on the skull it was not as much of an ordeal as I at first feared. I then went to Paddington Station, where I caught the train to Oxford. It was quite a relief to pass my precious burden to Le Gros, as he was always called, and watch his delight as he examined it.

My trip bore all sorts of practical fruit. Le Gros very quickly produced an interim report on the *Proconsul* skull and this, with the press coverage, helped persuade the Kenya Government to support the Expedition with grants that continued right through the 1950s. Also, I was able to meet and show the skull personally to our benefactor Charles Boise, who turned out to be a charming man. He was deeply pleased by the great find which his generosity had made possible. His satisfaction took the form of yet another generous cheque in support of our future work. As for the skull itself, after much discussion with Le Gros it was decided that it should be placed on long-term loan in the British Museum of Natural History in Kensington, and a very popular exhibit it proved when it eventually went on public display there in 1949. When this loan to the British Museum was arranged, the Chief Secretary of the Kenya Government wrote to confirm it, stipulating, however, that the loan was temporary and that the skull remained the property of Kenya and could be recalled at any time in the future. There was a sequel to this. When my son Richard became Director of the National Museums of Kenya many years later, he requested the return of the skull now that the National Museum in Nairobi was properly equipped to receive it and house it safely among the many other Kenyan finds of international importance. The British Museum claimed that *Proconsul* had been not a loan but a gift, and they refused to return the skull, which they said they had accessioned. All Richard's vigorous efforts during the 1970s failed to achieve the skull's return. But in 1982 my own secretary, Hazel Potgieter, found in the National Archives a copy of the Chief Secretary's letter of 1948, of which the British Museum had denied all knowledge. When I was in London I had a frosty telephone conversation on the subject with the Keeper of the relevant department. Even then, Kenya had to wait several more months before a meeting of the Trustees of the British Museum took place at which the skull could be 'deaccessioned', something which the Trustees alone had power to do. One might have hoped that a special meeting could have been arranged a little more rapidly. I am delighted to say that the *Proconsul africanus* skull is now safely back in Kenya, where it quite certainly belongs.

When I got back to Nairobi, Louis decided to spend Charles Boise's latest gift on a motor launch of our own for the Miocene Expeditions. After some searching, he found a suitable boat, with twin engines, which we named the *Miocene Lady*. The only trouble was that she was lying at Mombasa and it took a long time to get her to Kisumu and Lake Victoria. So long did the overland rail journey take, in fact, that her timbers shrank in the dry heat and as soon as she was lowered into the water at Kisumu she began to sink. Fortunately she was quickly rescued and, after this inauspicious start, she served us well for many years. Now at least we were self-sufficient for transport on land and lake: there was no longer any problem about getting to Rusinga or Mfangano, and we could now travel along the coast to look for new sites by water rather than on land. We could also return to Kisumu when necessary to collect mail or stores, or if anyone were taken ill.

The *Miocene Lady* needed an experienced skipper, and someone to care for her at Kisumu between our expeditions, and for this Louis recruited the resourceful and charming Hassan Salimu, who soon became almost one of the family on our expeditions to the lake. The boys got on very well with him. On one occasion, Richard, still quite small, and not yet able to swim, fell overboard head first from the *Miocene Lady* and sank instantly. He and Jonathan had been fishing from the boat while Louis and I were resting in the cabin after lunch and Hassan was on shore. We rushed out when we heard the splash, but while we were still wondering what to do Hassan had rowed out in the dinghy and rescued Richard. Had he but known it, he was rescuing a future employer, for when Richard was directing the East Turkana expedition in the 1970s and kept a boat at Koobi Fora to use on the lake, he put Hassan in charge as easily the best person for the job.

Another regular local member of the staff whenever we were on Rusinga was Agustino, the cook. He was from the area and had been lent to us for our stay by the local chief the time we arrived by dhow in 1942. Ever afterwards he always came to join us as soon as we arrived: he was slightly bibulous but a most amusing character and an excellent cook.

We often arranged to be on Rusinga over the Christmas holidays, and the children always had plenty to occupy them. After the earliest years, they required less and less looking after by me, and in any case I feel strongly that children should learn from as early an age as possible to provide their own amusement. In different ways, that had been the up-bringing of both Louis and myself, and neither of us ever regretted it. Philip of course was only a baby during our visit over the 1949 Christmas holidays, but it was not so long before he was keeping his brothers company rather than clinging to me.

Apart from joining us in fossil hunting, the boys would fish, with increasing success as they grew older, and play with the local Rusinga children, who taught them to make ingenious toy boats from rushes, folded and secured with thorns. There was also excellent bathing, if one discounted the fact that the waters of the lake around Rusinga had some crocodiles. Louis had a simple solution for this: when we were all ready to bathe he would fire both barrels of a shotgun into the water, which in his view would secure safety for at least fifteen minutes, because the crocodiles know about guns through having been hunted for their decora-tive skins. Only recently, when we were remembering this, Richard said that we should really have experimented to see whether gunshots could actually be heard under water at all. . . . But we never had any trouble from the crocodiles while swimming.

There were, of course, plenty of alarms, illnesses and minor disasters of the kind one would expect, though I cannot pretend to remember in what order they came. In those days there were no roads on any of the islands, even though they were quite densely populated and we got round on the well-established network of footpaths. Rusinga got its existing roads be-cause of the late Tom Mboya, a brilliant Kenyan politician who sadly was assassinated in 1969: he was born and raised on Rusinga, and when he became Minister of Economic Planning and Development, he did all he could for the island's amenities. On these trips we walked great dis-tances, and on one walk through a swamp on Maboko Island, all of us except Philip were attacked by parasites that give one bilharzia, a nasty lingering disease which used to require long treatment involving doses of antimony, to which I proved to be highly allergic. The parasites enter through the skin and infest the intestines or liver, or any other part of one's interior. Philip escaped because he was still small and was carried on Louis's shoulders. On another occasion, Louis went down with serious gall-bladder trouble, and at the end of our 1952 season I got acute appen-dicitis just after we had docked at Kisumu, and had to be rushed to the hospital. I know it was 1952 because Louis was away acting as interpreter at the trial of Jomo Kenyatta, of which I will say more later. I also know it was shortly before Christmas, because I can recall the sisters in the hospital handing out generous tots of whisky to all the patients. It was generosity touched with a certain self-interest. Very soon afterwards, they all rushed off to a Christmas party, leaving us in an alcoholic haze of well-being.

Though nothing could surpass in importance the skull of *Proconsul*, Rusinga and Mfangano islands produced other remarkable fossils. Perhaps the most extraordinary was the head and neck of a large lizard, with scales, eyes and ears perfectly preserved and the tongue hanging sideways out of its mouth. There were many fossils of large mammals and small rodents, but to me more interesting were the fossil insects, fruits and seeds. The insects included beetles, spiders, ants, grasshoppers and even soft-bodied caterpillars, one still looped like an inch-worm as though it had been in motion when it became fossilized. These insects are now composed of calcite, but the precise method by which they became fossilized – clearly with great rapidity – remains a mystery. Another fascinating discovery that I made was a complete tree ants' nest containing all the categories of ants from eggs to grubs, soldiers and workers that go to make up the population of an ant colony. I believe this is one of the earliest known examples of a social insect community.

Then there were multitudes of fossil seeds and fruits – even squashy fruits belonging to species of the cucumber family. Like so many of our discoveries Louis and I found the fruits and seeds quite by accident. We had spent a hard morning searching the exposures, hoping that we might perhaps find some pieces of the fossil apes. For our mid-morning break we sat down to smoke a cigarette each and suddenly noticed that all around us there were what seemed to be small pebbles, many of identical shape and size. We soon saw that they had recognizable structures faithfully repeated over and over again. There could be no doubt that they were seeds, some of which were reminiscent of their modern counterparts.

It would be totally confusing if I tried to give this account on a year-by-year basis and the only reasonable approach is to take the various subjects one at a time, even if not in strict chronological order. In 1950 we all went to England again on leave for a few months. We were lucky enough to get a free air trip again, for the whole family this time, from BOAC, in return for their taking our photographs for publicity purposes: I need hardly add that it was Louis who made this arrangement. We travelled in a flying-boat that started on Lake Naivasha and eventually got to Southampton with several stops *en route*. It was one of the most comfortable and pleasant air journeys I have ever made.

In England we stayed in a pretty Surrey village called Ewhurst, and during our stay there we became involved in a rather unexpected piece of archaeological fieldwork. A neighbouring landowner, Mr (later Sir) Edward Beddington-Behrens, had been unable to interest British archaeologists in the flints of Mesolithic type that he kept finding on his land, and when he learned who his temporary neighbours were he begged Louis to examine the site. This led to our conducting a proper excavation there and uncovering what we interpreted as a pit-dwelling of Mesolithic age, an extremely rare find in Britain. It was also during our stay at Ewhurst that we met Alex Wenner-Gren, who had set up the Wenner-Gren Foundation for Anthropological Research, based in New York. The Foundation, formerly known by the much more romantic title of the Viking Fund, was to help us the very next year, and that it did so arose out of this chance meeting, which took place at a dinner given by Edward Beddington-Behrens at his home, Abinger Manor, while Alex Wenner-Gren was on a visit to England.

During this leave, Louis and I went to France leaving the two younger boys with my aunts at Ewhurst and taking Jonathan, who we thought old enough at ten to enjoy the trip and to be a sensible travelling companion. The principal purpose of our visit was to join Charles Boise, who was already in France, and take him to see some of the great French archaeological sites, particularly some of the painted caves in the Périgord, for, in addition to his other interests, he was a collector of paintings and was anxious to learn about the remote as well as the more recent history of art. We wanted to give him this guided tour as a thank-you for all his generosity to us over the past three years, and for me it would also be something of a sentimental journey back to places I had visited with my own parents when I was about Jonathan's age. A highlight of our tour of the painted caves was Lascaux, still a relatively new discovery, where Louis arranged, through his contacts among French archaeologists, for us to have a private tour one evening after the cave had been closed to the public for the day. Jonathan was old enough to be deeply impressed by the magnificent paintings there, which have since so often been illustrated in books, yet never in a way that quite captures the impact they make on a visitor to the cave itself. At Pêch Merle we found the Abbé Lemozi in excellent form and not too much changed by the 25 years that had passed since I last saw him, and he was delighted to show us round. We went also to Cap Blanc, Niaux and other famous French sites, before going on into northern Spain to see the great paintings of Altamira, so different in style from those of Lascaux.

Charles Boise was both fascinated and greatly pleased by all of this and before we parted from him it was agreed between the three of us that early the following year, 1951, he should come out to visit us in East Africa, where we would show him Olduvai and also, especially, the Tanzanian rock paintings at Kisese and Cheke, and perhaps some of our

Kenyan archaeological sites too. He also gave us to understand that he would certainly be continuing his financial support of our work.

There was one other very pleasing event during our leave in England. This was the award to Louis of an Honorary Degree by Oxford University, in recognition of his work in East Africa, especially that on the Miocene sites. Wilfred Le Gros Clark had organized the putting forward of Louis's name, and the ceremony coincided with the holding of an international congress of anatomists in Oxford. Just over 30 years later, the University conferred a similar honour on me.

Charles Boise's planned visit to us in East Africa took place early in 1951 and he did indeed get to both the rock paintings and Olduvai. During his stay he indicated to us that his promised continuation of support, now that the Kenyan Government had taken over the financing of the Miocene Research, was to take a most generous form: a substantial payment by covenant for each of the next seven years, particularly for us to do further work at Olduvai. This was wonderful news. It seemed impossible not to make some small practical gesture of thanks to Charles without his immediately putting one deep in his debt again. So many researchers, quite apart from ourselves, have cause to be grateful to him, through the Boise Fund, which he later set up in the care of Oxford University to assist work of many kinds in Africa.

This particular promise of help to us marked something of a turning point in our work at Olduvai, because hitherto we had gone there whenever an opportunity arose and concerned ourselves mainly with exploring the Gorge in general – recording the existence of sites, making a first assessment of them, and endeavouring to establish a first understanding of the overall stratigraphy. With Charles's gift we could begin a more planned and concentrated kind of research to tackle particular problems in much greater detail, and we decided to concentrate on Bed II, where we already knew that several rich sites existed. But before we began, something quite different remained to be done, to which I was particularly looking forward. The Wenner-Gren grant had come through, and I could at last return to make the fuller study and record of the Tanzanian rock paintings that Louis and I had promised ourselves as long ago as 1935.

Those three months at Kondoa-Irangi, July to September of 1951, will always count as one of the highlights of my life and work in East Africa. They have been much in my mind recently, because at last it has been possible to bring together the records we made then into a book, *Africa's Vanishing Art*. In 1951, we had every intention of publishing them forthwith, but our grant was a single one to cover only the fieldwork, and even Louis could not raise the funds to finance what would have been a very expensive volume to produce. From one point of view the delay has been beneficial, because the standards of reproduction of colour plates have improved out of all recognition in the past 30 years. On the other hand, Louis, who loved the paintings almost as much as I did and made my work in 1951 possible, not to mention all the practical help he gave, never lived to see the volume in print. As it was, a selection of the copies of the paintings that I made in 1951 has been displayed in the Museum at Nairobi for many years: to that extent at least they were made available to the general public, and have aroused a lot of interest.

There were many reasons why I so much enjoyed the work on the rock art. The beauty of the paintings themselves was certainly one of the most important, together with the fascination and excitement of disentangling the figures from each other, because often they were superimposed in what would at first sight seem a completely bewildering mass, in which both human and animal forms could vaguely be made out. But when I had extracted, so to speak, each figure or each group of figures making up a scene, it was possible to get a glimpse of the Late Stone Age people themselves, and of incidents in their lives. There were details like clothing, hair styles and the fragile objects that hardly ever survive for the archaeologist – musical instruments, bows and arrows, and body ornaments depicted as they were worn. For the past several years I had been working largely on bones and stones and, for all the dramatic nature of the finds we had made, maybe I needed a change of occupation. No amounts of stone and bone could yield the kinds of information that the paintings gave so freely. Even at Njoro River Cave, where we had found the textiles, the decorated wooden vessel, and the beads, we had been excavating a cemetery, a place of dead people: here were scenes of life of men and women hunting, dancing, singing and playing music. And there was another thing that made the artists into real people having direct continuity with ourselves: they had lived not among extinct species of animals but among the same kinds we see around us today. And they had been acute observers not only of their distinctive features but also of the way they behaved. One painting of two rhinos illustrates both points: not only could we tell at once that they were the white rhino rather than the black, but also that they were clearly engaged in courtship, having reached the stage where the female pursues the male closely at a lumbering gallop. Many other familiar animals were depicted, including elephants and antelopes; zebra and giraffe; lions, ostriches and snakes. Sometimes a particularly striking or characteristic feature of an animal would be deliberately exaggerated by the artist: kudu, for example, were shown with as many as eleven twists to their horns, when in fact they have just three.

Apart from the paintings themselves, there were other things about this expedition that delighted me. The exceptional beauty of the wooded slopes had already greatly impressed me in 1935 and again during the short visit with the Congress excursion in 1947, and this was one of the best times of the year to enjoy it. I had a great sense of happiness and well-being, working on the paintings by myself in that setting while Louis, Giuseppe della Giustina and some of the men prospected on foot for new sites. Who could guess what they would find next? Around me and below were the sounds of the Warangi herds of cattle, sheep and goats, the animals moving at their own lazy pace and the herd-boys playing their pipes to themselves and their animals. All sounds seemed to carry for great distances. The current team of Dalmatians always came with me to where I was working and they too loved the place, but what they liked most about it was the abundance of baboons to chase. In fact, baboons are highly dangerous to dogs on account of their huge canine teeth, which can cause terrible wounds; there were also leopard around, so when the excited barking broke out I had to abandon my work, leap from whatever precariously constructed scaffolding I was standing on, and rush off to the scene, shouting loudly. As it turned out, the dogs invariably emerged from these encounters relatively unscathed.

Apart from the idyllic setting for our work, there was the very real challenge of devising appropriate techniques for the recording of the paintings. Finding sites was never a problem: they were extremely common all over this region and we decided not to expend our time and energies in a superficial study of a very wide area but to set reasonable limits and then try to record everything within them. The best and most important examples I would then trace, aided particularly by Giuseppe della Giustina. At the selected sites we would first make full-scale tracings on sheets of clear cellophane, and then return to camp, where we would transfer them, reduced exactly to half-scale, onto drawing paper tinted grey or buff – white paper proved to have far too much contrast for the finished reproductions, making their colours look completely wrong. With our outlines on the tinted paper we would then go back to the site and make careful copies of the figures themselves, in colour. We used poster paints, which we mixed to reproduce accurately the reds, blacks, yellows, white and oranges which the Late Stone Age artists had made by grinding ochre and other natural substances into powder and mixing them with grease. Later on, when the Museum displays were set up, the drawings were transferred onto moulded surfaces that reproduced the contours of the rock surfaces, thereby giving a much more realistic effect. If you wonder why we did not use photography, in the first place we had no adequate cameras and no money to buy any. But there was another reason: we needed to pick out individual figures from the superimposed masses, working out which belonged with which and in what order the paintings had been done, both to reconstruct specific scenes and also to understand the sequence of changing styles. With that, a camera could not help for it would merely have recorded the whole jumbled mass. Tracing and colouring by hand were in fact the best way to work; often it was necessary to gently wet the surface of the rock to bring out the more obscure and faded paintings.

These methods worked splendidly apart from the one time, which I have described in my book on the rock art, when a particularly violent whirlwind struck the site where we were working and also our camp nearby, where some of our tracings were stored in a tent. We had to watch helplessly while the fruits of several days' work were ripped into pieces and sent spiralling up into a blue African sky to drift down gently over an area of some square miles, so that we had to start all over again.

The expedition to the rock paintings began in early July. For the first few weeks the boys stayed in Nairobi, for by 1951 the two elder ones were attending school. When their term was due to end, Louis went back to Nairobi and brought them down to join us, turning the whole thing into one of those Leakey family working holidays that were such a feature of our life, particularly in the 1950s. Jonathan was ready to take a serious interest in the paintings and searched by himself for new sites, with considerable success. One of his best finds was a painting of what appears to be a gourd full of honey, with bees flying around it. Being just two, Philip was really too small to enjoy the trip as much as his brothers. He would get tired after a certain distance and keep saying 'Poor me, poor me!', which became something of a family catch-phrase at the time. Louis often carried Philip on his shoulders, when he really was tired as opposed to just saying 'poor me', and just as that mode of transport had saved Philip from bilharzia on Maboko Island so here it also helped him when one evening Louis trod firmly on an engorged python which he thought was a log of wood – just the sort of thing people do in books, but this was real. Richard too was involved in various incidents. On one occasion Louis was driving the car across country through long grass and struck a concealed tree stump with a loud bang and a bump. Richard was very startled and concluded we were all now actually dead – it took us some while to convince him that this was not the case. But the best-remembered incident was his firm and decisive action to stop Louis choosing rather too frequently for breakfast a kedgeree mixture of rice, tinned sardines and hard-boiled eggs. Of the four of us only Louis and Jonathan were fond of this dish. Instructed firmly to eat his helping, Richard did so and then deliberately pushed his fingers as far down his throat as he could reach, with predictable results. I think I am right in saying that Louis abandoned that recipe not merely next morning, but for ever.

During these three months in 1951, we camped in several different places as we covered our chosen area. First we were at Kolo, then at Chungai in the old rest-house there, and finally at Kisese, near the rock shelter Kisese II, which was one of our chief sites. From these bases we covered outlying areas – places like the Chora Valley, where there were traces of abandoned settlements. Our staff for the expedition included Heslon Mukiri, a few of our best regular workmen brought from Nairobi, and three or four from the Rusinga project, but we also employed four of the local Warangi people. They became so interested and involved in the work that they agreed to keep an eye on the sites after we had left. Louis found money to pay them for a while, but they continued to look after the sites voluntarily after the money was exhausted. Throughout our stay we received much courtesy and help from the Warangi, who at that time regarded the paintings with reverence, as of great importance, haunted by powerful spirits. For that reason we had to pay for a goat to be sacrificed at the Kolo cave when we first arrived, to propitiate the spirits before we could begin work – and incidentally to provide the elders with a first-rate dinner of roast goat. Even so, there was talk of one particularly fine painted shelter, too sacred for its whereabouts to be revealed to us. I never found out whether the rumour was true or not.

I have set out the archaeological results of our work in my book on the rock paintings and will not cover the same ground again here, beyond saying that we recorded a total of 186 sites, and selected 43 of them as having paintings worth copying; the total of individual figures we traced exceeded 1,600. On the results of all this work we suggested a probable sequence of artistic styles which between them may well span several thousand years. During our stay in 1951 we dug trenches at selected painted rock shelter sites, recovering Late Stone Age material, but obtained no useful evidence to date the paintings themselves. In 1956 Ray Inskeep, now at Oxford University, dug much more extensively at Kisese II and showed that pieces of colouring matter like those used for the paintings were present in the deposit in levels dating back at least 29,000 years, though this does not actually prove that any of the existing rock paintings were necessarily that old. Those that survive today, exposed to the air, are unlikely to be more than a few thousand years old at most.

I had to store away my reproductions of the Tanzanian rock art when it became clear that no money was available to publish them in full. It was my daughter-in-law Meave, Richard's wife, who came across them, almost forgotten, in 1980; and Richard persuaded the Rainbird Publishing Group in London to undertake a fully illustrated book, whose preparation renewed for me the pleasure of that 1951 expedition. While preparing the book, I revisited some of the sites to take photographs, with my friends Alan and Joan Root and Patti Moehlman, and later with John Reader, whose fine photographs appear in the book.

Things were much changed since 1951, though one of our faithful Warangi workmen, Issa, was still there. The area now is much more densely populated and seems to be one place where the Tanzanian Government's policy of *Ujamaa* (bringing scattered populations together into more concentrated and organized communities) has had a beneficial effect for the people concerned. Healthy crops are growing and there are clear signs of prosperity. But with the paintings, all is far from well. Awe and reverence for them has been dissipated and the herd-boys now deface and scratch them merely to amuse themselves. Some of the finest sites are now almost totally destroyed. At a few of the shelters, protective cages of pig-wire were erected by the Tanzanian Antiquities Department, but the doors, their bolts and hinges were soon stolen and the remaining wire merely calls attention to the sites and ruins their setting without offering any protection.

Away from the archaeological front, the 1950s and 1960s were busy and important years for us, with all kinds of new things happening on the domestic scene. They all became possible for one basic reason. In 1952 we moved from our cramped home in the Curator's bungalow to Langata, an outer suburb of Nairobi some twelve miles west of the city centre. Louis bought a five-acre plot, and a house was built for us on it to our own design. The whole family participated in the planning, arguing long and vigorously over the exact sizes and positions of the rooms, and the work was carried out by an Asian builder using local African craftsmen and labourers. Langata today is a busy suburb, but when the new house was built our only neighbours were the British Legion (whose telephone line we shared) and Armand and Michaela Denis, the wildlife photographers.

Our garden, mainly a grassy lawn, sloped down from the front windows, the thick hedge that surrounded it leaving a clear view west to the Ngong Hills, over which the sun set. There was also a broad view of the plains, quite empty of buildings in those days but with plenty of game, including rhinoceros, cheetah and giraffe, to be seen. Game animals came a good deal nearer than that, however. One particular giraffe, known as George, lived permanently at Langata and spent his time wandering about the roads. Lions often came around the house, not least because we kept horses, and the lions would try to get at them. On one occasion Richard, returning home in the evening from a party, found himself confronted by a whole row of lions staring at him through our gate. Another time several lions broke into a place not so far from our house where ducks were kept, and killed no less than 80 of them. In fact, even at the end of the 1960s, and perhaps later still, it was by no means rare for lions to penetrate well into the outskirts of Nairobi proper: there was a famous occasion when they disrupted a Ladies' Golf Championship by taking up residence on the Karen Country Club Golf Course.

I shall not attempt to write in detail about the origins of the Mau Mau or the political significance of this chapter in Kenya's history, though it was of great importance to Louis, who produced two books on the subject, written with deep feeling and urgency, *Mau Mau and the Kikuyu* (1952) and *Defeating Mau Mau* (1954). Louis, it must never be forgotten, thought of himself as a Kikuyu. Mau Mau was the violent side of the Kikuyu people's legitimate desire for independence and of their grievances, mostly real, about the European seizure, domination and exploitation of land that should have been theirs. The movement was also connected with the emergence of African leaders of considerable political skill, ability and knowledge, who were endowed with a fierce determination to free their people. Not all the individuals possessed all of these qualities, but Jomo Kenyatta, the acknowledged leader, certainly did. There were many leaders who were ready and willing to use violent means to free their country from British rule, and to indulge in whatever amount of bloodshed might be necessary to achieve this. Others, however, were moderates, and would have preferred to achieve the same objective by negotiation. As so often happens the aggressive element inevitably imposed its will on the rest, and a violent episode in Kenya's history was the result. Sadly, the vast majority of the victims of the violence were the rural Africans: the number of white civilians killed was minute by comparison – less than 40. If Kenyatta had the status and authority to prevent the growth of Mau Mau at the start, I doubt whether he or anyone else could have controlled the level of violence within the country once it got going. But in any case, in 1952 the British Government in Kenya arrested him and other nationalists whom they regarded as ringleaders, and put them in custody. After that, the terror and the killing could only spread.

It was a very worrying time for all of us, because Louis was necessarily deeply involved, through his unique situation. For the terrorists among the Kikuyu, he was a prime target – the supreme example of a prominent European working against Mau Mau in spite of his own Kikuyu connections, which went back also to the previous generation in Canon Harry Leakey and his wife. For the Kenya Government of the day, he was one of the few people with the local knowledge and understanding of the Kikuyu, plus fluency in their language, who could perhaps combat the trouble from inside. Therefore they set him to do much the same kind of work as he had done in the war: broadcasting propaganda to the loyalists and gathering intelligence about Mau Mau groups and their leaders. And, if all that were not enough, he had to spend several months from the end of October 1952 acting as the official interpreter at the Kenyatta trial, a capacity in which he was seen to be of far more use to the prosecution than the defence.

During this unhappy time Louis had a constant bodyguard and wore a revolver at all times. Everyone, including myself, had to carry arms, and I had a .22 pistol on my belt in the evenings and under my pillow at night. The wearing of a revolver or pistol was referred to as 'European national dress'. We had guards at our new home in Langata by day and by night. I am not sure how effective I should have been with my pistol if I had ever had to use it in an emergency: perhaps not too bad, judging by my success in target practice using empty tins bobbing up and down in the water off Rusinga Island. We could still get away to our work there from time to time, and a blessed relief it was to escape to a part of Kenya where there was no violence: life on Rusinga continued unchanged. The nearest I ever came to using my pistol in Nairobi was one evening while we were still at the old house, when I nearly shot our gardener while taking the dogs for their nightly walk: I just realized in time who he was. Everyone was very jumpy indeed after dark in those years, and a few people actually did shoot members of their own domestic staff by mistake.

It was entirely because of the violence of the time that the basic plan of our new house was designed and still exists today: a hollow square, with central patio. The point of this was that the dogs should be able to go out at night without leaving the building. All the windows on the outside were protected with heavy wire mesh. Precautions of these kinds were only too necessary. We all survived, but others were less lucky. Perhaps partly because they could not get Louis, the Mau Mau selected his elderly cousin, Gray Leakey, who farmed at Nyeri near Mount Kenya, for a particularly brutal ritual murder: he was buried alive, having first been made to watch while his wife was strangled. His step-daughter only just managed to escape and later to raise the alarm. Gray Leakey had trusted his Kikuyu staff and had refused to carry arms or keep his house locked and barred. The worst thing that happened directly to us was an attempt to sabotage the Chevrolet car we had at that time by loosening a U-bolt. In fact it was I who was driving when we discovered it, on a journey from Nairobi to Kisumu. If the bolt had come adrift at speed, the results would certainly have been disastrous.

After four tense and frightening years the troubles gradually died away. Louis had always maintained that they would only come to an end when Jomo Kenyatta was freed from imprisonment, and he was right, though Kenyatta served his full seven-year sentence. Louis had known him long before the start of the emergency; indeed, I remember we had both once met him in 1934 during one of our surreptitious lunches together in Bloomsbury, when Kenyatta was studying at the London School of Economics. After his release Kenyatta did indeed lead Kenya to *Uhuru*, full independence as an African state, which was finally granted in December 1963, and he became Prime Minister. Louis was distinctly nervous about meeting him again, because his own part in the trial had certainly helped to secure a conviction and he had not spoken to Kenyatta since. It was Malcolm MacDonald, in his capacity as Governor-General, who brought the two together again, and at once Kenyatta went out of his way to be friendly to Louis and thereafter remained an admirer of his work. Later, Kenyatta specially arranged for Louis to meet Emperor Haile Selassie of Ethiopia, when he made a State Visit to Kenya. As a result of the Emperor's interest in what Louis told him on that occasion about early man in Kenya, the international Omo Research Expedition was born which, in 1967, set out to provide Ethiopia with some early fossil hominids of its own, with Richard leading the Kenyan contingent. And out of that expedition came Richard's discovery of the infinitely more rewarding sites in northern Kenya, on the east side of Lake Turkana, and all that he achieved there in the 1970s.

Our move to Langata, with all its extra space, made possible all sorts of new activities and meant that we could have far more animals, including horses. There were always Dalmatians, and in the 1950s there were more than ever, because in 1949 Louis and I had founded the Dalmatian Club of East Africa and were now breeding and showing Dalmatians. Before 1949 they could only be entered in the general category of 'Any Variety Non-Sporting' at the dog shows organized by the East Africa Kennel Club. For a long time these shows were held in the open air, at the old Nairobi Race Course, where exhibitors would bring picnic lunches and sit round on the grass trying to keep their dogs clean by making them lie on blankets. Later, the East Africa Kennel Club built its own premises near Jamhuri Park, where the dogs were benched properly in buildings I designed while I was secretary of the East Africa Kennel Club. For several years we were responsible for running the dog shows in Nairobi, and Louis became president of the East Africa Kennel Club in 1959. Several of our dogs won prizes and one of the proudest moments of my life was when Victoria, perhaps our most beautiful Dalmatian of all, was judged Best in Show in 1957.

At a slightly different level in the Dalmatian world I must mention one who was with us both at the old house and at Langata: the unforgettable Bottom Biter. He earned his name by attacking in exactly that manner an intruder he saw trying to break into the Museum. The man's body was well greased, and he escaped. Next morning the police rounded up several likely suspects and a highly specialized identity parade was held. One man did indeed have a recently bitten bottom, and the size of the bite precisely matched Bottom Biter's mouth! The suspect was promptly arrested, and confessed. Bottom Biter was a dog of great character, and on one occasion, after a visit to Olduvai which he enjoyed immensely, he disappeared from our home at Langata. Several days later he was found –

purposefully crossing the Athi Plains, well on his way back to Olduvai.

It was during the 1950s at Langata that the family took to riding with great enthusiasm, though our first purchase was hardly an unqualified success. We bought a dun pony called Shandy for Richard, who ever since his second visit to Cornwall, when he rode for the first time, had been begging for a pony of his own. On his very first ride, when he was not wearing a hard hat, Shandy broke into a gallop and Richard fell off, fracturing his skull and suffering severe concussion. He was ordered complete rest for six weeks afterwards.

We therefore got Susie, a grey mare, who was temperamentally much better suited to Richard, and I took over Shandy myself. For Jonathan, we obtained a large bay gelding called Smash, who came from Kajiado on the Athi Plains. We heard that the District Commissioner there was being transferred and was looking for a good home for Smash as his new posting was somewhere quite unsuitable for horses. He sent his own syce over to bring Smash to Langata, and we at once decided to have him. Philip soon became just as keen as his brothers on riding and his pony was a bay called Storm. The head syce, in charge of our stables, was Mutevu, an old-style member of the Wakamba tribe who had followed his people's custom of filing his teeth so that they looked like pointed sharks' teeth. It was through Mutevu that I first employed Wakamba staff to assist my excavations at Olduvai, since at my request he chose and recruited sixteen helpers when we began to dig the *Zinjanthropus* site in 1960. They were so good that I have employed Wakamba workmen ever since.

There was excellent riding country round Langata in those days, and as other families moved into the area there were more and more children with ponies. We would meet groups of them, or often little girls alone, riding rather aimlessly round the roads. It seemed to me that it would be a good idea for us to get together so that we could all ride on the beautiful open country beyond the Mbagathi River, where the children clearly could not go without an escorting adult, a role I was quite prepared to fulfil. I had heard of Pony Clubs but never belonged to one myself owing to my childhood being spent mostly out of England. Louis, as always, fully supported my idea and we made inquiries as to how we should set about forming a Pony Club at Langata. The response was not encouraging. At the time we already held gatherings of children with their ponies on Sunday mornings, either to ride on the plains, practise jumping or otherwise amuse ourselves. At our request we were visited by several knowledgeable horsey ladies who informed us that the ponies were dirty, the children improperly dressed, and our activities totally unacceptable by Pony Club standards! This was rather a blow, but the advantage of complying with the rules, which would enable the children to compete at Pony Club events, seemed to outweigh our inclination for independence.

And so the Langata Pony Club was born. It is now the largest and most successful in Kenya, but it could never have got off the ground without the goodwill and hard work of a very large number of Langata residents.

I remember we had a children's drag hunt, which met twice at our house. On one occasion the hounds broke away from the scent and found a lioness instead – I well remember the rage of the Master, Robbie Barcroft, that the scent should have been laid through country where there were likely to be lions. He was so like everyone's image of a peppery MFH that he sometimes seemed almost a caricature of one. A little later on, Jonathan, Richard and I used regularly to follow the Limuru drag hunt. We also did a great deal of riding as a family and had our own sport of chasing jackals with the Dalmatians as our pack. In all of this I greatly enjoyed my own riding on Shandy, even if there was the odd embarrassing moment. Once, when escorting a Pony Club ride, Shandy and I suddenly encountered a large bird-eating spider. It had spun its web across the footpath we were following and was poised in the centre exactly at my eye level. Spiders, even small ones, are repulsive to me and my shriek of horror on this occasion caused Shandy to rear, throw me off and fall over backwards himself. No harm came to either of us, but the incident greatly entertained my following of children.

As for the other animals at Langata, I could fill a whole book with them, but a brief account must suffice here. All three boys attended the Duke of York School in Langata, Jonathan as a boarder and Richard and Philip as day-boys. I don't think any of the three paid serious attention to the classroom work at any stage (though who am I to criticize on this point?). One reason was that their minds were on animals, and the remarkable menagerie that accumulated at our home. This was mainly true of Jonathan and Philip; Richard's mind was usually busy working out plans to ride Susie.

In Philip's case, the main attraction was hyraxes, and the first ones he brought home started a family tradition of having hyraxes at Langata which still continues today. They are attractive house pets, being furry creatures somewhat larger than guinea-pigs: there are tree-hyraxes and two kinds of rock-hyrax. Ours were always free to roam where they wished at Langata, but they were usually to be seen around the house. The rock-hyraxes love warmth, and like to bask in the sun. Our tame ones would also frequently try to get into the bed of any member of the family who they thought worth a try, with a view to sleeping curled round the occupant's neck. Alternatively, they would snuggle up to one of the dogs, who all treated them with great tolerance. Philip caught many tree-hyraxes in the forest near his school, and rock-hyraxes could be found in a rocky gorge not far from our house. Among our earliest pet hyraxes I remember especially Midge and Big Boy and Miss Campbell. Big

Boy and Miss Campbell both liked to chew cigarette stubs and were also particularly fond of a drop of gin, so if guests were being given drinks it was never long before they appeared. Miss Campbell was also fond of early-morning tea, and would follow the tray into our bedroom when it arrived. It was absolutely necessary to pour her some in a saucer, with sugar and milk, because if one didn't she would dance about on the tray and knock everything over.

Hyraxes have very clean habits and they actually prefer to use the lavatory in the same way as their owners; no training was required for this. New visitors to Langata had to be instructed always to leave the lavatory door open at night for the hyraxes. The Chairman of the Board of Trustees of the Museum at the time of our move to Langata was Sir Ferdinand Cavendish-Bentinck, later Lord Portland, and he also had hyraxes in his house. His secretary had special instructions to visit his house at times when he and his wife were away and flush the loo on their behalf. Very rarely did this useful detail of hyrax behaviour cause us any problems, but I did come across recently a letter which I wrote to Louis in March 1965, which contains the following passage:

> 'The reason why the bath water got so peculiar is because the hyraxes got a bit mixed up in the plumbing. They have been using both the storage tanks as *choos*.'

The mention of Sir Ferdinand Cavendish-Bentinck will serve neatly to introduce another favourite pet of ours at Langata, an African eagle owl who was called Ferdy after him, although in fact she was a female. The reason for this choice of name dated back to when Philip was quite small and was playing one day with his toy cars under a showcase in the Museum near where I happened to be working. Sir Ferdinand, who was rather inclined not to look where he was going, accidentally kicked Philip, who was most indignant, and later told Louis that he had been kicked 'by a man with six beards' – Sir Ferdinand had bushy eyebrows and also some surplus hair around the ears and nostrils. It was later on that Jonathan found the owl, fallen from a nest in an abandoned stable near our house and half-drowned after a heavy storm of rain; but the Cavendish-Bentinck story had not been forgotten in the family, and the typical tufted ears of the little eagle owl decided at once what its name should be. Ferdy became a delightful and entertaining bird, making herself a nest at the top of a cupboard from torn-up paper. She was terrified of other owls, and clearly thought herself one of us. Early each morning she would fly in with food caught specially for Philip, whom she regarded as the baby of the family and whom it was clearly her duty to feed: she brought mice, lizards and even small snakes, all of which Philip had to pretend to swallow, for the sake of peace. When I left Langata and moved to Olduvai, Ferdy took up residence with one of our neighbours, who enjoyed her company as much as we had.

With Jonathan, snakes were the big attraction, from a very early age; and what began as a hobby turned into a profession. On one of our leave visits to England in the 1950s, Jonathan brought his pet house-snake, which travelled in a bag tucked inside his shirt. It was one of those long journeys by flying-boat, and at Khartoum the snake was taken to the gents' and given a bath to refresh it. In London it was exercised in Kensington Gardens. That time we all went on a camping trip to France, and the snake finally escaped somewhere near Bayonne. At Langata, Jonathan had his own snake enclosure, which he kept well supplied. When I went to visit him at school on Sundays there was usually a bag containing at least one snake for me to take home and release to join the rest. Once, when the bag was not properly done up, the snake escaped into the car, wriggling around by my feet before escaping through a hole in the floor. Jonathan had a pet python for a long while, and he had also been given a present by a friend in America of several rattlesnakes, who lived in a cage near the telephone and invariably rattled in alarm whenever the telephone rang. Not infrequently there were telephone calls from fortunately tolerant neighbours to say that the python had escaped: 'Oh, Mrs Leakey, that big snake of yours is on my doorstep again – could you possibly come round and collect it?' It was something of a relief when, soon after leaving school, Jonathan founded and stocked the Nairobi snake-park, which is still a big tourist attraction, situated in the gardens near the Museum.

The list of creatures already given would be more than enough for most households, but we had many more, even if not all at once. There were the two duikers (small antelopes), Dicky and Dora, who were with us for many years. Dora kept her babies under our bed and came into the bedroom twice daily, no more, to suckle them. For a while there was an eland calf, which Richard found abandoned by its mother on the plains, and as company for it we had an orphan wildebeest calf that we brought back from one of the Olduvai visits. When these grew too large to keep, David Roberts took them to join his herd of tame eland at Lake Baringo: he was Jonathan's neighbour when Jonathan went to live there. We also looked after a baby baboon – not an easy character to cope with, and he too could not be kept when he grew up. Longer-term residents were the two genet kittens, Timmy and Tommy. Genets look very cat-like, with their spotted flanks and striped tails, though they are not really cat family at all. Timmy and Tommy were hand-reared by us and became very tame; they would sit on our laps and purr, and they got on very well with the dogs. They also relied on us for their food, but since genets are nocturnal creatures it was usually at about 2 am that they wanted to be fed: they would jump onto Louis and wake him by pounding on his chest until he got up. Later, I too had genets at the Olduvai camp. They came to be fed but never became really tame.

In fact we had a houseful of various animals, all of whom got on remarkably well together and gave Louis and I and the children infinite pleasure. I mentioned in an earlier chapter that my aunt Toudy came out to Kenya when in her seventies, and spent the last year of her life with us. She saw nothing odd at all about the collection of animals she found on her arrival at Langata. On the contrary, she took as much pleasure in them as we did and although she was a very particular person, even the raw minced rats kept in the fridge for the owl did not horrify her. She and her sisters had had a tame fox during their childhood in Italy and she had always remembered it with pleasure. So when a bat-eared fox was brought in to us in need of care, Toudy at once adopted it and she further insisted that another be found to keep it company. The foxes would often wander off and lie up during the daytime in holes on neighbours' land; many evenings were spent by the entire household locating them and shepherding them back to sleep in Toudy's room.

It was about this time that I had the strange experience, to which I referred when describing our dig at the Njoro River Cave. We were all living at Langata at the time and one morning I was driving, with Philip beside me, along a stretch of road where the side-road from Langata meets the main road to Nairobi in a T-junction. As we approached the junction I saw an old-fashioned car – a Model A Ford or something similar – travelling towards Nairobi, apparently driverless. Philip, too, saw the vehicle, and was as astonished as I was. We later mentioned the incident to friends in Langata and learned that we were not the only people to have seen an ancient and driverless car on that stretch of road. To this day no one has been able to explain that strange phenomenon.

To return to professional matters: two major discoveries marked turning points in my life, the finding of *Proconsul* in 1948, and the finding of Zinj in 1959, with which I will end this chapter. Ever since Louis and I came out to East Africa in 1937, we had never let slip any opportunity of a visit to Olduvai Gorge, where such an outstanding wealth of early archaeological material was known to exist. There were sites and whole stretches of the Gorge that remained just as we had observed them on the 1935 visit, waiting until we had time and resources to explore them properly. The generosity of Charles Boise in 1951 had made a certain amount of more systematic work possible, including excavations at two sites in particular, BK and SHK, both in Bed II, but at the time we could only spend short seasons with small teams of helpers, working intensively until the money ran out.

During the 1950s, we camped in tents under the thorn trees down in the Side Gorge, not too far from the sites where we were working. This was a much handier location than our old camp, but we still had to travel nearly 30 miles whenever we needed to replenish our supplies of water. Heslon Mukiri directed the digging staff and our regular helpers included Jonathan, with a school friend, Nick Pickford; Richard, with Ian McRae, a Pony Club friend, and Jane Goodall and Gillian Trace, who were volunteers and also helped at the Museum. On one of our expeditions Louis got bad heat-stroke one afternoon and was really very ill indeed with it. His hair turned from brown to white, literally overnight, something I had heard was possible but never expected to witness. He aged considerably in appearance as a result.

Apart from the money given regularly by Charles Boise, Louis occasionally managed to get special grants to purchase equipment, notably from the Wilkie Brothers Foundation and from Wenner-Gren, but if we were ever to make real progress, funding of a quite different order of magnitude would need to be forthcoming, and it was hard to see where that might be found, unless perhaps we could make some really dramatic find that would capture the public imagination. Yet even hominid remains eluded us almost entirely, for all that the deposits in which we were working preserved animal bones extremely well, and we were finding living-floors that were undisturbed, containing huge numbers of artefacts.

In 1951 Louis's book *Olduvai Gorge* had at last appeared, having been delayed many years awaiting a promised study of the faunal remains which Louis had left with A. T. Hopwood at the British Museum of Natural History. Before the book had long been in print our work at the Gorge had put it seriously out of date. One thing that we had shown was that Hopwood's conclusions were quite wrong and the lower beds at Olduvai were far older than he had allowed – Lower Pleistocene rather than Middle: Louis's own guess in 1935 had been right after all. In the 1951 book Louis had pointed out that some of the human industries at Olduvai were too early and too primitive to include hand axes, and belonged to a tradition that he called Oldowan, which at that time was not known to exist elsewhere. Sometimes we got remarkable insights into the life and abilities of early man, for example when we found at BK a place where a herd of *Pelorovis* had apparently died after having fallen, or been driven, into a swamp. Many of them had been butchered. If their death in the swamp represented a hunting episode it would have required bravery, skill and co-operative effort, for *Pelorovis* was an animal of buffalo type, but far larger than any modern or recent buffalo, the spread of the horns being about six feet.

During 1951–58, we concentrated our efforts on Bed II, second oldest of the five major units that were recognized as comprising the overall stratigraphy of the Gorge. We had made progress and altered existing ideas, but we did not have sufficient resources to open large enough trenches to solve all the problems of stratigraphy and correlation. It was time for a change of scene. Early in 1959, therefore, we made a trip to look again at the Laetoli deposits, to which we had been taken in 1935 by Sanimu and where we had noted large numbers of fossil bones. But, as in 1935, we could find no trace of associated stone tools, so we decided not to start excavation there. The Laetoli trip used up most of the 1959 money in our Olduvai research account and we returned to Olduvai for only a short stay, determined to turn our attention to the oldest levels there, those belonging to Bed I. But where, among all the many miles, should we make a start?

At that point, in July 1959, we had what seemed to be the first stroke of luck for some while. Heslon Mukiri, inspecting Bed I sites on foot some way down the east end of the Main Gorge, came to MK, a *korongo* named after Donald MacInnes, who had found it during the 1931 expedition. There Heslon found a hominid tooth in a block of limestone, and after the matrix had been removed it was found to be still in place in a fragment of lower jaw. Since MacInnes had originally reported that there were stone tools at MK, this seemed an excellent and promising place to begin our investigation of Bed I. I was not fully convinced in 1959 that there really were Oldowan stone tools contemporary with Bed I, but MK would be a test case. We would have started at once, but for one thing. At Langata we had as near neighbours Armand and Michaela Denis, who made African wildlife and topographic films which had proved popular, especially their 'On Safari' series, which was then being shown on British television. Their cameraman was Des Bartlett, whom we also knew well, and we had promised to let them come to Olduvai and film one of our excavations from the start, just as soon as we had a site that looked promising. MK seemed to fit the bill, so we held back the start of work there until Des Bartlett could arrive. There was plenty more prospecting at Bed I exposures that could usefully be done, and only a day or two to wait. Des was to bring his wife Jen and their small daughter Julie, and he would also give a lift down to Richard, whose school term was about to end. It all fitted in nicely. Then Louis got an attack of 'flu and retired to bed, and so it came about that on the morning of 17 July I went out by myself, with the two Dalmatians Sally and Victoria, to see what I could find of interest at nearby Bed I exposures. I turned my steps towards a site not far west of the junction of the two gorges, where we knew that bones and stone artefacts were fairly common on the surface of Bed I sediments. The site was known as FLK, one of the two that Louis had named after Frida, before I knew him.

There was indeed plenty of material lying on the eroded surface at FLK, some no doubt as a result of the rains earlier that year. But one scrap of bone that caught and held my eye was not lying loose on the surface but projecting from beneath. It seemed to be part of a skull, including a mastoid process (the bony projection below the ear). It had a hominid look, but the bones seemed enormously thick – too thick, surely. I carefully brushed away a little of the deposit, and then I could see parts of two large teeth in place in the upper jaw. They *were* hominid. It was a hominid skull, apparently *in situ*, and there was a lot of it there. I rushed back to camp to tell Louis, who leaped out of bed, and then we were soon back at the site, looking at my find together. Louis was sad that the skull was not of an early *Homo*, but he concealed his feelings well and expressed only mild disappointment. *'Zinjanthropus'* had come into our lives. Though we were not immediately aware of it, the whole nature of our research operation at Olduvai was about to alter drastically, and we ourselves were going to be profoundly affected. We covered the skull carefully with a protective pile of stones and waited even more impatiently than before for Des Bartlett to arrive.

10

The impact of 'Zinj'

THE REASON WHY 'Zinj' was so important to us was that he captured the public imagination rather than merely exciting the human palaeontologists and stirring up scientific controversy. If we had not had Des Bartlett and his film camera on the spot to record the discovery and excavation of the skull, this might have been much harder to achieve. Zinj made good television, and so a very wide public had the vicarious excitement of 'being there when he was dug up'. It was the general popular impact of the new skull, combined with the tremendous scientific importance of such a find *in situ* on a rich undisturbed living-floor (for that is what the FLK site proved to contain), that convinced the National Geographic Society in the United States that Louis and I and Olduvai were worth financial support on a scale that exceeded our wildest dreams, starting with $20,200 in 1960. That was what they decided to give us, to carry out a proper excavation at FLK, in return for exclusive American publishing rights for the *National Geographic Magazine*, and the right to send a writer and photographer to cover the dig.

There was probably no one in the world better able than Louis to exploit the publicity value, and hence the fund-raising potential, of a find like Zinj. Once we had resources of that kind at our disposal, we were able to work on a scale appropriate to the archaeological sites and the geological problems, and we could import the best specialist advice available as and when we needed it. Therefore further outstanding discoveries were made and continued to be made, and so the National Geographic Society continued to support us, year after year, with great generosity, and is still doing so. Other institutions were also anxious to become involved and, as the research expanded and gathered strength, so too established scholars and hopeful students alike were all wanting to come and work at Olduvai. This snowball effect lasted right up to the world recession that began in the middle 1970s, and even in the leaner years since then I have been extremely fortunate in the level of support I have enjoyed. Yet it is in no way fanciful to assert that the start of it all was my happening to notice that fragment of skull on a morning in July 1959 when, but for a promise to friends who wanted to make a film, I should instead have been starting a small trial dig at a quite different site away down the Gorge.

Given that events were to turn out the way I have just indicated, with Louis and myself becoming celebrities whose names were known all over the world, it is curious to recall that when Louis first saw what I had found he was rather disappointed. The reason for this was that the general form of the skull, and the great size of the teeth, showed the fossil to be an australopithecine of some sort rather than an early example attributable to the genus *Homo*, for which Louis was always hoping, since he firmly believed that the australopithecines were not on the direct line of human ancestry, but merely a side branch that eventually became extinct. He soon perked up, however, when he saw how much of the skull was preserved and that, although in many pieces, it was in excellent condition and not distorted by earth pressure. We devoted the rest of our time at Olduvai in 1959 to extracting it, recovering every fragment we could find by sieving and washing the soil, and to demonstrating that it was indeed *in situ* on what was clearly part of an extensive living-floor with many stone artefacts and animal bones. Our trench also yielded a hominid tibia (a leg bone), which Des Bartlett found, and we assumed it belonged to Zinj himself. Sieving the deposit on the erosion slope below the Zinj level produced some skull fragments and the crown of a tooth, which was certainly from a different individual since Zinj already possessed that particular tooth himself. As I had done just over ten years before with *Proconsul*, I again devoted myself to the task of fitting the fragments of the skull back together. Then we packed up our camp and Louis and Richard left with their precious cargo for Nairobi on the usual road via Arusha, while the Bartletts, Philip and I, with the Dalmatians and another pet of mine, a crippled cat, set out in three Land-Rovers to try an alternative route back to Nairobi via Lake Magadi — a route across country, of which we had recently heard, which would be new and different and should take us through beautiful country.

It was all those things, but it was also a great deal more than we had bargained for. Enquiries of local Masai had confirmed that there was indeed a track to Lake Magadi, but we had not taken account of the fact that *magadi* is the Masai name for *any* soda lake, and it was Lake Natron that they meant. Therefore we quickly got ourselves thoroughly lost, since our track kept drawing us towards the volcano Oldonyo Lengai, which seemed to us not at all the right direction. It was extremely hot, which neither the dogs nor the little cat appreciated at all; and in places the roads were very rough indeed, so that Julie Bartlett, still very small, kept falling forward and hitting her head on the windscreen. Jen Bartlett was close to desperation, and we were all in the state known in her native Australia as 'bushed'; lost and exhausted and not knowing what to do next. There were sand-rivers to cross, which are fine if you take them fast and keep going, but if your vehicle stops you may have grave difficulty in getting it moving again. Eventually we met a Masai, who directed us to an old road which would take us up the side of the Rift to the plateau. It had once been a highway, built by the Germans early this century, but decades of use by herds of cattle had worn its profile to a narrow V-shape and the Land-Rovers were sometimes scraping both sides at once as we struggled up. On the plateau there were many animals and we nearly lost the dogs when they jumped out of the vehicle to chase zebra. As a final disaster the pictures Des Bartlett took of our adventures never came out because the winding mechanism in his camera had not been working. But one good thing did come out of the trip. On the southwestern side of Lake Natron I noticed some promising-looking Pleistocene sediments: four years later, my son Richard went there to check my report on them, leading an archaeological expedition for the first time, and accompanied by Glynn Isaac. At Peninj, some 30 miles north of where we had been, in January 1964 they found an important fossil mandible, belonging to an early Pleistocene hominid like Zinj, and also a horizon that yielded early hand axes.

I have referred to the newly found skull as 'Zinj' because Louis, when he had studied it, decided it was not after all a straightforward species of *Australopithecus* but a new genus within the hominid family, which he decided to name *Zinjanthropus*, the 'Zinj' part of the name coming from an ancient Arabic word for East Africa. To denote the species to which this first member of the supposed new genus belonged, Louis chose the name *boisei*, in honour of Charles Boise, who had given us such valuable support and financial aid over the previous twelve years. He quickly wrote an article for the journal *Nature*, announcing and naming the new find. This should have appeared in mid-August, but one of those printing strikes in which the British seem to specialize delayed publication until early September, and the press release accordingly had to be held back until the technical announcement had been made. The delay in the appearance of *Nature* also meant that care had to be taken when Louis announced the discovery verbally to an excited audience of his colleagues in African archaeology at the Third Pan-African Congress, held at Kinshasa (then Léopoldville) in the Congo, beginning in late August. He and I both attended this meeting, and we flew there from Nairobi, I with Zinj on my knee in a box, rather as I had taken *Proconsul* to London. Nowadays, we should never expose a unique and fragile find to such hazards – an accurate cast would be sent instead; but in 1959 we set out optimistically, and later the same year Louis also flew to London with Zinj, who, by then, was known to his immediate circle of admirers as 'Dear Boy'.

At the Congress, Zinj attracted enormous attention, and small groups of delegates came to our room for a privileged close examination. Already, grave reservations were being expressed at Louis's identification of a new genus, since robust forms of *Australopithecus* had long been known in South Africa; but Louis was unconvinced. Raymond Dart was particularly pleased and delighted with our discovery. He had been the discoverer of the first australopithecines in South Africa, at Taung and in the Transvaal during the 1920s, and he very charmingly said how happy he was that this great discovery had been made by Louis and me. Among others who came to see the skull was another South African physical anthropologist, Phillip Tobias, who had succeeded Dart in the Chair of Anatomy at the University of Witwatersrand in Johannesburg. After discussion with me during the Congress, Louis offered Phillip the task of preparing the technical report on Zinj, which he accepted with amazement and delight.

In his report, Phillip put Zinj back firmly and formally into the australopithecines, and used his opportunity to sort out the whole tangle of nomenclature surrounding that genus. He allowed Zinj to be a new species of *Australopithecus, A. boisei*, and by then Louis was quite prepared to accept this, though he had his reservations about Phillip's view of the broader picture of hominid evolution. The general public, however, did not care one way or the other about such niceties, beyond noting that the scientists had been having a good old fight among themselves. To them, what really appealed was Phillip's phrase 'Nutcracker Man', casually given to Zinj at the time of the Congress in Kinshasa, because of the huge size of his molar teeth. That caught the popular imagination, and to many people Zinj has been 'Nutcracker Man' ever since.

In February 1960 the new series of excavations at Olduvai got under way, and that first season, which began with the excavation of the FLK Bed I site where Zinj had been found, lasted for no less than twelve months. A permanent camp was established, on the north side of the Main Gorge, nearly opposite FLK, and I stayed there almost the whole time, with only short visits to Nairobi. Louis, with the Museum's affairs to run in his capacity of Curator, stayed in Nairobi and visited us at weekends and other times, just as often as he could. Already the effects of the Zinj publicity were bringing him extra work, and he was also involved with many other things that were going on, such as further work on the West Kenyan Miocene deposits. Inevitably, therefore, he could not be with me for more than a small part of the time, and I missed him very much. At the end of 1960 he went again to the United States for a long and tiring lecture tour, as he was to do at least once a year for the rest of his life. The American audience loved him, and could not get enough of him. Although in the early 1960s the main purpose of his going was always to carry an exciting report to our financial benefactors, and thereby persuade them to continue their support, there is no doubt that he greatly enjoyed the hospitality he received, the packed and enthusiastic audiences, the ecstatic applause at the end of each lecture, and the local and national television appearances. As the years passed, his reception in at least some parts of the States turned to outright hero-worship.

At Olduvai during 1960 we logged more man-hours in concentrated work than had been expended hitherto in the whole history of the research at the Gorge, thanks not least to the energy of the Wakamba workmen. The principal site studied at first was that where Zinj had been found, and we exposed some 3,600 square feet of the living-floor, noting a curious arc of empty space in the otherwise dense distribution of material, which we thought might indicate the position of a simple windbreak, though no structural traces remained. It was Desmond Clark who first made this suggestion. We also found more hominid remains: a fibula, another tooth, and some fragments of a skull whose structure was much thinner than that of Zinj. Jonathan had now left school and came down to Olduvai to help for a few months. It was actually he who spotted the hominid fibula at FLK: he was sitting above the baulk that I had left standing in the centre of the excavated area, holding a plumb-bob to help me draw the section and watching the workmen uncovering an area of bones a little way away. 'Does any animal have a long thin bone like this?' he asked, tracing the shape he could see with a finger in the air. I said that I couldn't think of one. 'Oh, then I think it must be hominid,' he said, casually. I dropped my drawing and we rushed round to see. He was quite right. But that was only a start.

Not content with helping at the Zinj excavation, Jonathan liked in spare moments to wander by himself in search of interesting fossil bones. One day in mid-May, near the north end of the series of gullies that make up FLK, he found a fragment of the mandible of a sabre-toothed cat. This was a rare enough species to make it worth sieving the deposits on the surface where Jonathan had made his find, to see if there were more fragments. There were none, but instead the sieving produced a hominid tooth, and shortly afterwards a terminal phalanx – the end bone of a finger or toe. We therefore dug a trench at 'Jonny's site' as we called it, though its proper name was FLK NN (FLK North North). Jonathan himself directed the dig and during the course of it, in early November 1960, he personally found some important new hominid material, *in situ* on a living-floor, representing remains of two individuals. Of one, a juvenile, there were not only substantial parts of the skull and the lower jaw but also no less than 21 of the small bones that together make up a hand. The other was an adult, probably female, and the most important finds in this case were twelve associated bones that were components of a foot. The group of foot bones I found, but almost everything else was found by Jonathan himself, and it should be stressed that these were no casual items picked up on an erosion surface but were found *in situ* on a datable living-floor.

These new discoveries were very exciting for a number of reasons: they were complementary to Zinj and in many ways more important. The two sites were less than 100 yards apart, which meant that correlation between them was very easy since certain key levels within Bed I were present at both. Thus we knew that the new hominid finds occurred a foot or so below the level of Zinj and in a different deposit, and were therefore a little older. The fragments of the new skull indicated that it was quite different from that of Zinj, even allowing for differences between juvenile and adult. Here was a creature with a larger and better-developed brain, contained within a skull shaped rather more like a modern one, and with thinner cranial bones than Zinj. And then there were the hand and foot bones – a completely unprecedented find for this opening period of the Early Stone Age.

It is one thing trying to work out from the size and shape of a skull, and by estimating brain capacity, how skilled an early hominid *might* have been with his hands, but if you can examine directly the degree of mobility of the hand itself, a quite different order of evidence becomes available. Again, if a few fragments of limb bones are all you have on which to base your judgement of whether or not a given hominid type could walk upright, then the sudden availability of much of a fossilized foot is enormously helpful. That particular point did specifically occur to me soon after I began to excavate the foot bones and more and more of them kept appearing. By the time Phillip Tobias had made a preliminary study of the skull parts and lower jaw, and John Napier and his colleague Michael Day, experts on human palaeontology from London, had between them examined the hand and foot bones, we knew for certain what we had guessed from the start: Jonathan had found a quite different type of hominid from Zinj, but one who was contemporary with him, and indeed had been present at Olduvai before the *Zinjanthropus* living-floor had accumulated. And it was a hominid which in terms of human physical evolution seemed to be one of a far more 'advanced' type, relatively larger-brained, able to walk fully upright, and possessing considerable manual dexterity. We were now able to attribute to it most of the hominid remains other than the Zinj skull itself, which we had found at the FLK site – those found on the living-floor, and those we had recovered by sieving on the eroded surface a little way below, which had almost certainly been derived from the floor itself. But what were we to call our new hominid type, and what was his relationship to Zinj?

Louis was predictably delighted by the new finds. In 1959 he had regarded Zinj as the maker of the artefacts at FLK, but here was a far better candidate in terms of both brain and hand. This was right in line with his own theories of *Homo* evolving during the earlier Pleistocene. This had to be *Homo*. He directed his considerable powers of eloquent persuasion towards Phillip Tobias and John Napier, and when the three of them made the formal announcement naming the finds, in an article in *Nature* in 1964, they claimed that the material belonged to *Homo habilis* – that is to say, to a new species within the genus *Homo*. The name *habilis* was suggested by Raymond Dart, to denote the hand was capable of a precision grip: there is no very suitable equivalent word in English, so the press and the popular books have usually made do with 'Handy Man', which is about on a par with 'Nutcracker Man'.

Louis restrained himself from using the term *Homo* in print until this 1964 article. The outcry that followed came from those of his colleagues like Sir Wilfred Le Gros Clark (he had been knighted in 1955) who felt that the individuals concerned were australopithecines, at the gracile end of the range represented in that very broad genus. Zinj they saw as being at the opposite extreme. But the press did not have to wait until 1964 for a sensation. At the time of the original public announcement of the skull from FLK NN, which came at one of Louis's lectures in America early in 1961, they pounced on his description of a certain fracture in the centre of one of the parietal bones and cornered him into agreeing that it could have been made with a blunt instrument. That was enough: here was evidence of 'the first ever murder'. The occurrence of Zinj himself on a living-floor in the presence of remains of a higher hominid, who was assumed to be the tool maker, also came in for some colourful comment in the mid-1960s, when those who liked the idea of cannibalism were able to exercise their minds.

The excavations at the Zinj site and at Jonathan's site of FLK NN did not account for all our finds in that long first season. Our geologist at that time was Dr Ray Pickering of the Tanzania Geological Survey. While he was digging a small pit about half-way between the Zinj site and Jonathan's site to check the presence of one of the important 'marker' horizons, on which we depended for correlations between exposures, he found a concentration of stone tools and bones which became site FLK North, at which we carried out a very productive excavation, mainly in the 1961–62 season. Louis in particular did not get on well with Pickering, who was rather a nervous person, and he regarded Pickering's conclusions with grave mistrust. On 2 December 1960 he accompanied Pickering to a site in the Side Gorge, the other side of the tongue of land that separates FLK from the Side Gorge. At an exposure of Bed II deposits at LLK (Louis Leakey Korongo), Louis found the greater part of a massive hominid calvaria (the top part of the skull) on the surface of the small gully. (From a distance he had thought it was only a modern tortoise carapace, something that had often raised our hopes in the past.) This was an excellent discovery, and is still one of the earliest known examples of *Homo erectus*, an important stage in human evolution which comes after

Homo habilis. All things considered, we had given the National Geographic Society excellent value for their support since 1960.

The whole campaign of large-scale excavations at Olduvai, of which 1960 had been the first year, continued until the end of 1963. During this time we concerned ourselves with Bed I and a selection of sites in Bed II, and at the end of that time I was in a position to stop and write up the archaeology of these two beds. With a contribution on the geology from Richard Hay and a faunal list from my daughter-in-law Margaret, my report turned into quite a large volume, and since the detailed work on the finds was a very long process it was 1971 before it was finally in print, as the third volume in the new monograph series. Having in this chapter recounted the first season in some detail with all its important and exciting hominid finds, I shall not do more than pick out one or two highlights from the discoveries of 1961–63.

The site that Ray Pickering had found, FLK North, must certainly count as a highlight, though parts of it consisted of clay and were extremely difficult to excavate. There were no less than five separate stratified Oldowan levels in the top part of Bed I, and one of them was clearly a butchery site, where much of an elephant skeleton was found in close association with stone tools. The skull and tusks of the elephant were the only major parts missing. At FLK North we also cut a trench back into the side of the Gorge above the upper limit of Bed I and found that there were yet more occupation levels in deposits belonging to the lower and middle parts of Bed II. Among these was another butchery site, not quite so well preserved, where remains of a *Deinotherium*, a large creature distantly related to the elephants, was associated with artefacts. We cannot be sure at either of these butchery sites whether the people who made the stone tools were themselves responsible as hunters for the animal's death, or whether they were merely scavenging the carcase of an already dead animal, but there can be no doubt that they were capable of using stone tools to cut off meat, and these are still among the earliest known occurrences of that activity.

FLK North produced only a single hominid bone, the terminal phalanx of the big toe, but by chance it was one of the bones that had not been represented in the nearly complete foot from Jonathan's site. As such it was a useful piece of evidence, also probably attributable to *Homo habilis.*

Another site that produced remarkable evidence was DK (Donald's Korongo). It lay at the base of Bed I, situated only just above the black basalt that can be seen as the floor of the Gorge in many places today. Philip, then aged 12, dug a small trial trench here under my tactful but careful supervision, when he was with me at Olduvai during his Christmas holidays. His dig confirmed the richness of the site in both artefacts and bones, and we began a full-scale excavation in 1962. There was indeed an extensive Oldowan living-floor, and on it we found a circle of loosely piled lava blocks, which appear to have been the base for some simple hut structure, probably made of branches and roofed perhaps with grass or animal skins, like those used today by a few surviving nomadic peoples in various parts of Africa. This was a completely unprecedented find for an Early Stone Age site and therefore wholly unexpected, so much so that when one of our trenches first began to expose the lava blocks we removed them, and only when we saw that they formed part of a low wall surrounding an empty area did we realize their significance: it was Heslon Mukiri who first pointed out that they really did look like part of an Iron Age 'hut circle'. Fortunately, I had plotted the position and drawn on a plan each of the stones we had removed, so when we expanded our excavation to reveal the whole of the structure, the final site plan was complete. This circle of blocks at DK is believed to be the oldest known human structure in the world.

During these years we lived comfortably in a camp above the Main Gorge on its north side – a site now occupied by the permanent camp of the tourist guides. We had a large *banda*, which was our combined living- and work-room; it had a work table at one end and a dining table at the other. It also housed a refrigerator that ran on kerosene. There were tents for those who came to join in the work, or just to visit. I slept in a tent at first, and then for a while in the truck-caravan which Charles Boise had given us, and later in a grass hut that was built for me. To this camp came many people, some only once and briefly, and others, who were to become close friends and colleagues, many times.

We started having visitors as soon as we began the 1960 season. Matthew Stirling, the archaeologist on the Research Committee of the National Geographic Society, came in the capacity of an observer for the Society. In the course of his visit, Jonathan showed him round almost the whole Gorge, and he took away a favourable impression of its vast potential for future work. Sir Julian Huxley came, with his wife Juliette, who, when we met again not so long ago, reminded me of the occasion and their great enjoyment of their stay: by luck, they were with us when the find of the *Homo habilis* hand bones was made. Raymond Dart, Camille Arambourg (a senior French palaeontologist) and Desmond Clark came as a group, officially invited by Louis to inspect progress on the excavation of the Zinj site. At the time of their visit we were carrying out experiments on the breaking open of modern marrow-bones to see if the resulting debris resembled that on the Olduvai floor, for it looked to us as if the early hominids had smashed bones deliberately to get at the marrow. Raymond Dart, never one to lose an opportunity, delightedly ate the raw marrow from some of the bones we broke.

Another specialist visitor was Jack Evernden, a geophysicist from the University of California at Berkeley, who came briefly to take samples from some of our volcanic deposits for the then new dating method known as potassium-argon (or K/Ar) dating. This is one of those methods that depend on the presence of a radioactive isotope which decays at a known, constant and measurable rate to form a different isotope which is retained inside the sample. In this case, an isotope of potassium in a volcanic rock decays to form argon, which is a gas. If you know the decay rate and can measure the amount of argon that has accumulated in your sample, you should be able to work out how long ago the parent rock was formed. Naturally, it is much more complicated than that in practice, and requires elaborate laboratory equipment, but Olduvai offers quite re-markable scope for its use because of the close association of undisturbed archaeological sites with deposits of volcanic origin, some of which yielded samples appropriate for K/Ar dating. In 1960 there were still teething troubles over the use of this method on deposits of Pleistocene age. It was more often used by geologists to establish the ages of rocks that were hundreds or even thousands of millions of years old. For rocks of Pleistocene age, contamination of samples was a difficult problem, and some of the results were erratic. Shortly after Evernden's visit the K/Ar dating work was taken over by Garniss Curtis, an extremely careful and scientific worker, also from Berkeley. Garniss himself came to Olduvai in 1961 and took numerous samples, from which reliable and surprisingly old dates soon began to emerge. It greatly startled many of our colleagues to learn that the basalt of the Gorge floor was no less than 1.9 million years old, while the hard tuff which overlay the DK hut circle site dated from about 1.75 million years ago. Quite a sharp controversy sprang up for a while. And not surprisingly. Before potassium-argon dating, people could only guess the age of the start of the Pleistocene, and the conven-tional estimate had been about one million years ago. Since our fauna in Bed I was Lower Pleistocene, it followed that the Pleistocene itself had begun at some point earlier than the formation of our 1.9 million-year-old basalt, or, in other words, was twice as long as everyone had assumed. This is another example of the dramatic nature of the results that poured from those excavations of 1959–63. I should perhaps add that various other direct dating methods have since been used at Olduvai, confirming Curtis's first conclusions.

It was through Garniss Curtis that there also came to Olduvai, for the first time in 1962, someone who has become one of the chief participants in all the work that has been done over the last 20 years: Richard Hay, who has been a key figure throughout our work at Olduvai, as well as a colleague and close friend. Louis, who had found it almost impossible to work with Ray Pickering, asked Garniss if he knew of a suitable replacement – 'a good field man who also knows how to write,' I remember him saying. That was certainly what he got. Garniss was based at the University of California at Berkeley, and Dick Hay was one of his colleagues within the Earth Sciences Faculty. Louis sent off a letter, and Dick came. I have followed with the greatest admiration his work at the Gorge, which has been of fundamental importance to my own understanding of the archaeological sequence. There has hardly been a year since 1962 when Dick has missed a visit to Olduvai or, later, to Laetoli. His definitive report on the Geology of the Olduvai Gorge was published as a book in 1976.

Other colleagues came for shorter periods, to direct the excavation of a site or sites. John Waechter, whom we had known for many years and who had been a great help to us during the first Pan-African Congress, and Maxine Kleindienst, an American archaeologist, both worked on Beds III and IV during 1962–63 while I was still occupied with earlier levels. John also took charge of the camp and the dogs for me at times when I had to be away. There were also some who were not professional archaeologists when they first asked if they could come and help, but who later became close friends. These included a girl who even became my daughter-in-law for a while: Margaret Cropper. Margaret was still a schoolgirl when she first came down in July 1961, and she worked first with us on Jonathan's FLK NN site. That she was not afraid of hard work or uncongenial conditions she showed both then and even more so the following year when FLK N was being dug. Not only was it she who laboured at my side on the elephant bones, but in the evenings she would help me by the light of a pressure lamp at the monumental and scarcely entrancing task of sorting and classifying the tiny rodent bones and teeth, of which there were many thousands from the several levels of that site. I remember that sometimes one of our neat heaps of sorted bones would suddenly begin to move slowly across the table – enough to make one give up drink for life, or at least stop work for the day, the first time it happened. In fact it merely meant that a mass of tiny brown beetles had penetrated into the pile and were on the move.

Margaret's sharp eyes were not only good for the sorting of microfauna: it was she who in 1962, at VEK, found a hominid skull, or much of one, that had eroded out of Bed IV only to be trampled to fragments by a herd of Masai cattle. She was one of the best assistants I ever had, and later, in Nairobi, helped me write up the reports of the finds.

It was in the school holidays of 1960 too that Shirley Coryndon first came to Olduvai, bringing her young daughters Anna and Virginia. While Margaret was a novice when she first came to work at Olduvai, Shirley Coryndon was an experienced palaeontologist, having worked extensively on the Miocene fossils from West Kenya. She was married then to

Roger Coryndon, son of Sir Robert Coryndon, who had been Governor of Kenya from 1922 to 1928, and after whom the Coryndon Museum was named. Having a young family, she was not free to spend such long periods at Olduvai as Margaret could, but she came as often as possible and proved to be a delightful companion and a great help to me in identifying fossils and running the camp, of which she took charge while I was away. But it was really in the middle 1960s that I got to know her best, when she gave me great assistance in the detailed study of our finds from the excavations, and we became the closest of friends. Through her own research, Shirley became an expert on fossil hippos, and she studied all the main Pleistocene examples from Olduvai as well as material of much earlier date. She had first studied palaeontology in the Museum at Nairobi and when working as an assistant to Donald MacInnes at the Miocene sites, including Rusinga, from 1950 onwards. Afterwards, when she returned to England, she was for some years on the staff of the Department of Palaeontology at the British Museum (Natural History). Her second husband, Robert Savage, is a geologist and palaeontologist at Bristol University in England, and on one of her later visits to East Africa he was able to accompany her and they worked together in North Kenya. I felt a very deep sense of loss when she died of cancer in 1976, and I still miss her greatly both as a friend and a colleague.

Life in our 1960s camp at Olduvai had a special quality of its own, and during the excavation season was usually lively, with frequent visits by Louis at weekends and the presence of visiting colleagues and a variety of students and others assisting us in the fieldwork. But you would hardly by now expect a Leakey camp to be populated solely by humans: there were Simon the monkey, Oliver the wildebeest calf, the current team of Dalmatians, the cripple cat who had taken part in that difficult journey to Nairobi via Lake Natron in 1959, and sundry others. Of all these, Simon and Oliver are most likely to be remembered, or maybe I should say least likely to be forgotten, by those who encountered them.

Simon was a Sykes monkey that Richard saw being hawked around the streets of Nairobi and took pity on. In our family at that time there seemed to be a universal notion that if you acquired an animal and were then unable to look after it yourself, you gave it to Mother. Anyhow, Simon took up residence at the Olduvai camp and set himself to play every conceivable trick he could, and to satisfy as much as he could of his limitless curiosity. One of those driven nearly frantic by Simon was the usually calm Dick Hay, who had a set of coloured pencils which he used in recording his geological observations, and which Simon thought were one of the best things ever invented. He also liked to unpack the suitcase of anyone foolish enough to leave one unlocked; the hoped-for prize in any such search being a bag of lipstick and toilet articles belonging to one of the girls. He would also sit for ages on the shoulder of my neighbour and friend George Dove, fingering George's famous waxed moustaches, which absolutely fascinated him.

Poor Simon – drink was his undoing; but that happened when I moved back to Nairobi, taking him with me. The cage from which Simon could not escape has, I am sure, still to be invented. So too, perhaps, the drinks cupboard into which he could not find his way. Not even Simon could hope to mix his drinks (or, rather, our drinks) like that and stay sober. When he recovered, he found himself on the way to the Nairobi animal orphanage: yet for all his tricks, we remained very fond of him.

Like Simon, the dogs had the free run by day of the surrounding countryside, where they loved to hunt, chasing hares, dik-dik and anything else they could find. It was a risk, since there were leopards about, but there was no way of restraining them, and they all survived, although one frightening day they were away hunting for nine hours. Oliver, the wildebeest calf, also had the free run of camp. He was an orphan, or perhaps just lost or abandoned by his mother, and had followed Louis's Land-Rover down the lower slopes of Ngorongoro. Wildebeest congregate in huge herds during the migration and the calves are all born then, within a very short space of time. When the herds stampede for one reason or another, calves often get separated from their mothers and never find them again: often they trail pathetically along behind the column of adults. Whenever we encountered a calf in that situation we would try to rescue it, because otherwise it would inevitably starve or be killed by predators. When my grass hut was built at the camp, I actually had an extra enclosure added to it as a stable for wildebeest calves – necessary at night, as had been shown when a calf was taken by a leopard.

Oliver, however, was not the sort of calf to languish or die in captivity. He enjoyed himself thoroughly and gave the impression of being highly intelligent, if perhaps not quite certain what sort of animal he was. Brought up with the Dalmatians, he liked to walk and run with them and once, when by himself, he chased a hare and caught up with it, as any self-respecting Dalmatian would. But he then had no idea what to do next, and didn't in any case have the right sort of mouth, so it got away while he was pondering the problem. His other favourite sport was to charge headlong through the flaps of any tent in which he could hear someone taking a bath. He always chose the girls, apparently on the grounds that they could be counted on to give a satisfying scream. He clearly knew which tents contained girls, and he also knew from the sounds of the water when was the right moment to attack – the audience could watch him waiting. Margaret Cropper was one of the many who bolted out of the other end of their tents seeking to retain some semblance of modesty with a hastily grabbed towel.

Not all our encounters with animals were with camp pets, I need hardly say, and some took place between the main digging seasons, when only a few people were at Olduvai. Leopards, lions and hyenas disturbed us most. I recently re-read some letters that I wrote to Louis from Olduvai during periods when he could not visit me there, for example in the spring of 1963, when he was in California for a term as Visiting Professor at the University's Riverside Campus. Perhaps two short extracts will be better than any attempt of mine at long-range memory:

> 'Nights are most disturbed. Again last night lions round 3 times. Ben barked every 15 mins. regularly. I have now put the bitches in the car and the dogs with me, for tighter control.... Last night was the worst in living memory: the leopard squatted under the bushes near the banda all night. Lion roared, plovers shrieked and Ben never stopped barking. I got so *furious*. Finally, I threw firecrackers in various directions, but they are all used to bangs and did not mind at all.'
>
> (22 Feb 1963)

> 'The leopard has been around for nights and Mollie and I have had v. little sleep. So last night we both got tin cans and beat a tattoo on tins as soon as the dogs started barking – Mollie in her 'shorties' with a red blanket draped round her and myself in a dressing gown. All quiet afterwards. Jonny will be joining the percussion band tonight, I expect.'
>
> (25 May 1963)

The Mollie referred to was Mollie Knights-Rayson, who at the time of the letter was working with me at Olduvai and had recently become Jonathan's fiancée: they were married in December of that year. How I wish there were still leopards around camp to disturb us at night as I write this, almost exactly twenty years after that second extract, but they have been poached to virtual extinction on the Serengeti. An equally tragic loss from the same cause is the rhino. I see that in a letter of mine to Louis of slightly later date, April 1965, I reported that Richard had counted no less than 55 rhinos in the immediate area of the Gorge. On that occasion he had gone out on foot to count rhinos to help John Goddard, a zoologist who was studying them in the Olduvai area, and during the course of the day he had to take refuge in a tree from a pride of no less than 20 lions, who kept him there eight hours. Not everything has changed, however: in my present camp we are still quite often disturbed at night by lions roaring, and they occasionally jump over the thorn fence and come into the camp compound, but I no longer have to throw firecrackers in self-defence. I did earlier this year throw my bedroom slippers at a porcupine who was keeping me awake by rustling and rattling around outside my hut.

Our relationship with the local wild animals did, however, occasionally

135

pass well beyond passive resistance. On one occasion Richard experimented by playing to the lions a tape recording of their own voices, but that merely infuriated them because they took the sounds to indicate intruders in their own territory. Of quite a different nature was the gentle Olduvai sport, during the digging seasons, of spring-hare chasing. These animals are not really hares at all, but charming nocturnal creatures, who proceed by a series of kangaroo-like hops. After dark we would take vehicles out and drive slowly along until we could see a hare in the headlights, and then chase it on foot trying to catch it and hold its tail for a minute before releasing it. The hares did not seem to mind this unduly and hopped away quite happily when let go. Sometimes those who were driving would get so involved that they would leap out to take part in the game leaving the Land-Rover to drive itself slowly across Serengeti, until the engine stalled or someone ran and caught it up.

In the first half of the 1960s, the work at Olduvai was certainly the most important thing I did, and it dominated my life during these years; but there were other events from time to time, some of which took me on journeys outside East Africa. Occasionally the travelling was only loosely connected with the Olduvai discoveries, or even had nothing at all to do with them, but often I was going to see sites or archaeological material that was highly relevant to gaining a better understanding of the finds we had made in Beds I and II. The need to make such working trips continued through the 1960s while I was preparing the monograph on Beds I and II, but working visits of that sort always have their social side and are a pleasant way of visiting old friends and making new ones. For example, I went to South Africa and Israel on very enjoyable visits that produced a lot of useful information.

South Africa was generally regarded as the home ground, so to speak, of *Australopithecus*. Raymond Dart had found the first specimen as long ago as 1924, at Taung in Cape Province, just across the border from the Transvaal: it was a juvenile skull of a gracile individual, which he named *Australopithecus africanus*. Many dozens of australopithecine fossils were subsequently discovered at caves in the Transvaal, notably in the Sterkfontein Valley. The first specimen of *Australopithecus robustus* was found by a schoolboy at Kromdraai in 1938 and identified by Robert Broom: it represented an altogether more heavily built species, which, of the two, seemed closer to our Zinj. In the late 1950s, stone tools had come to light at the Sterkfontein cave itself, and new excavations there that began in 1966 under the direction of Alun Hughes and others produced more. C. K. Brain, known always as Bob Brain, had also found stone artefacts among material from the Swartkrans Cave, across the valley from the Sterkfontein, which he wanted me to study. I was also anxious to see certain other material in which Raymond Dart was an ardent believer, which he had named (with tongue at least partly in cheek) the 'osteodontokeratic culture' of the australopithecines – or, in less classical language, fragments of bone, tooth and horn which he was convinced they had used as simple tools. In an impassioned address he had put forward this theory at the Kinshasa Pan-African Congress in 1959, the same one to which Louis and I had taken Zinj. Dart's speech was hugely enjoyed by the audience, but it left them unconvinced. Now I needed to see the objects for myself.

I visited the Bernard Price Institute in Johannesburg, and the Transvaal Museum in Pretoria, and was taken to see the main sites, including a visit to Hughes's excavations. I too came away unconvinced by Raymond Dart's supposed bone tools, which were not at all like our few but rather more impressive worked or deliberately broken bones from Olduvai, but the stone tools I was shown certainly seemed to me close to types we had encountered at Olduvai in some of the Bed II sites.

In December 1963, Louis and I went briefly to another part of South Africa for the wedding of Jonathan to Mollie Knights-Rayson. This was the first wedding in the family, so it was quite an occasion. Before long, Jonathan moved with Mollie to Lake Baringo, a lake in the Rift Valley north of Nairobi and beyond Nakuru, where he had rented a piece of land and where they lived in a prefabricated wooden house, surrounded by enclosures for the snakes.

The following year I made my first visit to Israel. The reason for going was to visit the early Palaeolithic site of Ubeidiya, in the Jordan valley, which had been discovered in 1959 and was producing what seemed like Oldowan artefacts. Louis had already made several visits because a condition made by the foundation that funded the work was that he and I should keep an eye on the progress there. Israel is a small enough country for one to be able to see most of it in a short stay, and I found it very attractive. It was not possible at that time to get access to the Old City in Jerusalem, but I did see it on a later visit and found it profoundly impressive, unlike the tourist trap that Bethlehem had already become. I stayed with my hosts in a kibbutz, and in a letter I wrote to Louis at the time I said that I found the kibbutz system repugnant, particularly the way children were brought up in age-group 'child houses', and only allowed to visit their parents for two hours each evening. At the same time, I admitted that I had never seen healthier, happier children, and that the kibbutz system had brought much prosperity to Israelis. I also liked Jewish cooking, the 'real' parts of an Arab market, the wonderful wild flowers in the limestone hills near Nazareth, and the enchanting early Christian mosaics in the little church of Capernaum above Lake Tiberias that is said to be on the site of the miracle of the loaves and fishes. Predictably most of my letter is about the Ubeidiya site and the finds,

which impressed me greatly, as did the skill of many of the Israeli archaeologists, several of whom later visited us at Olduvai at one time or
another.

It was in 1962 that I made my own first visit to the United States. Louis
and I had been jointly awarded a great honour, the Hubbard Medal of the
National Geographic Society, and we were to receive it together in
Washington. Jonathan accompanied us. In later years I have been so often
to the States, and made so many kind friends there, that it is quite hard to
remember on which occasion I first met each of those who seem to have
become so much a part of my life. This first visit made a great impact on
me, though the whole occasion was dominated by my absolute terror at
having to be on the platform in Constitution Hall in Washington D.C.,
which held perhaps 3,000 people, under glaring spotlights and television
cameras. I didn't have to speak – Louis did that for both of us – but I still
had to get up and receive the medal, and I was very nervous. That safely
over, I was borne along on a wave of American hospitality, and it was a
pleasure to meet so many of our kind friends and sponsors in the National
Geographic Society. The President was Dr Melville Grosvenor, and I
think it was probably he who first introduced me to bourbon whiskey and
American seafood, both of which I have never ceased to enjoy when they
have been available. Dr Leonard Carmichael, Secretary of the Smithsonian Institution, gave us a lightning tour of that remarkable place.
Melville Grosvenor also introduced us to Dr Melvin Payne and his wife
Ethel, from whom I later received a standing invitation to stay with them
at their home in Bethesda when visiting Washington; I have often done
so. They have both always been kindness itself to me and Ethel, in fact,
has become one of my closest friends. There were also Mary Griswold
Smith, one of the Society's photographic editors; Joanne Hess, their lecture organizer; and Bill Graves, a staff writer of the National Geographic
Society. So many of these people became real friends and visited us
sooner or later at Olduvai or at Laetoli. Mary Smith in fact visited us
within a year of this first meeting, and was one of those who suffered at
the hands of Simon the monkey.

I will end this chapter by mentioning a visit Louis and I made within
Tanzania in 1965. It was to Dar-es-Salaam, and its purpose was to attend
the ceremony of the arrival of Zinj himself at his final resting place in the
National Museum there which had been enlarged and modernized and
where the Tanzania Government had built a special air-conditioned
strongroom to house him. President Nyerere and several senior members
of his government were there and I, as the finder, was given the honour of
handing Zinj to the President. To my great relief I only had to say a few
words; Louis made the main speech on our behalf to the large international audience of distinguished scientists. Afterwards, we took almost

the whole of the National Geographic Society's Research Committee on a visit to Olduvai and showed them the sites they had so generously helped us to excavate.

The years that followed the discovery of Zinj had brought Louis and me fame, if not exactly fortune, and had given us the opportunity to travel half-way round the world as well as making many important finds on our own doorstep. Yet, by 1965, a period of change was beginning; perhaps with hindsight, I should say that it had already begun in the Third World, and Kenya and Tanzania had by then both achieved independence. In the Leakey family, individual members were achieving independence in various ways: Jonathan was married; Richard was now 21 and was soon to become engaged to Margaret Cropper; Philip would soon be leaving school. Louis had begun a pattern of annual international travel that took him away for months at a time, and I had spent long periods down at Olduvai, leaving the others to look after themselves while I worked. Before the decade of the 1960s was complete, our own pattern of family life had completely changed.

11
The partnership breaks down

I COME NOW to what is quite certainly the hardest section of the story for me to tell and, if the truth be known, I would much rather draw a veil over at least the years 1968 to 1972, which turned out to be the last four years of Louis's life. But that would be impossible, because they were also four years of my life, and I cannot just omit them. It was all very sad and painful at the time, after so much happiness before, and it remains sad in the remembering. Ten to fifteen years later, perhaps the best approach is to try and understand what happened, and why. The basic facts are clear enough: our marriage, which in its best years had been an idyllic partnership, had by 1968 begun to deteriorate and, for the last four years of Louis's life, although there was no official separation, we lived apart and met only for brief periods. For my part, I had to watch Louis decline from the height of his intellectual powers and the fullness of his charm, to become irritable and irrational, someone for whom his colleagues had quite frequently to cover up, out of respect for what had once been: to watch, and to be powerless to bring him any help or comfort or support. He became someone utterly different from the Louis I had married and loved and admired, the Louis whose stature in his profession had perhaps never been equalled. And I have no doubt at all that he thought I, too, had changed, had become cold and uncaring, had abandoned him when he needed me most.

At the end of the last chapter, I was stressing the growing independence of members of the family – myself included. I also described how the snowball effect that began with the discovery of Zinj had profoundly affected our lives; so, if you like, Zinj was one of the root causes of all this too. It was inconceivable, given all that had happened to us as archaeologists in East Africa, that Louis and I should have regarded the finding of Zinj and *Homo habilis* as anything other than a triumph, a series of discoveries to be followed up regardless of the amount of effort required until every possible piece of information had been extracted. That is what we set ourselves to do, and the cost included elements that we had not considered. Louis did not simply decide he would go off to America and elsewhere for increasingly long periods in addition to all his other work: it was forced upon him, and once caught in the net he could not escape. Nor did it ever occur to me that I would go off on solo research visits to places around the world, but that was what inevitably happened. So our increasing independence of each other did not originate in a conscious choice, even if in the end we let it go to its logical conclusion. Hitherto we had done everything together unless some good reason prevented it. Now our paths were necessarily diverging, for eminently practical reasons as it at first seemed.

Then again, so far as the matter of professional independence was concerned, it was not only Louis and me who were involved, for a powerful new professional force was suddenly appearing in our midst: Richard, young, able, ambitious and direct to the point, in those days, of outright tactlessness. On leaving school he had at first deliberately turned his back on prehistory and palaeontology as a profession, determined not to ride upon his parents' shoulders. With his usual enterprise and resourcefulness he had made himself a living by such things as trapping animals for zoos, collecting animal skeletons for zoologists, and running a safari company, first alone and later in partnership with Alan Root, the wildlife photographer. Since he has given his own account of his early life, I need not here go into the reasons why he changed his mind. As regards the timing, I have already noted in passing that the first archaeological field expedition he led was to Natron and Peninj in 1963–64. By this time he had learned to fly and had his own aeroplane, which perhaps reflects the pace at which he liked to move and get things done. Richard was always a competitive person, and when he entered a new field it was with the intention of getting to the top, and the sooner the better. And who at that time was in possession of the summit, needing therefore in due course to be displaced? Louis. Add to that the curious but undeniable fact that Louis had never really been as fond of Richard as of the other two when they were boys, and had visibly treated him with less indulgence than he had shown to Jonathan and Philip, and you begin to realize the potential strength of the disruptive forces at work within the family, and to see that sooner or later Louis would inevitably begin to feel threatened. Once there was any such feeling in his mind, then I myself would also seem to be a threat, since achievements that would once have been seen as his and mine jointly were increasingly being seen as mine alone, because I was actually leading the research at Olduvai and was responsible for publishing the results.

Nor was that all. Louis's health began to fail, though not to the extent it was to do later. His troubles began with the worsening of an arthritic hip, reducing him to the use of a stick and then two sticks, though he fended off until 1968 the necessary operation to put in an artificial joint.

All his life Louis had been a field archaeologist, and work in the field was his greatest love. From 1960 onwards, the need to raise funds for so many different projects, and the increased burden of administration, were acting to reduce his time in the field to a minimum, and that was bad enough. The painful hip made things even worse, and in the later 1960s he could hardly hobble round sites at Olduvai or elsewhere on occasions when he did get there. His long trips abroad became feats of endurance, but he would never disappoint an audience or cancel a trip, except on the various occasions when he did actually collapse; so, things never got any better, only worse. Later there were more serious medical problems than the hip, but it was the hip that began it. I doubt whether, after about 1966, Louis was ever wholly free from pain, but so often he contrived to conceal it.

Had the situation been only as I have described it so far, I am sure I should have been able to stay at his side and help him to cope with these . problems. But so far I have only been describing causes rather than their effects. The latter were such that I ended by losing my professional respect for Louis; and it had been very great indeed. Once that was so, I was no longer able to offer the concurrence and unquestioning adulation he now seemed to demand. Accordingly, he began to seek it elsewhere, in directions that appalled me, while I became the opposite of a comfort to him; a cause of exasperation, a harm to his self-esteem. So I judged that it was kinder to remove myself to Olduvai, taking with me very much lingering affection. Of all the places where Louis could count on the adulation he craved in these latter years, nowhere exceeded the levels reached in Southern California. His audiences there loved him anyhow as a person and a visiting super-star, but the local archaeological community worshipped him even more because he gave them, with the guarantee of his personal infallibility, what they had always wanted: Early Man of their very own. And it was Louis's attempt to fulfil this desire at Calico Hills in the Mojave Desert that was so catastrophic to his professional career and was largely responsible for the parting of our ways.

I shall not dwell on the details of the Calico dig, which continued for the next five or six years, and indeed sporadically long after that. I visited the site with Louis when we were in California together, and I saw the finds, which mainly consisted of fractured pieces of chert, found *in situ* in an alluvial fan laid down by various processes including mud-flows. This deposit was certainly old, and could well have been much older than Louis and his local geologist, Thomas Clements, were arguing. Within the fan deposit there were rounded boulders and angular blocks of chert which, when the fan was in a mobile state, could hardly have avoided coming into frequent and heavy contact with one another. Of course there were flakes of chert incorporated in the deposit – in such circumstances, how could there fail to be? Some of them, if found on a true working-floor, would certainly have been accepted as genuine knapping debris: the casual flakes produced by nature and by a human tool-maker can by no means always be distinguished, but on a human working-floor there will always be products that are beyond the scope of natural processes.

That Louis and I should argue in a friendly way, or agree to differ on some archaeological point, was nothing new; but this was something quite different, which shows all the ways in which Louis had changed. However meticulous the excavation, he was still arguing in a completely unscientific way, by not considering all the processes that *might* have produced the pieces he regarded as artefacts. To me, it was the treatment of the finds that was most shocking. In the dark ages of prehistory it is true that only *belles pièces* were retained by the excavators. Waste material and artefacts that did not catch the eye were discarded. At Calico, this process was carried even further. The chert fragments from each square – carefully kept according to their appropriate levels – were set aside. Dee Simpson, who directed operations in Louis's absence, then sorted through each heap and selected certain pieces as possibly pleasing to Louis. Later, whenever Louis happened to be in California next, he would take certain pieces from the selection kept for him and pronounce them to be artefacts. The proportion of pieces that finally made the grade was infinitesimal compared to the whole.

In 1968 Louis called an international conference of experts, everyone he could get to come, to consider the site and the finds and pass judgement on them. After various delays this took place in October 1970, by which time Louis was a sick man, recently recovered from a serious heart attack. I was not asked to go: I had made my opinion clear enough already. There was quite a large attendance, including many senior and experienced geologists and archaeologists, who were shown everything and listened to reports on every conceivable aspect of the site and the finds before being invited at a final session to give their opinions. As various of those who attended have told me, no one really cared to get up and make a strong outright condemnation of the evidence, because it would have been equivalent to saying that Louis had lost his capacity to think scientifically – which, I fear, was perfectly true. But there was too much affection for him and respect for what he had achieved in past years, and a feeling that his health was too precarious to stand much emotional strain. Therefore many gave no opinion at all, and others confined their rejection to asking searching questions and expressing guarded dissatisfaction with the answers or suggesting other tests that needed to be made. The session ended with what the delegates thought was a verdict of 'not proven', but Louis apparently had no doubts that his assessment of the Calico site had been approved, because he held a conference for the local press representatives which resulted in articles in the next morning's papers stating on his authority that the existence of Early Man at Calico Hills had been confirmed by the international experts, and that the age of the site was likely to be 80,000 years.

I remember that I met him at the airport on his return, and that he told me, 'It's all right; they all accepted the evidence.' I said nothing, because colleagues had already informed me that this was by no means the case. My own belief is that his faith in the site had probably been seriously shaken, but that he would never admit he had been wrong or let down his faithful followers in California. I cannot recall hearing him mention Calico again. It was all so unnecessary and so sad when one thinks that Louis still had the world of prehistoric man at his feet here in East Africa. It grieves me particularly to think that he entirely missed the significance of Laetoli, that spectacular Pliocene site in Tanzania, 3·75 million years old, where he had actually worked on two occasions and where the unique hominid footprints were found only six years after his death. At Laetoli no fewer than fifteen new species have emerged as a result of the work carried out between 1974 and 1981, possibly a record for a single site, and that would have delighted him beyond measure.

Calico Hills was without doubt the main cause of our basic disagreement and virtual separation, but there was another event not without significance. At the instigation of Phillip Tobias, the University of Witwatersrand in South Africa had resolved to confer joint honorary degrees on Louis and myself, and late in 1967 the Vice-Chancellor wrote to Louis to find out whether this would be acceptable. But the relations between Kenya and Tanzania on the one hand, and South Africa on the other, were as prickly then as they are now, and Louis, who felt himself (with justification) to be a figure of some importance in East Africa, considered that he should refuse, as a gesture against the policy of *apartheid*. He expected me to do the same. My own view was different. It was true that the University of Witwatersrand had ultimately been compelled to exercise racial discrimination in its admission of students, but it was doing so under strong protest, having spoken out boldly. As recently as 1982 the University nominated Nelson Mandela, an African Nationalist leader who has been in detention on Robben Island over twelve years, for the office of Chancellor.

There were universities in South Africa with which I would not have wished to have even the most tenuous connection because of their support for *apartheid*, but Wits was not one of them and I saw no reason for administering a rebuff to Phillip, one of our best colleagues, for that is what it seemed to me to be and indeed he was greatly upset. So I told

Louis demonstrates his talent for making stone tools to Gertrude Caton-Thompson during the 1955 Pan-African Congress.

PREVIOUS PAGE: A historic moment. Presenting *Proconsul* to the world's press at Heathrow airport in 1948.

TOP LEFT: Starting to uncover the 'Zinj' skull in 1959, accompanied by Sally and Victoria.

BOTTOM LEFT: The 'Zinj' site at an advanced stage of excavation in 1961. The dividing wall of undisturbed deposits provides a reference section for identifying the levels of individual finds.

ABOVE: Louis and I delightedly display the palate of the 'Zinj' skull, shortly after it was discovered.

RIGHT: The 'Zinj' skull after careful piecing together. The lower jaw was never found, and the sides of the reconstruction shown here are probably too long.

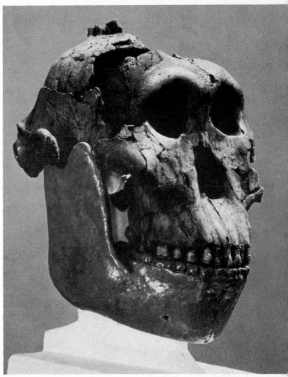

ABOVE: Simon, the incorrigible Sykes monkey, was great friends with all my Dalmatians, especially Victoria.
BELOW: There are times when boisterous wildebeest calves can prove quite a handful.

ABOVE: This photograph of Ferdinand, our tame eagle owl, was posted in our local shop at Langata with a notice requesting anyone finding him to telephone our house.
BELOW: Lisa, the orphan cheetah, who 'adopted' us at Olduvai.

ABOVE: The Honorary Degree conferred by Yale University gave me particular pleasure. After the ceremony, the honorands were photographed with Dr Kingman Brewster, President of the University and later US Ambassador to Britain.
RIGHT: Another great honour was receiving the Linnaeus Medal from King Gustav of Sweden in 1978.

Louis I proposed to accept. He was furious about it. Again, instead of accepting a decision of his with unquestioning loyalty, I had opposed it with a reasoned judgement of my own. So I went ahead and on 30 March 1968 received what was, in fact, my first Honorary Degree, at the University of Witwatersrand in Johannesburg.

My daughter-in-law Mollie, who was staying at Langata at the time, told me afterwards that while I was away on this trip Louis listened for hours to the local radio, apparently expecting to hear of some hostile reaction to my going. I simply do not know what he could have been expecting, but it certainly never came. Meanwhile, I greatly enjoyed being an academic VIP on my own for the very first time.

In 1961 Louis had resigned as Curator of the Coryndon Museum in return for a salary, guaranteed by the National Geographic Society, which would enable him to work on research. In 1962 he got the Trustees to agree to the creation of an ancillary Centre for Prehistory and Palaeontology, and became its Honorary Director, with a duty to raise funds for its staff and its work. The Centre was where I worked in Nairobi, and therefore where I did the bulk of my laboratory studies for the monograph on Olduvai Beds I and II. Space was quite extraordinarily cramped at first, when the Centre occupied old buildings, adjacent to the Museum, which had formerly been the offices of the East African branch of the Desert Locust Control. In 1964 the Wenner-Gren Foundation gave money for a new building, the Fejos Laboratory, named in memory of Paul Fejos, their Director of Research. Sadly, he died while it was being built. His wife Lita succeeded him as Director of Research and officially opened the new laboratory. But the Fejos Laboratory could not solve all the Centre's space problems, and even after it was built I was still working on the mass of Olduvai material in space that amounted to little more than a cupboard. Fortunately, we had a visit at about this time from Melvin Payne and others of our good friends from the National Geographic Society, who agreed to fund a new laboratory for me to work in. To my great relief and gratitude, it was ready by the end of 1964.

In case anyone should think that we were also financially prosperous in our family life at this time, I will quote a letter I wrote to Louis during one of his periods away in America. It is dated 1963, but I could have written something similar at almost any time in the 1960s:

'I certainly *do* hope you can do something about cash. Things are pretty desperate. I have not been able to pay Mike or Mollie [assistants at Olduvai] last month and will not be able to this month, or myself. There is not enough to get more petrol or pay more deposit accounts in Arusha, all of which are now exhausted. Also, no *duka* [Asian traders' shops] bills have been paid. The telephone is 700/- and Philip's school fees for this term just 1000/-. I am quite desperate. If Richard had not been able to lend us *all* (including Shirley and Mrs

M – [Louis's secretary]) I don't know how we could have got through. You must realise that I cannot meet school fees, light, telephone, wages, food and all the extras out of my 2000/-, even if I get it.'

Louis's mind was clearly on higher kinds of finance. He was never practical about his own money, or that of his family, however much his institutional fund-raising might prosper.

So life went hectically on during the late 1960s, against the deteriorating background that I have already described. But if Louis was beginning to totter on his pinnacle, Richard was already starting to scale the heights. After the successful Peninj expeditions with Glynn Isaac, and his marriage to Margaret Cropper, Richard worked voluntarily with Louis and me at the new Centre, though his income still came from his safari company in partnership with Alan Root. Margaret also worked at the Centre, devoting most of her time to helping me on the Olduvai material. She also went with Richard on a further successful field expedition, to work on Middle Pleistocene sites in the Baringo basin, not far from where Jonathan and Mollie were now living. The deposits there produced important faunal and archaeological remains, and a lower jaw of *Homo erectus*. Glynn Isaac had been the first Assistant Director of the Centre, under Louis, and held that post until he left Nairobi in 1967 to go first to Britain to complete his doctoral dissertation on Olorgesailie, and afterwards to take up a post at Berkeley, California. His departure left the post of Assistant Director of the Centre free and Richard was appointed to it as the ideal person to act as Louis's deputy. From there he moved the following year, while still only 23, to become the Administrative Director of the National Museum. Louis gave his full support to this appointment, and was delighted, though he made quite sure that he himself retained full responsibility for the Centre.

But it was in the field that Richard had really been showing his prowess, for in 1967 he had been the leader of the Kenya contingent of a three-nation expedition (Kenyan, French and American) to the Plio-Pleistocene deposits in the Omo Delta area of southern Ethiopia. This was the expedition that arose directly out of Louis's meeting with Emperor Haile Selassie a few years before. Strong financial support was given by the National Geographic Society – and it was needed, because the country was wild even by the standards members of the Leakey family were used to. Transport and communications were a major problem, and that is how it came about that a helicopter was used.

During that season some business matter arose in Nairobi that demanded Richard's presence, and in response to a radio call he was flown down and back in a light aircraft, since the overland trip would have taken some days. On the return journey, the plane took a route along the east side of Lake Turkana (then Lake Rudolf) to avoid an area of bad weather, and Richard saw from the window deposits of what looked like ancient lake sediments traversed by eroded gullies, between the present lake shore and the volcanic hinterland. Like Louis, he was not one to leave an exciting possibility unexplored if any means lay to hand, and just such a means was indeed available in the form of a helicopter that could be borrowed. Richard therefore made a quick reconnaissance trip to the eastern shore of the lake, about which he kept fairly quiet, and satisfied himself that the deposits were of the kind he had supposed and did indeed contain fossils. I suppose in a way it was an episode like Louis's and my following up the news of fossils at Laetoli while we were at Olduvai in 1935, though the speed and ease of Richard's reconnaissance in contrast to ours reminds one that over 30 years separate the two episodes.

Early in 1968, Richard accompanied Louis to the States on the usual fund-raising pilgrimage, and it was expected that in reporting to the National Geographic Society the results of his 1967 Omo work, he would ask for another year's funds in order to continue. But without consulting Louis in advance, he instead asked for the grant to be given to him to go with a separate expedition to explore his new East Turkana area, leaving the Omo joint expedition to the French and Americans. This bold stroke threw Louis completely off balance and he argued forcefully against it, though it was just the kind of tactic he might himself have deployed in earlier days. The outcome was significant: Richard's arguments won the day. Later that year he led his first expedition to East Turkana, and so began a series of discoveries that were to prove as spectacular and important as anything Louis or I had found. As the years passed, a staggering amount of information emerged about Early Man and his environment. Funding and research assistance poured in. The count of individual hominids represented among the East Turkana fossil finds rose rapidly into three figures and included an unsurpassed number of magnificent fossil skulls and parts of skeletons. But there are always problems, and there was a major one even in the spectacularly successful East Turkana project. In this case it was a matter of dating: there was a level of volcanic ash known as the KBS Tuff (named after Kay Berehnsmeyer) that was critical for correlating sites in different parts of the vast expanse of the East Turkana fossil beds. Potassium-argon dating of this tuff, carried out by a Cambridge laboratory under the direction of Drs Fitch and Miller, gave a date too old to be compatible with the faunal evidence if this were tied in with the faunal sequence at the Omo valley at the northern end of Lake Turkana. The Omo site had been firmly dated and had yielded a fine sequence of fauna, although the hominid finds were disappointing.

Garniss Curtis of the Berkeley Laboratory, who had been responsible for the Olduvai dating, maintained that the Fitch and Miller date of 2.6 million years for the KBS Tuff was erroneous, and too old. Arguments continued for a number of years and at times became quite heated, but never descended to the personal level that has since become prevalent in certain quarters. Finally, with Richard's permission, the Berkeley Laboratory was supplied with a series of samples scrupulously collected by Thure Cerling, a former student of Dick Hay's, and Garniss was able to prove conclusively that the KBS Tuff was either 1.6 or 1.8my old, and not 2.6my as claimed by Fitch and Miller. Taking other lines of evidence into consideration there seems every reason to believe that the date of 1.8my is correct. Throughout all the years of arguments Richard staunchly, one might almost say obstinately, supported the Fitch and Miller date and even developed a distinct coolness towards me when I became sceptical of it. This state of affairs is now happily over and we are once more as good friends as we were before.

By the end of 1968 my own necessary path, for Louis's good as much as my own, had become clear in my mind. A new campaign of excavations could be begun at Olduvai whenever I was ready: the analysis of the finds from Beds I and II was approaching a state of readiness to go to press, but Beds III and IV were still guarding their secrets. One did not go to Olduvai just to live: one went to work and live. Since I was starting a new campaign of fieldwork at Olduvai Gorge, I would have to spend long periods of time down there as I had during the exploration of Beds I and II, so of course I took the dogs with me. At the time it never occurred to me that this would be the beginning of the final break with Louis, but in fact it was so.

12
The end of a chapter

IT WAS ABOUT FIVE YEARS since I had lived at Olduvai, as opposed to making short visits there, and since 1963 the place had joined the tourist route, as was bound to happen after all the publicity of the early 1960s. Those were great days for the tourist trade: *safaris* were still cheap, game was abundant, the roads were in reasonable repair, petrol was easy to obtain and inexpensive, and Kenya, Tanzania and Uganda enjoyed friendly relations and economic co-operation. If one drove from Nairobi to Olduvai, the border crossing at Namanga involved little more formality than the signing of one's name. Even the currency notes and postage stamps of Kenya and Tanzania and Uganda were interchangeable. Small wonder that the tourists came in large numbers, bringing prosperity to many areas and receiving superb value in return as they stayed in spectacularly situated and well-run hotels, where they were well fed between their not-too-arduous drives through some of the most beautiful scenery in the world. Olduvai was a natural port of call between the central Serengeti, where there were safari lodges at Seronera and Ndutu, and Ngorongoro, where the Crater was a world-famous attraction. How very different things are today in Tanzania, though the tourists still come and travel as best they can between run-down and crisis-stricken safari bases, not knowing what basic commodities will be unobtainable at each next stop. It says much for the natural beauties of Tanzania and its wildlife that they still come, and for the ingenuity of the people of Tanzania that the tourists still get to see a great deal.

But in 1968 the tourists had never had it so good, and therefore I moved my camp some distance from where they arrived at the Gorge, some of them clearly expecting a hominid fossil under every stone and a lion under every tree. In some ways I was delighted that there should be tourists because they contributed to our research fund, and in due course I did my best to see that they should have literature and postcards available, good guides to show them the Zinj site and the open-air museums we had made, a small museum explaining the geology of the Gorge with casts of the main hominid fossils and a selection of stone tools, and an open-fronted grass-roofed *banda* with a magnificent view over the Gorge, where they could eat their picnic lunches. But that did not mean that I wanted them waiting concealed outside my hut to photograph me through the window when I had just washed my hair, as happened on one occasion. Nor did I react kindly the time when a group of about 30 came upon Dick Hay, Shirley Coryndon and myself down near the MNK site and encircled us against the steep site of the Gorge so that we could not escape from their clicking shutters and peering eyes. Finally Dick rounded on them and sent them scurrying off.

By now we also had our own airstrip at Olduvai, a great benefit for bringing in stores, or distinguished visitors who had no time to travel down by road, but that in its original position began to attract uninvited airborne visitors of the kind who expected one to drop one's work and confer a prolonged welcome upon them, even if they were complete strangers. I used to estimate, with disgust, how much each such party had paid for its safari by the width of the leopard-skin bands on their hats. And now we have no leopards left. After the border between Kenya and Tanzania was closed in 1977, tourist flights to Olduvai ceased and I therefore closed the old airstrip and opened a new one handier for my camp, where only personal friends could come. In 1968 I was still very shy of having to give lectures to completely strange audiences. I had no patience with well-meaning, but to me stupid, questions, and above all I wanted to be left in peace to get on with my work at Olduvai, choosing my visitors carefully when I wanted any at all. Some people might say I have not changed so much in all these respects since then, although public speaking now presents no problems to me.

The new camp was across the Main Gorge from the old one, on the level land not far from where the Main and Side Gorges meet. Here a large grass *banda* was erected as a living-room, dining-room and place to work, close to a fine flat-topped acacia. My own hut, odd as it may sound, was one of those round 'Uniport' metal structures that are made in sections and are easy to assemble. Painted green and given the addition of a double verandah and a large thatched roof of grass, it created no scar on the landscape, and, with the advantages offered by a proper door and glazed windows, it has been my real home ever since. The camp also included a kitchen and quarters for my camp staff, some of whom are still with me today in Nairobi. There were also what house agents call 'the usual offices', but since 1968 several buildings have been added – work-rooms, simple laboratories, storage for excavated material, visitors' huts and others to which I will refer later. It was Richard, with his usual energy, who organized for me the move of camp in 1968, and the setting up of the buildings. He understood very clearly that this was to be a semi-permanent home, and he made an excellent job of it.

The main work-room looked south across the Side Gorge to the great extinct volcano Lemagrut, which is the dominant feature in almost any Olduvai landscape, changing its hues with the passage of each day's sun, sometimes hazy and distant-looking, sometimes extraordinarily sharp and clear. The original grass hut has now been replaced by an enlarged version with stone walls, but on exactly the same site, positioned to give plenty of light through its open front without the sun ever shining directly in. My own hut stands only a few yards from the edge of the Main Gorge, and looks southeast with a view across the Main Gorge itself, against a backdrop that includes the whole mass of the volcanic highlands – from Lemagrut on the right, past Sadiman, Oldeani and the caldera wall of Ngorongoro to Olmoti, Embagai and finally, 50 miles or more away, a glimpse of the truncated cone, clad in white ash, that is Ol Donyo Lengai, the last volcano of them all that remains active. These are Masai names with descriptive meanings. For example, Oldeani is the place of the bamboo; Olmoti is shaped like a cooking pot; and Ol Donyo Lengai is the mountain of God, so named because it is still active. At any time of the year I can watch the dawn from the windows of my hut. Behind my camp, the view beyond the Gorge is very different: the acacias and thorn trees quickly end and the flatness of the Serengeti stretches away to the horizon, broken here and there by inselbergs, sudden isolated or clustered outcrops of the very old basement complex rocks – some of them a thousand times as old as our earliest Bed I sites in the Gorge.

The object of my new campaign was not the early levels on which we had previously worked, but the later half of the sequence, Beds III and IV, and the divisions that Dick Hay had proposed to replace what was formerly called Bed V: the Masek, Ndutu and Naisiusiu beds, all named after local topographic features. This is not to say, however, that we ignored Beds I and II. Far from it. In the very first season, in October 1968, one of my workmen, Peter Nzube, found a crushed but nearly complete cranium of *Homo habilis* some 300 yards east of the DK hut circle site. It was in a block of limestone that had been worked loose by erosion, but we were able to trace its position conclusively to between the basalt at the base and the hard marker tuff, which had been dated to 1.75 million years ago, so it cannot have been far in age from the hut circle itself.

The higher beds at Olduvai represent a very different situation from that which prevailed when Bed I and the older parts of Bed II had been laid down. Then there had been a lake, and many of the Oldowan sites were close to its margins; the faunal evidence included such creatures as crocodiles, hippos, water-fowl and many fish remains. By the time of Bed III and afterwards, the local topography had been changed by faulting and the lake filled a different depression, with the whole drainage pattern changed, so that we found ourselves concerned with a plains environment in which there were stream channels, with which the archaeological sites were associated. The sites in these upper beds are therefore less numerous, and since the stream beds underwent phases of violent seasonal activity, the archaeological material has usually been disturbed to at least some extent, often considerably. Apart from the material filling the channels, large parts of the accumulated deposits consist of volcanic ash in one form or another.

That I can express these points about the Olduvai stratigraphy in just a few short sentences is entirely due to the long years of fieldwork spent at Olduvai by Dick Hay, whom I mentioned when I wrote about the campaigns that began in 1960 and whom I was delighted to have with me again in 1968 and for some part of almost every year since. Apart from the fact that Dick's work enabled me to achieve some understanding of the stratigraphy of the later beds, and thus of how the different archaeological sites related to each other, he was such a pleasant and reliable colleague and a splendid person with whom to discuss new ideas. Few things stirred him to anger, though the tourists I mentioned were one.

As regards the archaeology of Beds III, IV and Masek, we began with two disappointments and a success. The success was in that extraordinarily prolific locality FLK, which had already given us the Zinj site and Jonathan's *Homo habilis* site and all the material from FLK North that I mentioned. This time we were working high up in the side of the Gorge, in the Masek Beds, only two or three hundred yards from my new camp site. Here a fragment of hominid mandible had been found, and though little was to be seen on the surface our excavation uncovered a fine Acheulian site about 400,000 years old, in which almost all the tools were made of a white quartzite obtainable from the Precambrian inselbergs that were clearly visible a mere mile away to the north. The hand axes made from this rock were large and beautiful, and their symmetrical narrow pointed shapes had been repeated by their makers with a degree of precision that argues remarkable technical control.

The two disappointments were at sites where very prolific spreads of hand axes and cleavers had long been known to exist, and where much material had already been collected from the surface. Louis had believed these sites to be within Bed IV, but we found that in fact they were incorporated in superficial deposits of much more recent age, a circumstance that made it impossible to tell what original stratigraphic position the implements had occupied, and therefore what their real age was.

Other sites which we dug in these years in Bed IV were in parts of the Gorge known as PDK, WK and HEB. Between them they produced a great amount of material which I shall not attempt to describe in detail here. HEB yielded several different levels with hand axes. In 1962 John Waechter had excavated here a fine industry, with many elegantly shaped implements fashioned from green phonolite, a lava whose source we discovered to be Engelosen, a small volcano rising from the plains about eight miles away. In other levels the scarcity of flaking debris accompanying the hand axes suggested to us that the implements had been blocked out at the quarry sites where the rock for them had been obtained, and then brought to the site for completion. At a site known to us as Hippo Cliff, WK yielded a large skeleton of *Hippopotamus gorgops*, almost complete and associated with a few stone tools, and this seemed to be a kill or butchery site. Not far away was the main WK site, where a large number of hand axes and cleavers lay within a stream channel, disturbance being only slight. There, we were delighted to find *Homo erectus* remains lying at the same level as the implements, and they included the first ever *H. erectus* pelvis, though some years later Richard found another at one of his East Turkana sites and a further example has come from Tautavel in France.

The Bed IV sites I have mentioned so far have all been Acheulian, with many of the typical hand axes that are so widely distributed over the Old World as the hallmark of Acheulian industries. Their dates range from Lower to Early Upper Pleistocene. Where there is any proper association of Acheulian material and hominid remains, the hominids seem to be *Homo erectus*, as at WK, or for the younger Acheulian industries in some parts of the world, primitive forms of *Homo sapiens*. Previously, when we excavated in Bed II, we had been able to show that the oldest Acheulian material at Olduvai was contemporary, from the middle of Bed II onwards, with industries that were developed forms of the Oldowan tradition. In my view at the time, these two series of tool kits had been made by different populations, and probably different hominid types, though some of my colleagues preferred the perfectly reasonable alternative notion that the tool kits differed merely because they had been made to fulfil different functions. When we began our campaign in Bed IV we found, quite against expectation, that in these younger levels too there were sites that appeared to be Developed Oldowan rather than Acheulian, though clearly of closely similar age. It was not just that the industries *looked* different from those of the Acheulian; when studied technologically, or when the pieces were measured and analysed statistically, major differences could be pinpointed. I would dearly have liked to find hominid remains at one of these Bed IV Developed Oldowan occurrences, to see whether my idea that a different hominid type was their maker held good – something to compare with the *H. erectus* remains from WK. But it was not to be, and the reason for the contemporary occurrence of such different tool kits still cannot be stated with certainty.

Bed III, in the eastern and central section of the Gorge, is a very striking feature, being bright red in colour. When one comes to think of it, it is to the sporadic patches of Bed III sediments contrasting with the greys, whites and buff colours of the other beds, and with the greens and bleached yellows of the vegetation, that the Gorge owes its very great beauty, especially in the early evening light. But colour is not a useful criterion for field geologists, and Dick Hay's predecessors in that role had assumed that all of Bed III was red, and also that all red sediments were Bed III. Both beliefs turned out to be wrong, and when Dick was able to show this he made a major contribution to our understanding of the overall geology and stratigraphy of the Gorge. The redness of Bed III appears to reflect a set of climatic circumstances and chemical processes like those operating today to turn certain localized areas of the sediments red at Lake Natron, where fresh-water streams flow across highly alkaline soda-flats. Only one area of the Gorge has produced archaeological sites within Bed III, of which those at JK are the most important. Stone tools were found and some hominid remains with them, but the material seems to have been reworked by stream action and one cannot be sure which items really belong together.

But also at JK was one of the most remarkable and unexpected sites found anywhere in the Gorge: a complex of pits and connecting runnels which seem to have been scooped by hand out of a silty deposit, then soft but now rock hard. There were many other indentations in the same surface in the area we exposed. Some could be animal trampling and one looked very like part of a human footprint. Nothing like this pit complex had ever been found before at any Lower Palaeolithic site in the world, and I was faced with the problems of convincing sceptical colleagues that the pits were artificial in the first place and explaining their function in the second. I am not sure I have by any means succeeded yet with many people. Richard put it in a nutshell when he flew Louis down to see the pits in April 1972. The two of them stood in front of the JK pits in utter silence, which lasted for some minutes. Then Richard said: 'You know, Mother, when there is complete silence in this family it means only one thing: some member of the family is in serious trouble.' It was me he meant.

When the geologist W. W. Bishop visited the site he was at first convinced that the pits were of purely natural origin. Bill Bishop had been a friend of ours ever since he came to study African palaeontology with Louis on his way to take up a post in Uganda. Later he did much good work in the Baringo area, and was still working there when he died at a tragically early age from a heart attack in 1976. But I showed Bill Bishop how the runnels were flat-bottomed, with a profile that no naturally formed runnel could ever have, and how the pits were not smooth-sided as they would have been if they had been pot-holes formed by a natural scouring process. Indeed, the walls of some bore curious parallel grooves, which looked very much as if they had been left by human fingers. With these observations Bill could only agree. Others who were sceptical about the artificial nature of the pits and runnels suggested that they could have been made by tree roots, or by animals trampling at a salt-lick, and this is probably true of the smaller holes; but I remain convinced that the larger pits are the work of man.

The only real clue I can offer regarding the purpose of the pits is our discovery that they contained traces of a deposit very much richer in salt than the one into which the pits and runnels had themselves been dug. Were they perhaps a system by which salt-bearing water was trapped and channelled into scooped-out hollows, where it could evaporate, leaving a salty deposit to be scraped from the walls by human fingers? Salt is an important commodity in hot arid climates like that of the Olduvai area in Bed III times. No doubt its presence would also have attracted animals, but I do not think that animals' feet can account for more than a proportion of the features we excavated. Recently, while flying in a light aircraft over North Kenya not far from Isiolo, my youngest son Philip saw a complex of pits and channels of modern age, very like those of JK, and known to be in use for salt extraction. I am making plans for these to be visited and studied in case they can cast any light on our discovery. Whatever the reason for the existence of the JK pits there can be no doubt of their age: they are *in situ* in Bed III sediments.

While all this archaeology was going on between 1968 and 1972, various geophysicists were engaged in studying the Olduvai sediments from the point of view of the palaeomagnetic polarity record. It has been well known for many years that at various times in the past the direction of the earth's magnetic field has undergone periods of reversal. In the simplest possible terms, if a reversal happened now, compass needles that point north would swing round and point south – though in fact such reversals do not take place instantaneously. To the great benefit of geologists and archaeologists, when certain kinds of rock form, notably volcanic lavas and ashes deposited under conditions of great heat, they preserve for ever the polarity direction that prevailed at the time. In a sequence of deposits, many of volcanic origin, covering a long period of time, which is exactly what we have at Olduvai, one can therefore hope to read off a long record of consecutive periods of 'normal' and 'reversed' polarity. All that is interesting enough, but it becomes a great deal more so when one remembers that the very same types of rock are often directly datable by isotopic methods, particularly the potassium-argon method to which I have already referred. From work of this kind, all over the world, the situation has come about that a complete record of the numerous polarity changes, with accurate dates, is now known for the last several million years. Merely to find a 'reversed' deposit is to narrow down at once the range of possibilities of its age, and other evidence such as isotopic dating, fauna and archaeological remains may assist in pinpointing the age more accurately.

Significant parts of the early work in this field were done at Olduvai, and, starting in the period I am describing, various geophysicists came to work alongside Dick Hay, including Allan Cox, a Professor of Geology at the University of California, Stanford, and Andrew Brock, then a lecturer in Physics at Nairobi University. There is even an event of 'normal' polarity within a 'reversed' epoch that was first found at Olduvai and is named the 'Olduvai Event'. As with all scientific methods, great care has to be taken over the material studied. If a rock has been reheated above a certain critical temperature then it will lose its original polarity record and take on the one prevailing at the time of the reheating. Only in extraordinary circumstances could such a critical temperature be reached. But I well remember Allan Cox's excitement when he thought he had located a certain very rarely preserved brief reversed event within the normal sediments of the Ndutu Beds, only to find that it was an effect of modern lightning strikes!

While all these things were happening at Olduvai I was also making periodic visits to Nairobi to attend to family affairs. The main situation with which I had to cope was Louis's steady decline both in health and, from my point of view, personality. But there were other quite separate issues. In 1969 Richard and Margaret had a daughter, Anna, a most delightful child. But Anna's parents were not happy together and before the end of the year they had separated, after less than four years of marriage. I was sad, especially for Anna. I was, and still am, very fond indeed of Margaret, but I had never seen her and Richard as temperamentally compatible, and so it proved. I was delighted that Margaret stayed on to work at the Centre, so I did not lose her or Anna, though some years later they went to live in South Africa. With the strains of marriage removed, Richard and Margaret could meet quite amicably, even after he married Meave Epps in October 1970. Meave was a zoologist who had completed her doctoral work while assisting Louis on one of his primatology projects. She had joined Richard's 1969 East Turkana expedition, and they had quickly become inseparable. Meave and I have got on well together from the start, and our mutual affection and friendship have been further cemented by working together on *Africa's Vanishing Art*, my book on the Tanzanian rock paintings. Meanwhile Philip, to keep his end up, made a marriage to a Californian girl, Lynn Bailey, early in 1970, which all of us except Louis thought hasty and ill-considered. It lasted just a few weeks.

Louis continued his hectic fund-raising visits to the States, though in 1968 an event had taken place in California which should have eased the pressure. This was the institution of the L.S.B. Leakey Foundation for Research Related to Man's Origin, set up for Louis by his friends in Southern California, under the inspired leadership of Allen O'Brien. I myself had very little to do with it at this stage, though I did after Louis died. Allen and his wife Helen became close friends of mine, and his early death in 1980 in a plane crash was a great sadness to me and to many people. He was an enthusiast in the nicest sense of the word and never lost his boyish love of adventure. We first met him as a safari client of Richard's, and then he took part in Richard's section of the Omo expedition in 1967, and afterwards joined Clark Howell and the American team. Oceans and rivers always fascinated him, and on the Omo he descended rapids in a rubber boat and swam among the crocodiles to his heart's content. He virtually adopted Louis, who was the epitome of everything he wished to be, and he fell gladly for the local 'Early Man' hypothesis. Allen ensured that Louis's lecture fees were commensurate with his box-office value, something that had never occurred to Louis himself, who was one of nature's financial innocents. The Foundation from the start tended to have a second existence as an élite social club for the higher ranks of Californian hostesses, but there can be no question of their devotion to Louis, and they certainly organized his programme for him even if they tended to pack in more than was really desirable. That side was run by Joan Travis, whom I also later came to know quite well.

In 1970, for a change, it was Richard and I who went to America early in the year to raise funds and report on our work, while Louis stayed in Nairobi; and it was while we were away that he had his first heart attack. Unfortunately, he either misunderstood, or simply ignored the pain, and insisted on flying at once to London *en route*, he said, to join me in Washington as a spur-of-the-moment idea. Not surprisingly he got no further than intensive care in a London hospital, where he survived a second coronary. He afterwards spent a long convalescence in the flat of Vanne Goodall, mother of Jane Goodall, one of Louis's best known and most successful primatologists. One way and another, Vanne Goodall found herself caring for Louis on many occasions and in various capacities during his later years, and I am sure he derived from her kindness and friendship much of the support that I myself could no longer provide. In his last two years, he survived a number of serious falls, two of which actually resulted in blood clots on the brain, high blood pressure, various bladder infections, and an extraordinary attack by a swarm of bees, in which he received several hundred stings. Through all this he drove himself relentlessly on, never giving his body the spells of complete rest that just might have allowed a real recovery.

Aware as Louis was of his failing health, of my withdrawal, and of the encroachment of others on his professional territory, can it surprise anyone that he spent most of his life at the end in a ceaseless struggle to prove that his powers were not waning? Hence the refusal to rest, the quest for new projects, the acceptance of every invitation to lecture, to make a film, to visit a university, to receive some wealthy visitor; hence perhaps even the ultimate need to pull in the funds, to show what power his name still carried. And, at a more human level, hence his women, some of whom were girls barely out of their teens, who gave him tenderness and attention. On this I do not wish to dwell. Of course I knew, and of course I minded, and perhaps what I minded most was the deplorably low standard, as it seemed to me, of his choices in some cases. Therefore, it was painful, but not really a surprise, if once or twice when I arrived at Langata I found him not alone, though he tried to be discreet.

I do not mean to give the impression that from 1968 to 1972 Louis and I were never together, for that would be quite untrue; indeed there were happy times when, so to speak, the old Louis would briefly reappear when he visited Olduvai to see how work on Beds III and IV was progressing, and when he and I visited Addis Ababa in Ethiopia in 1968 for him to receive a special gold medal and cash prize awarded by the Emperor himself, the Haile Selassie I Award for African Research. Louis and I were in Addis Ababa together again three years later for the Seventh Pan-African Congress in the series Louis had begun in 1947. The Eighth, incidentally, was held in Nairobi as Louis had greatly hoped, and although he died before it took place he knew that it was to be there and was very glad.

The meeting at Addis had its hilarious aspects, notwithstanding all the efforts of its Vice-President, who was none other than my old friend Thurstan Shaw. The great conference room where the sessions were held had no projector, and if it had possessed one there would have been no means of darkening the impressive circle of windows all round the hall, just below the ceiling. The Emperor was present at the principal reception, seated on his throne: a small man, who expected the ultimate in formality and protocol, to whom everyone was introduced, whether or not Thurstan could remember their names. The Emperor smiled only when his two pet dogs came up to him and burrowed under the throne on which he sat: tiny Chihuahuas of impeccable lineage, actually wearing diamond-studded collars – I cannot imagine what my Dalmatians would have thought of them. When not under the imperial throne, they ranged around the room getting under people's feet, and Thurstan did his best not to trip over them, an enterprise in which I fancy he was not wholly successful. This was the last time that Louis and I were together at a large professional gathering of our friends and colleagues, and we thoroughly enjoyed it.

I also remember with pleasure that the last evening I spent with Louis was a strikingly happy one. Richard was there too, and it was 26 September 1972. We were all three at ease with each other, and Louis was happy for two quite specific reasons. First, he had just completed the extrication of his son Colin and his family from Uganda: Colin had a post as lecturer at Makerere University, and the reign of terror in Uganda under Idi Amin was about to begin. Colin Leakey was one of the last Europeans to leave in time, and Louis had actually met him at Nairobi airport and taken him and his family to Langata to spend the day before they flew on to London that evening. Louis himself was due to fly to London a few days later, *en route* to California to begin another of his long tours, so he would soon be seeing Colin and his family again. The other reason was that Richard had just returned from East Turkana for a mid-season visit to Nairobi, bringing his latest star find, something he very much wanted his father to see. This was the famous hominid skull known as '1470' (which is its Kenya National Museum registration number) – by far the best-preserved skull of *Homo habilis* to be found anywhere. It came from below the KBS Tuff, then believed to be 2.61 million years old. So on that day Louis was able to rejoice in his own son's discovery of just what he himself had been predicting and seeking for 35 years: a really early example of something that would have to be recognized as *Homo* rather than *Australopithecus*, thereby proving a major point in his own view of human evolution. As the dating then stood, this new find of Richard's looked likely to be late Pliocene, let alone Lower Pleistocene. Louis was excited, triumphant, sublimely happy, and his mood communicated itself to me and to Richard. It was almost like old times, as we spent the evening at Langata together before Richard drove Louis to the airport to begin another round of the kind of travel he so much enjoyed, however tiring it was.

As the car left, I thought something I had thought on more than one previous occasion; that I would never see him again.

Next day, Richard and I went our separate ways, he back to East Turkana and I to Olduvai. The next Sunday afternoon, I was in camp at Olduvai talking with Amini Mturi, the Director of Antiquities in Tanzania, who had looked in to pay one of his regular visits to see how we were getting on. Suddenly there came the sound of a light plane passing low over camp as a signal of intention to land, and it came straight in: Philip, in a hired plane. Once before, when Louis had been rushed to hospital and was on the danger list, Philip had flown down like this to tell me, for there was no other sure way of getting in touch in an emergency. I knew what to expect, as I drove out to the airstrip. He came towards me. 'Another heart attack?' I said, 'Or is he dead?' 'Dead,' said Philip.

Louis had had a massive coronary that morning, at Vanne Goodall's flat in London: he had been rushed to hospital but had died soon after admission. When something long expected finally happens, the shock is not lessened. Within the hour I had collected a few things and was flying back with Philip to Nairobi.

13
Picking up the threads

LOUIS'S DEATH WAS NEWS around the world, as was only to be expected. Letters and tributes, official and private, poured in – several hundred in all. They spoke with unfeigned warmth of his achievements and his stature in the world of anthropology, and their number and the variety of sources from which they came showed once more one of Louis's great qualities – his ability to make a profound impact on people of every kind, even those he met only briefly. 'Charisma' is a much over-used word, but it is exactly what Louis had, from quite an early age right to the end.

By the time I reached Langata, Richard had returned from Koobi Fora and had begun to arrange for Louis's body to be flown from London to Nairobi. Our old friend Sir Malin Sorsbie, who had more than once got us free return flights to London twenty years before, generously undertook to pay the cost of Louis's last journey. I went with Jonathan, Richard, Philip and Mollie to the airport to meet the flight, and President Kenyatta did us the honour of sending his social secretary to be with us, as a sign of his respect and affection for his old friend; he also sent a personal wreath to the funeral. It was rather ghastly waiting around at the airport and trying to think of things to say while crate after crate of ordinary cargo was unloaded before the coffin could be reached. The funeral was held on 4 October at the little church at Limuru, where both Louis's parents were buried as well as his aunt Sibby and also Archdeacon Owen, that splendid character of whom Louis and I had been so fond. It was just a short service, in a churchyard that is as English as any in England itself. I had wanted it to be for members of the immediate family only, but we had to include one or two official representatives and somehow there seemed to be far too many other people there as well. I have always looked on death as a very private matter, so the day was inevitably a tense and wearing one, not eased by the fact that I arrived late at the church after Jonathan took a wrong turning when driving me up to Limuru from Nairobi.

Two days later there was a big memorial service in the Cathedral in Nairobi; absolutely packed for the occasion and rather too much of a social event for my own taste. There were formal addresses, including one from Louis's brother-in-law Leonard Beecher, the Archbishop of East Africa, and also from the pastor and the Attorney General, Charles Njonjo, who had known the Leakey family from childhood. With that event over, we were left more or less in peace to sort ourselves out, and I was very glad indeed to have the companionship of Shirley Savage, who flew out from England to be with me, arriving the day after the memorial service. Later that month another memorial service was held, in the Chapel of St John's College, Cambridge, where Louis had been an undergraduate and a Research Fellow and latterly an Honorary Fellow. By all accounts it was a beautiful service, which Louis himself would greatly have appreciated. Frida Leakey was able to attend, with Colin and Priscilla and their families, and a large number of Louis's English friends and colleagues.

Meanwhile, we in Nairobi were assessing the situation in which Louis's death had left us and deciding how to resume lives that seemed suddenly to have changed in various ways, not all easily definable. Louis had left no Will and named no executor; he had left very little money, either, if it comes to that, because he spent most of what came his way on one or other of his research projects. In any case, there was no Will and his bank accounts were frozen since no one had power to sign on his behalf. Fortunately, by now, all three sons were fully independent, and my own needs could in the immediate future be met out of the annual honorarium I received from the National Geographic Society. The funding for my current work at Olduvai was also secure for some little way ahead. The burden of dealing with Louis's various research projects was mainly inherited by Richard, so far as Kenya was concerned, and by the Leakey Foundation as the main source of finance for projects outside Kenya. Over the next year or so, some were run down and some continued under new arrangements, but none of that really involved me.

The question of what should happen to the house at Langata was solved by Philip, who wisely took a longer-term view. It would certainly have been expensive to maintain the house just as it was to serve merely as an occasional base for myself when in Nairobi, and Philip saw that with a certain amount of building two guest houses could be made to yield good rentable accommodation and hence bring me in an income which would at least pay for rates and services and maintenance of the whole property. He therefore designed the conversion of a house and an outbuilding, making them into nice small houses with two bedrooms, kitchen and bathroom. Philip organized the whole operation, bringing in African workmen from his own safari camp to do the building, and very successful it proved, since I have never had difficulty in finding tenants and a useful amount of income has resulted, without any alteration or division of the main building itself having been needed.

As for myself, I returned to Olduvai as soon as I could. There was never any question of my moving back to Langata at this time. Olduvai had become my home, and it was a much nicer place in which to live. I had left a programme of work, which I was being paid to carry out and which would take a year or two yet to complete. Endless other research possibilities existed at the Gorge after that, if I wished to remain there. Remote though Olduvai was, access to Tanzania was easy and travelling was cheap, so I had no lack of company, what with field teams, long-term visits by colleagues helping in the research, and casual calls by friends from all over the world *en route* to their own fieldwork. There were also various safari parties, made up of members of learned societies or academic institutions. Most of the archaeological material I was studying was stored actually at Olduvai, and from that base in those days it was easy enough to travel to Nairobi or anywhere else I might need to visit.

Louis died eleven years ago, and if I were to try and give an account of those years with all the events in chronological order, the result would be an impossible muddle and very dull reading. Only now that I look back, with the writing of this book in mind, does it occur to me just how busy those years have been. There has been my research: not only the fieldwork, first at Olduvai and then at Laetoli, but also all the follow-up effort of laboratory work, and the preparation of the publications without which the whole operation would be useless. Then there has been my foreign travel, much of it in the States, which increased steadily through the 1970s and in the early 1980s was becoming almost too much to cope with, though Louis would probably not have thought so in comparison to his own travels. During these trips abroad I had to become a lecturer to mass audiences, a performer on radio and television, and a successful fund raiser, all to an extent the mere thought of which would once have appalled me. Then again, there has been a great change in the circumstances of life at Olduvai, reflecting not only East African political events but also the deepening world recession. There have also been many events within the Leakey family which are part of my story, while the development of my own work and the resulting widening of my geographical horizons have caused me to meet many remarkable people and make many new friends. Under each of these headings, at least a little and often a lot happened in every year, and I don't think I could possibly write the account chronologically myself, let alone expect anyone else to follow it.

When I returned to Olduvai in October 1972, it was as I have indicated to the task of completing my study of the upper part of the sequence, Beds III and IV and the beds that follow them. There was no inkling that before three years had passed I should be well embarked on a new and quite different project, at Laetoli: one that was to produce some of the most important and startling discoveries with which I have ever been associated. By 1974 we had finished all the digging that was needed at Olduvai, and the remarkable pits at JK in Bed III were being prepared for permanent exhibition to visitors. I could begin in earnest the writing up of the results of the work, which had started in 1968. Much of the analysis of finds I should be carrying out myself, but other aspects were being studied by specialists among my colleagues in many parts of the world, and it would therefore be some while before the complete text of the new monograph would be ready to go to press. Though no time at Olduvai is ever really slack, perhaps it was not too inconvenient a moment when certain unexpected finds drew my attention to Laetoli.

Laetoli lies away to the south of Olduvai, some 30 miles by road, a little beyond the beginning of the Side Gorge and close to the watershed between the Olduvai and Eyasi drainage basins. The name is the Masai word for a certain kind of red lily which grows there. I have already mentioned two previous visits I made there with Louis: the first in 1935, as an interlude during my first visit to Olduvai, and the second in 1959, shortly before the discovery of *Zinjanthropus*. On those occasions we had collected many fossils and puzzled over their age, without being in a position to reach any useful conclusion. In 1939 a German explorer, Ludwig Kohl-Larsen, had visited the area with his wife and collected much material from the surface, including a fragment of hominid maxilla, with two teeth in place, and also another tooth. But Kohl-Larsen had no geologist with him, and little geological expertise of his own: he assumed that the deposits, and therefore the fossils, were all of one age. This posed problems because, when the fauna was studied in Germany, it appeared to be a mixture of early and late types – the different kinds of elephant, in particular, could hardly belong together – but for lack of further information the matter rested there. In 1969 I went over for a brief visit from Olduvai, taking Dick Hay and Allan Cox. We found little of interest in the area of exposed sediments we looked at on that occasion, and it is interesting to recall that Dick was extremely doubtful that further work at Laetoli would prove worthwhile. In the course of his study of the geology of Olduvai he did, however, establish that certain tuff horizons which occurred in the Laetoli sediments were also represented in the Side Gorge, in a stratigraphic position which would make them older than even our earliest archaeological sites of Bed I.

The first thing that in 1974 turned my attention back to Laetoli was the finding by my neighbour George Dove of some fossils, including zebra and antelope teeth, in a load of sand that had been brought as building material to the Ndutu Safari Lodge, which he owned and where he was putting up an extension. George had been a friend of mine for many years; he was a delightful and colourful character, and I mentioned him earlier as the owner of the superb waxed moustaches which had so fascinated Simon, our pet monkey. We exchanged news and visits frequently, so that before long I heard about the fossils: I have described him as my neighbour, as in fact he was by Serengeti standards, although he lived at Lake Ndutu 25 miles away. The sand had come from the bed of the Gadjingero River, which drains down to Ndutu through the Laetoli area, and it seemed well worth a pleasant day out to go over and see if we could locate the area of sediment from which George's fossil teeth had been washed out. In fact his fossils were of relatively young age by Laetoli standards, but in the course of our exploration that day I came upon a large and productive area of the older sediments which, so far as I could tell, had not been visited previously. Over the next few weeks we made more visits there, usually at a weekend, coupled with a visit to George's camp, where I always enjoyed staying, and on the third trip one of my African staff, Mwongela Mwoka, found a hominid tooth, a premolar. This of course intensified our interest, and other visits followed.

By the end of that year, thanks partly to a short visit made to Laetoli by Kamoya Kimeu and other members of Richard's highly trained fossil-hunting team, we had found quite a lot more hominid material: two mandibles, part of a maxilla, and several more teeth. I was not prepared to venture an opinion at this stage on the nature of the hominid types we were finding, but it was certain that the remains were coming from that part of the thick deposits of volcanic material at Laetoli which were known as the Laetolil Beds – a name which Peter Kent had given them during our 1935 visit. At that time the area was called 'Laetolil' not 'Laetoli', an anglicization which the Tanzanian authorities later asked us to drop in the interests of accuracy. This we did, but following the formal rules of geological nomenclature we were bound to keep 'Laetolil' in the name of the stratigraphic unit. We did not know the age of the Laetolil Beds, but late in 1974 we were able to take samples for potassium-argon dating from lava flows that overlay the Laetolil Beds, and these were sent off to the laboratory of Garniss Curtis at Berkeley. Early in 1975 we had the result: the lava was in the order of 2.4 million years old and the Laetolil Beds, since they underlay it, must be an unknown amount older. This was extremely exciting news, for it meant that the hominid remains we had found were substantially older than any we had discovered at Olduvai, where the oldest finds in Bed I were a little less than 2.0 million years old.

On this basis I decided that a full field season at Laetoli was certainly called for, and I applied successfully to the National Geographic Society for funding, which they gave in generous measure. I had already written to Dick Hay to tell him what we had been finding in 1974, assuring him that our new exposures of the Laetolil Beds were in places 200 or possibly 300 feet thick, and far better than anything he or I had seen in 1969. I think he was still a bit sceptical, but at least he agreed to come out and see, which pleased me greatly. We made our plans to work at Laetoli in

July–September 1975, and in due course the team set off from Olduvai to a camp site south of Ndolanya Hill, not so very far from where Louis and I had searched for fossils just over 40 years earlier.

I shall devote the next chapter to an account of the Laetoli operation, which actually lasted into the 1980s, and I will also say something in it about the implications of the finds we made and certain controversies that have arisen in connection with them. I would like to end the present chapter, however, by saying a little more about George Dove, because he did something else for me in 1974, quite apart from the incidental part he played in bringing about my return to Laetoli.

George had been in East Africa much longer than I had: he had done many things, but chiefly he had been a well-known white hunter. You might suppose that his connection with hunting would have been enough to make me dislike him, but in fact I could see that although he was prepared to kill animals, in his own way he also loved them and had a profound respect for them. To George, the preservation and exhibition of an animal he had shot was the highest compliment he could pay it. I do not say I subscribe to his view on this, but at least one can understand it. Besides, George's kind of hunting was a very different matter from the indiscriminate slaughter of game animals by poachers in their ruthless quest for ivory, rhinoceros horn or leopard skin, which incensed George every bit as much as it does me. He was also invariably scathing about the scientists at the S.R.I. (Serengeti Research Institute), who had a project that involved attaching metal tags to the ears of lions: this he saw as an appalling insult to such magnificent creatures.

George Dove's attitude to animals is also shown by an incident in 1973, when we had a lot of trouble at Olduvai from a pride of eight young lions who had lost or been abandoned by their parents before they had learned how to hunt wild game for themselves. They attacked the local Masai herds, taking cattle, goats and donkeys, causing panic in the *manyattas* and eventually killing a child. They also attacked dogs, first killing a fine cross-bred Dalmatian belonging to our head guide, and afterwards coming right into my camp one night to get at my own Dalmatians, who were sleeping as usual with me in my hut. One lion jumped up at my window, shattering the glass, and I had the very frightening sight of a lion's head filling my whole window frame, kept out only by the metal grille on the inside. It was something that haunted my dreams for some nights afterwards. Just as everyone in the area was getting desperate, the lions moved off across the plains, and that brought them to Ndutu, where they arrived weak from hunger. George took charge of them and shot gazelle to feed them (quite against the law) until they had regained their strength and learned to fend for themselves. It is worth contrasting that story with the incident of Henry Fosbrooke and the lions at Engaruka in 1935.

There were always animals around George's camp at Ndutu, often mixing freely with the guests. I remember in particular that he had many genets living in his store, twenty or thirty of them, which is remarkable in itself since genets are not usually gregarious. George's genets would emerge in the evening to be fed, and he always gave them best breast of chicken, because he said they would eat nothing else. They would clamber around the rafters of the main safari lodge building while the guests were at dinner, the only snag being their habit as territorial creatures of descending to mark with a spray of urine the clothes of any guests present that happened to smell strongly of sweat.

George Dove was the kindest neighbour I could wish for and when, after Louis's death, it was clear that I would be living at Olduvai for a good while, he decided that I ought to have better facilities and he set out to build me a fine new stone-walled work-cum-dining room in place of the old grass-walled hut, together with a proper water supply. He provided the material and the workmen for this project himself. The building has been a tremendous success and it seems hard to believe that nearly ten years have passed since it was put up. The cost was borne by another good friend, Gordon Hanes, President of the Hanes Hosiery Corporation of North Carolina. He first came to Olduvai as a visitor and was delighted with everything he saw – except the flimsy nature of the chicken-wire constructions we had put up as protection for the display sites to which visitors were taken. Gordon sent us a generous donation to enable us to erect the solid buildings that now cover the same sites, and as a result of this kindness Louis and I got to know him well. When the new building in the camp was completed, we had a party there for George as a combined thankyou and house-warming. This he greatly enjoyed, having made only one stipulation when invited. 'Mary,' he said suspiciously, 'you're not inviting anyone from the S.R.I., are you? Because if so, I'm not coming.' Very sadly, this party was also effectively a farewell party for George, who left Tanzania for good later that year. This is how it came about.

In 1973, the attitude of the Tanzanian Government towards resident Europeans and other foreign nationals changed dramatically. Almost everyone was descended on without warning, by units of the army, and their premises were searched for illegal possessions such as ivory, rhinoceros horn or undeclared foreign currency. During this operation soldiers arrived at my camp at Olduvai, but they only wanted to see our fossils. George was less fortunate. By chance Dick Hay and I had gone over to have lunch with him at Ndutu the day several vehicles full of soldiers with automatic rifles burst into the place. We were ordered to leave; which we did, at gun point. George was then taken off to the police post at Ngorongoro, and after several weeks' delay he was fined several thousand shillings for being illegally in possession of ivory. This stupid charge related to an old elephant skull which had been left in a tree near the camp to please the tourists. To my certain knowledge it had been there since long before George went to Ndutu, and had nothing at all to do with him except that he was technically its owner. The skull didn't even have tusks.

This shameful incident so disheartened George, who really loved Tanzania and had done so much for its tourist trade, that he forthwith decided to sell the Ndutu Lodge and leave the country. Tanzania is the poorer for his going. The building work he undertook for me at Olduvai was done while he was completing his arrangements to leave, and not so very long after the celebration party he was on his way to Australia with his wife, son and daughter-in-law to start a new life. I hear that all goes well with them. For George's friends and former neighbours in Tanzania, the whole affair was deeply distressing. But it was a warning that, as time passed, Tanzania might cease to be the happy, carefree and prosperous place in which to live and work that it had hitherto been. Sadly, that is indeed the way things have turned out.

14
The Laetoli years

OF ALL MY MAJOR PROJECTS, Laetoli was certainly one of the most demanding and arduous, but it also proved one of the most worthwhile. Working out in the field at Laetoli with a large team is a very different matter from a similar operation at Olduvai, based on the excellent facilities of my own permanent camp. At Laetoli there were formidable logistical problems involved in feeding and transporting everyone. Our nearest source of good fresh water was something like ten miles away. The road from Laetoli via Endulen to Ngorongoro was long and in appallingly bad condition. More than ever I was grateful for the cheerful efficiency of my staff, and their astonishing ability to cope with the various domestic difficulties – particularly Kitetu Itumange and Kabebo Kimeu, both of whom have been with me at Olduvai and Langata for more years than I care to recall. Between them, they kept everyone remarkably well fed and it never failed to amaze us how they contrived to produce well-cooked meals for an endless number of people under such difficult conditions.

Even the climate at Laetoli was appreciably different from Olduvai, with temperatures falling rapidly in the evenings and often being as low as 40°F in the early morning, while in the middle of the day it would be baking hot. Our big camp-fires each evening were not only social gatherings but were really needed to keep people warm. Fortunately there was plenty of firewood to hand because the Laetoli area had been invaded by elephants since my previous stays there in 1935 and 1959, and elephants have a regular habit of pushing over trees or tearing off whole branches. If, by doing that, they performed a useful service for us, they did great damage to the trees and made a considerable nuisance of themselves in other ways – such as chasing people, or dragging away the plastic sheeting we used as part of the protection of our main excavation areas. Buffalo are far more of a threat to people. They are aggressive and dangerous creatures to have around and there were many of them at Laetoli. We also had more than a fair ration of trouble with snakes, in particular puff-adders.

Added to that, I was not really in the best of health myself when we began at Laetoli in 1975. Earlier in the year I had had a hysterectomy operation in London and, although that had been perfectly successful in itself, I had picked up an infection while in the hospital, and the effects of that lingered on. One of them was high blood pressure, and I know that at times it soared quite dangerously. I suppose one does not shrug these things off so easily when one has reached the age of 62 as one would have done earlier. All things considered, I ought probably not to have undertaken the Laetoli project when I did, but fortunately everything worked out quite well in the end. Other members of the team got ill during some of our seasons, and the proximity of the Austrian Mission Hospital at Endulen proved invaluable.

During the various campaigns at Laetoli, large numbers of people came out, either to be members of the field team or to advise or perform specialist tasks, and in certain years the long-term members of the team between them generated more in the way of personality clashes and emotional sagas of every conceivable kind than I have ever known at digs I have directed. Every archaeological field season has its own human interest side, but in some years at Laetoli the heights (or depths) reached were really extraordinary. It all added to the complexities of the operation and seems rather more amusing now than it did at the time.

In 1975, our main aims included the establishment of a proper geological sequence, a search for more hominid remains, a look at the palaeo-environmental evidence and, especially, the finding, if we could, of artefacts *in situ* in the deposits that were yielding the early hominids. This was of great importance. We already knew from the dates Garniss Curtis had sent that the Laetolil Beds were substantially older than our earliest Bed I sites at Olduvai. At Olduvai it had been clearly established that the making of a simple range of stone tools was common practice among the human groups in this area by a date not much less than 2.0 million years ago. The big question was: how far back beyond that could the manufacture of stone artefacts be traced? For the moment the oldest undoubted artefacts were certain specimens from the Omo valley, which were perhaps as much as 2.2 million years old, but these were rather unsatisfactory in themselves because many were just waste flakes and knapping debris. We were anxious to see if we could find something better at Laetoli, in deposits older than 2.4 million years.

As it turned out, we drew a complete blank on this, both in 1975 and in all other seasons, in spite of a lot of searching. There were no worked stones at all in the Laetolil Beds, nor even any unmodified stones that were foreign to the deposit. From this completely negative evidence one might conclude that we were dealing with a stage of hominid evolution in which, although man was bipedal (as we were later able to show so dramatically) and his hands were therefore freed for such activities as tool-making, perhaps his brain development had not yet reached a stage where he was capable of the necessary conceptual thought that artefact manufacture demands. However, we do not yet have enough evidence to say that this is certainly so. Since, as we found, the ancient environment at the time of deposition of the Laetolil Beds was an open one, lacking the presence of any such features as a lake shore or a permanent source of fresh water that might have led to man's establishing settlement sites, it may simply be that the early hominids only passed across this landscape occasionally in transit, and did not stop there to perform the kinds of tasks that required tools. If we could discover and excavate a contemporary living site (if such ever existed), we should have a better idea of whether or not they made artefacts.

But if we found no artefacts in 1975, in that year and the next we made a great deal of progress. In all, Dick Hay came out to Laetoli for five visits during our years of work there, and his first task was to clarify the general geological sequence. With this he made good headway in 1975. He showed that the Laetolil Beds themselves were at least 400 feet thick and he divided them into a Lower and an Upper Unit, the latter being the one we are concerned with when I refer to 'Laetolil Beds' in the ensuing pages. Overlying them, after a break in the sequence, came what he designated the Ndolanya Beds, after a local hill of that name – again with Upper and Lower Units, between which there was a break. Above the Ndolanya Beds, after another erosional gap, came the lava from which Garniss Curtis had obtained the date of *c.* 2.4 million years. This we named the Ogol lava and other stratigraphic units overlay it: the Naibadad Beds, Olpiro Beds and Ngaloba Beds. Only the last two of all these divisions contain fossils as well as artefacts of Pleistocene age. The Upper Ngaloba Beds yielded to us in 1976 a cranium of early *Homo sapiens* and artefacts of the Middle Stone Age, dating from about 120,000 years ago, but all our most important finds have come from the Laetolil Beds. At the start of the first season, we merely knew that the Laetolil Beds must be older than 2.4 million years, but since then their range in time has become reasonably well established through potassium-argon dating carried out by Garniss Curtis and Robert Drake, mostly using samples of biotite. A reading towards the top of the Upper Unit of the Laetolil Beds has given 3.49±0.6 million years. Our hominid remains were clearly very old indeed.

Dick Hay identified the Laetolil Beds as having originated from the volcano Sadiman, some twenty miles east of Laetoli. The whole deposit consists of erupted material, the large majority in the form known as 'aeolian tuff', which means volcanic ash redeposited by wind action. But within the Upper Unit there were a number of horizons of 'air-fall tuff', that is to say ash that had descended directly, without wind action. These air-fall tuffs were to yield our most important finds – the now-famous hominid and animal footprints. Dick also worked on the overall geology and geomorphology of the Laetoli region and showed that at the time when the Laetolil Beds were forming the area had consisted of relatively flat savannah grassland. Not until a million or more years afterwards had it been dramatically uplifted as a fault block to form the modern Eyasi Plateau, and it was only at that time that the present Lake Eyasi came into existence in the new Rift Valley below. We should imagine a semi-arid savannah landscape with a prolonged dry season each year and temperatures at least as warm as those of the present; a situation probably comparable in general terms to the eastern Serengeti of today.

Our field team in 1975 was large. My youngest son Philip came as camp manager, and brought with him his wife Valerie and their young daughter, Lara, who treated the field season with admirable equanimity. Dick Hay brought his wife Lynn. Philip selected a delightful-looking camp site under the fever trees, near the Garusi River, and Ron Clarke, who had worked for Louis and me as a technician at the Centre in Nairobi and also at Olduvai, directed the building of a living/work-room and various other huts. Hardly were the camp buildings completed before we had learned why the Germans called the Garusi River the *Vögelfluss*. The local bird population, which includes many rare species, is both prolific and tame and the birds at once started coming boldly into our huts.

Allan Cox was with us for some weeks in 1975, taking palaeomagnetic samples, and among the others were Sonia Cole, who had recently completed the biography of Louis (*Leakey's Luck*) which I had commissioned, and Mary Jackes. Sonia assumed charge of the cataloguing of finds, and she and Mary Jackes struck up a close friendship and indeed partnership, because Mary did the faunal identifications and classifications for her. Mary was an Australian, but was studying anthropology at the University of Toronto in Canada, and the previous year she had spent some while working with me at Olduvai, during which time she had discovered Olduvai Hominid 51, part of the left side of a mandible with a molar tooth and the roots of a premolar in place.

Despite not finding any dramatic hominid remains we were well satisfied at the end of the 1975 season with the start we had made, and it was clear that at least one more major season would be needed. Funding was obtained and plans were made accordingly. When we left in 1975, the local Masai population indicated their willingness to look after our camp, so we left it standing. We had got on well with them, and had been able to offer occasional medical assistance or if necessary transport injured Masai to the Endulen Hospital – those, for example, who had been trampled by buffalo. But when we returned in 1976, we found that the camp had been burned down. This had been done probably not by the local Masai, but by a wandering band of young *morani* (warriors) from some other area, who were on a mischief-making expedition of a kind that is only too common among that age-group. In fact we had found that the 1975 camp, though pleasantly situated, was altogether too far from that part of the Laetolil Beds exposures where we needed to spend most time. So, instead of rebuilding on the same site, we took the opportunity to move to a more convenient location, where there was a flat piece of ground, with some acacia trees to give shade.

This proved a good site, though it had its drawbacks, one of which was the extraordinary number of puff-adders nearby. Sometimes we killed two in a single day, and still more came. The birds used to give us warning of their presence, congregating in trees over them and drawing our attention to them with a chorus of loud alarm calls. The large flocks of Superb starlings were particularly helpful in this way; they used to come in their hundreds each day for an afternoon siesta in the trees near our main building. It was really entirely thanks to the birds that no one got bitten by the puff-adders, and in return we made a bird-bath and kept it filled, which they much appreciated. Another snag from my point of view at this second camp-site was the bush-baby population. I had a metal 'Uniport' hut to sleep in, like my one at Olduvai, because it was safer for the dogs. The bush-babies are nocturnal creatures and they used to feed in the acacia trees overhanging my hut on seeds which they took out of the pods. Unfortunately all night long the empty pods would be dropping onto my tin roof with loud pings. There were two more hazards at Laetoli. The first was ticks. We all had so many on us that it was simpler to remove them from our clothing with a brush several times a day than to pick them off singly. The dogs, of course, were absolutely covered in them. The other thing was a particular hazard to the dogs: a large kind of wild asparagus plant with vicious long hooked thorns, which would lacerate the dogs, tending especially to catch their ears. One of the bitches, Sophie, nearly died on two occasions from loss of blood caused by such injuries – only just managing to stagger back to camp, bleeding profusely after having her ears torn by these thorns on hunting expeditions.

In the end, our work at Laetoli from 1974 onwards gave us a total of no less than fifteen new species and one new genus, and I cannot help thinking how Louis would have loved that. The work went well in 1976, with a great deal more systematic collection of faunal remains.

There were some changes in the field team: Sonia Cole did not come, but that year saw the arrival, from England, of Peter Jones, a young man who came out on the recommendation of Kenneth Oakley and, as it transpired, was to remain in Tanzania right up until 1983 as my assistant at Olduvai. Since he had spent much of his early life in Afghanistan and travelling with his parents, Peter's formal education had been rather patchy, but he possessed a remarkable range of practical talents and was already one of the best exponents of experimental tool manufacture. In 1976 we were still hoping to find stone artefacts at Laetoli, and Peter would have been involved in the study of their technology. He also had other skills which were of the greatest value to us at Laetoli, including photography and the making of casts. Peter's arrival happened to coincide with that of two charming Austrian nurses at the Endulen Hospital, Barbara Leitner and Tina Pöschl, who were there for three years. They became frequent visitors to our camp, taking a great interest in our work and finds and arguably an even greater one in Peter. Another interested visitor once or twice at about this time was the local witch doctor, whose powers had a tremendous reputation. In fact, he was regarded as so powerful that later on, when the Tanzanian army was fighting in Uganda after the fall of Idi Amin, he was specially drafted there to help maintain the morale of the troops: when we knew him he was still wearing the Army boots with which he had been issued.

To return to the scientific side of the 1976 season: the most unexpected and exciting discovery was the existence of large numbers of fossil animal footprints, preserved in one of the air-fall tuff levels of the Upper Unit of the Laetolil Beds. As is often the case with important finds, the first of these animal tracks came to light in a rather unlikely way. Jonah Western, Kaye Behrensmayer and Andrew Hill were visiting us and one afternoon were returning to camp after a long walk around the principal exposures. For some reason they amused themselves by throwing lumps of dried elephant dung at each other and there was certainly plenty of it around in the flat open space where they were. Andrew fell down in the process and noted that he was lying on a hard surface which appeared to contain ancient animal footprints, including those of rhinoceros. He was right. The hard surface proved to be one of the three thickest air-fall tuff horizons in the Laetolil Beds, and the locality became known to us as Site A. Since then, literally tens of thousands of prints have been found in this deposit, ranging from the trail left by an insect, and the tracks of birds, to the footprints of large elephants. Site A, as we soon discovered, is only one of several exposures of what we termed the Footprint Tuff, though it is by far the largest. We calculated that Site A alone contained 18,400 individual prints. There are quite a number of sites in the world that have produced fossil animal tracks, though none in such extraordinary quantities or variety as Laetoli. The other unique aspect of Laetoli is that the deposits that contain the footprints also contain great numbers of remains of the kinds of animals that made them.

Dick Hay became fascinated by the problem of how the footprints in this tuff should not merely occur but should be preserved in such sharp and perfect condition over so long a period of time. He also noted that the Footprint Tuff, which was about six inches thick, consisted of a series of fine laminations. Only three air-fall tuffs in the Laetolil Beds are formed in this way, and we subsequently learned that the other two also contained footprints, though not in such prolific quantities as the Footprint Tuff itself. As for the age of the latter, we have a number of good potassium-argon dates from above, below and within it, which clearly establish its date as close to 3.5 million years ago, or perhaps just slightly older.

It took Dick several more visits and a lot of research before he solved all the problems, and I cannot here go deeply into the chemistry that is involved. Briefly, a main factor was the presence in the air-fall tuffs of the mineral carbonatite, various properties of which not only made the soft ash cohesive when damp, so allowing it to receive the prints clearly, but also served to cement it. That the footprints are preserved to this day is due to the fact that in the course of time the carbonatite was replaced by calcite to give an extremely hard and durable cast. By good fortune the prints seem mainly to have been made at a time of year when the dry season was giving way to the wet: we can even see the impressions left by raindrops. As for the laminations, it is quite clear that ash was coming from the volcano Sadiman in an intermittent series of short episodes, each represented by a single discrete layer. In the few millimetres' thickness of any one of the laminations, we are perhaps looking at just a few hours of Pliocene time and, in the whole thickness of the Footprint Tuff, at a mere few weeks. Sadiman was evidently building up to a much more substantial eruption and accordingly the Footprint Tuff was quite quickly sealed in by a thick layer of ash which covered it gently enough to do no damage and deeply enough to preserve it intact.

By the end of the 1976 season we had located four major exposures of the Footprint Tuff, and eventually this number rose to eighteen, that were worth detailed recording and plotting. It was clear, when we finished work for 1976, that more seasons would be required and, as it turned out, the best was still to come. In 1977, rather to my relief, we took a smaller permanent team into the field, though we had others who joined us for shorter periods.

In 1977, the detailed recording of footprints was clearly the main objective. We were joined that year for some time by my old friend John Waechter, who in his own recent campaign of excavations at Barnfield Pit, Swanscombe, in England, had come across an area of animal footprints preserved on the surface of a Middle Pleistocene loam, and had successfully made casts of them. This proved to be the last year of John's life; he died suddenly from a heart attack in 1978. We also had a short visit from Professor Henry de Lumley and his wife Marie-Antoinette, from Marseilles in France, both distinguished and experienced colleagues, he an archaeologist and she a human palaeontologist. They were extremely keen to come out and see the site. Michael Bird, a student of Bob Savage's at Bristol University, was another new member of the team, and he was with us for the whole season. That year we also brought in two Africans to help us identify the animal tracks. One was an elderly Musukuma who had been George Dove's tracker during his hunting safaris, and the other a member of the Hadza tribe, who are hunter-gatherers and skilled in the tracking of game. We could not explain to them successfully that some of the kinds of animals that had made the tracks no longer existed, and all their identifications were therefore in modern terms, but the exercise proved useful and interesting.

John Waechter showed Peter Jones the principles of making casts of the footprints using latex and silicon rubber and, assisted by Mike Bird, Peter soon began to obtain excellent results. They got even better in later seasons when he had perfected the technique after getting further advice from the casting department of the National Museum in Nairobi. At the end of the previous season, 1976, Peter and my son Philip had independently discovered a most unusual trail at Site A, consisting of four prints which we rather thought might be hominid, though they were not as clear as the best of the animal tracks. We had had a lot of discussion about these prints without reaching any firm conclusion. During their stay the de Lumleys photographed the prints and afterwards, working from a cast which Peter Jones took, they made a stereophotographic record from which to prepare computerized contoured plans. Henry and Marie-Antoinette de Lumley appeared to enjoy their time at Laetoli and I was delighted that they took such pleasure in the birds and animals around the camp. The only reservation I had about their visit concerned Henry's kindness in driving one of the vehicles back from Laetoli to Olduvai when he thought I was tired. I have since learned that his driving style is well known among his colleagues, but at the time I was inclined to take the view, shared I believe by Marie-Antoinette, that if one is following a track marked by intermittently placed large boulders, it is not strictly necessary to do so by hitting each one of them as you pass it!

The Nairobi Pan-African Congress was held in 1977 and we had two parties of Congress members down to visit Olduvai and Laetoli. That was a little less easy to cope with than it should have been, for 1977 was the year when Tanzania suddenly closed its border with Kenya and the delegates had to reach us by the extraordinary method of flying from Nairobi to Kilimanjaro airport via the Seychelles and Dar-es-Salaam. The closure of the border meant that office work in Nairobi more than doubled. Permits to cross to and from Olduvai had to be obtained for all members of the Olduvai staff and for our vehicles as well as for scientists coming from Nairobi. This may sound like purely routine administration but it requires great patience, perseverance and an unflappable temperament when lines of communication are tenuous at best. More often than not it is impossible to phone between Tanzania and Nairobi; cables frequently become 'lost' in transit; and even 'normal' mail deliveries are erratic and often depend on whether or not a bus reaches Ngorongoro – my nearest post office. If Hazel Potgeiter had not then joined me as my secretary and dealt with all these problems, to say nothing of the endless shopping lists and other requests, generally conveyed almost inaudibly over the telephone, it is doubtful if I would have been able to carry on the work at Olduvai.

For the 1978 season, largely because of the four curious footprints which some of us thought might be hominid, I asked Dr Louise Robbins to join the expedition. She worked in the Department of Anthropology at the University of North Carolina, Greensboro, and was an expert on footprints: she had been introduced to me by Gordon Hanes when I was visiting the United States during one of my lecture tours. We were also joined by Dr Tim White, whom I had first met when he was a graduate student working for his doctoral dissertation in 1975 and 1976, and had then invited to describe for publication the Laetoli hominids. At Christmas 1976 he had joined our family party at Olduvai, as he was on his own, and I also asked him to take part in our 1978 season at Laetoli. It was a large party again that season and others included Paul Abell from the Department of Chemistry, Rhode Island University, and John Harris, palaeontologist now at the Los Angeles County Natural History Museum and formerly on the staff of the National Museum in Nairobi.

Louise Robbins took the view that the four doubtful prints we had found in 1976 were indeed hominid; others did not agree. In fact, this matter has never been finally resolved, and some people believe that they might be those of an extinct bear. This is not so implausible as it seems since an extinct fossil bear is known in the Pliocene deposits of South Africa, dated about 5 million years ago. However, before very long these four prints were entirely eclipsed by the discovery of undoubted human footprints, some of which were of great clarity. The first of these was found by Paul Abell. Paul had worked for several years with Richard at East Turkana, and one object of his joining us was to try and lift a block of deposit with rhino prints to become a museum exhibit at Olduvai. In the course of a search for further exposures of the Footprint Tuff, Paul came upon what he thought was the heel part of a hominid print; erosion had removed the front part. He showed it to Louise, who was inclined to disagree, but when I saw it next day I agreed with Paul. Some careful excavation would clearly be needed to check the identification, and for this I selected Ndibo Mbuika, one of the most experienced of my Kenyan staff, who had found and excavated various hominids at Olduvai, including O.H.13, the skull known as 'Cindy', the safe recovery of which had required great care and precision. I knew I could rely on him, and before long, having excavated a small area, he brought his report back to camp. Ndibo not only confirmed Paul's identification but said that there were also two more hominid prints, one of them 'at least this long' – he held up his hands about twelve inches apart. We thought at first that he was exaggerating, but a visit to the site confirmed that it was just as he had described it. It seemed very likely that yet more hominid prints would be revealed when we excavated below the shallow covering of tuff and soil which here overlay the Footprint Tuff.

At this stage Tim White, whom I could never convince of the experience and ability as excavators of my Kenyan staff, decided that he ought to take charge of what would clearly need to be a careful and extremely precise excavation. By the end of the season, Tim had succeeded in uncovering what seemed to be two parallel trails of hominid footprints, extending over a distance of about 30 feet to a point where they were interrupted by a small fault line. However, a small trial excavation beyond the interruption confirmed that the prints did continue there, so clearly we could begin again next year with high hopes.

The discovery of the trails was immensely exciting – something so extraordinary that I could hardly take it in or comprehend its implications for some while. It was a quite different feeling from the discovery of a major hominid fossil – *Proconsul* or *Zinjanthropus*, for example – because that happens to you all at once, and within a short time you know exactly what you have found. The Laetoli hominid trails were something that grew in extent, in detail and in importance over two seasons. But then again, there *was* an immediate impact in the vastness of our discovery because from a very early stage it was clear that we had before us unique evidence, of an unimpeachable nature, to estabish that our hominid ancestors were fully bipedal a little before 3·5 million years ago – the kind of thing anthropologists had argued over for many decades, with no real hope of proving or disproving their views. The Laetolil Beds might not have included any foot bones among the hominid remains they had yielded to our search, but they had given us instead one of the most graphic alternative kinds of evidence for bipedalism one could dream of discovering. The essentially human nature and the modern appearance of the footprints were quite extraordinary.

As the 1978 excavation proceeded, we noted a curious feature. In one of the two trails, some of the individual prints seemed unusually large – just as Ndibo had observed at the outset – and it looked to several of us as if these might be double prints, though by no amount of practical experiment in the modern dust could we find a way in which one individual could create such a double print. In any case, Tim would have none of it: to him, the prints were all single, and he excavated them as such.

At the end of the 1978 season the *National Geographic Magazine* published an article about the hominid trails and in this was included a striking 'artist's impression' painted by Jay Matternes, showing two hominids walking across an ancient ash-covered African landscape.

In 1979 we had as large a team as ever. I remember that at the evening meal I found myself sitting at the head of a longer table than I could remember on any dig, with the line of faces on each side seeming to stretch away into the darkness beyond. Again there were old friends and some newcomers. Tim White was not there: he and I had ended the previous season on rather bad terms, for reasons that will become clear later. Bill Sands, from the British Museum (Natural History) was there, an expert on termites who had come out at my request to study some remarkable fossil termitaries we had found preserved in the Laetolil Beds at a level somewhat below the Footprint Tuff. There were various other scientists who had come to deal with one or other class of the fauna: Walter Auffenberg and Peter Meylan from Florida, Claude Guérin from France, and Paul Sondaar from Holland. It was an international gathering indeed, and for all its size it was a team that worked extraordinarily well and produced none of the personality problems that had tended to sour some of the previous seasons.

During 1979 we completed our excavation of the hominid trails up to another fault line, and then we left what might lie beyond for future researchers. The combined trail, in its final state, was 80 feet long and looked immensely impressive. Peter Jones's casting recorded as much of it as was possible and his casts were later used by Professor Russel Tuttle of Chicago University in studying the way in which these early hominids walked. The prints in one of the trails did indeed turn out to be double, as Louise and I and several others had suspected, and at last we understood the reason, namely that *three* hominids had been present. The first indication of this was provided by Alan Root, during a visit he made to film the trails. Alan compared what seemed to him to be the quite deliberate superimposition of one set of footprints on another to the habit of young chimpanzees when playing 'follow my leader'. This was a brilliant piece of insight and something that had simply never occurred to any of us. Technical assessments of the trails will be given in the Laetoli monograph and I will simply summarize here by saying that we appear to have prints left three and a half million years ago, by three individuals of different stature: it is tempting to see them as a man, a woman and a child. Whether or not this is so, the middle-sized individual was stepping deliberately into the prints left by the largest. The trail is crossed by the tracks of a Pliocene three-toed horse (*Hipparion*) accompanied by a foal.

When the excavation of the trails was completed we all felt that it would be marvellous if this extraordinary and unique find could be preserved complete as an open-air museum, and indeed a donation of $25,000 was generously offered for that purpose by Hubert Humphries, one of the Trustees of the L.S.B. Leakey Foundation. Unfortunately we eventually had to abandon the idea. Laetoli is more remotely situated than Olduvai in terms of access by road, and we could find no way of providing for the care and upkeep of a building, which would have needed to be guarded and maintained right through the year and not only in the main tourist season. We therefore took the only reasonable alternative, which was to bury the trails with great care, first hardening the individual prints and then covering them with alternating layers of river sand and plastic sheeting, with a final capping of heavy lava boulders. The location is permanently marked, so the trails could be uncovered again relatively easily if it were ever necessary: meanwhile, they should be safe enough. Accurate fibre-glass casts of the entire trail are available for those who wish to study the footprints.

1979 was the last of the five major seasons of fieldwork at Laetoli. In 1980, Bill Sands and his wife went back to the site to complete their work on the termitaries, and I merely went over to visit. We had found these termite workings as early as 1975, and various experts had been to look at them before Bill Sands but would not commit themselves to accepting the evidence. This consisted mainly of the tube-like sections of the tunnels and passages of the termite mounds, surviving because they were harder than the surrounding material of the ash-falls that had covered them. Bill Sands probed further and recovered examples of the distinctive 'hive' part of the nests and even two typical queen cells. These are the oldest known traces of higher termite workings. I have no space here to describe all the other remarkable things that were preserved in the ash of the Laetolil Beds – but they include remains of Pliocene mammals of all sizes from elephant to shrew, numerous rodent bones, hundreds of snail shells, tortoises (some virtually intact), monkeys, and some remarkably well-preserved birds' eggs, identifiable as those of guinea-fowl.

In 1981, a small party went back to Laetoli to check specific stratigraphic points in connection with the writing of the report, and for Dick Hay to complete his study of the nature of the Footprint Tuff. Four of us went: myself, Peter Jones, Dick and his former student Thure Cerling. It was a short, pleasant and productive season. Since then I and many others of those who took part in the Laetoli operation have been preparing our contributions to the monograph, and we and colleagues all over the world have been considering the implications of what must surely be one of the most remarkable bodies of evidence ever to be recovered. And between 1975 and 1981, while we had been so engrossed, the rest of the world had not been standing idly by. Other expeditions had been in the field and other extraordinary discoveries had been made, some of the most startling in Ethiopia.

Ethiopia was a relatively late addition to the list of African countries that possess outstanding palaeontological and hominid material in datable geological contexts. The Omo expedition had begun to demonstrate their presence in the extreme south of the country in the late 1960s, but it was during the period 1973 to 1977 that attention became focused on northern Ethiopia, on the valley of the River Awash and in particular on the area of Hadar, in the Afar Triangle, which is itself a widening of the Great Rift Valley just before it reaches the Gulf of Aden and the southern end of the Red Sea. Here some quite amazing hominid discoveries were made by an expedition consisting mainly of American and French researchers, led by Donald Johanson from the Cleveland Museum of Natural History, Ohio, and Maurice Taieb and Yves Coppens from France.

In 1974, Johanson found the famous early hominid skeleton known to the world as 'Lucy', and in 1975 he discovered an area where, on a single erosion slope, there were some 200 hominid fragments, among which at least thirteen individuals, presumably contemporary, were represented: these became known popularly as the 'First Family'. There were also some excellent upper and lower jaws containing teeth. In all, remains of at least 35 individual hominids, including the 'family group', were discovered in the Hadar region. Opportunities for potassium-argon dating were rather limited, but readings obtained from a nearby lava flow indicated that the earliest hominids were likely to be around 3.0 million years old and Lucy somewhat later. However, in 1979 it was suggested that they were something nearer 3.5 million, which, if correct, indicated general contemporaneity with our Laetolil Beds hominids.

I had known Johanson for some years, and we had exchanged news of our work from time to time, so at his invitation Richard, Meave and I flew up to Ethiopia in 1974 to visit the Hadar site. By chance we were just a day or so too early to be there when Lucy was discovered. In 1975, Johanson brought his 'First Family' bones to Nairobi to show to Richard and me, when his field season ended. As it happened, Tim White was at that time in Nairobi studying hominid mandibles and teeth for his doctoral research, and he had already worked on those we had so far found at Laetoli. This was the occasion on which he and Don Johanson first met – a rather fateful event, as it turned out, because Tim White became deeply involved in the study of the Hadar hominid material for publication and was co-author of two reports on it which appeared in 1978 and 1979. At that time Tim White impressed me as a good scientist and a hard worker, if sometimes a little naïve. The purely descriptive reports he produced for me on the Laetoli hominid finds were clear and admirable, making no attribution to any hominid type. However, his interpretation of the Hadar material was to prove very controversial.

Since the Hadar and Laetoli sites were being studied at much the same time, and were both yielding hominid remains of Pliocene age, it was not surprising that people should wish to make comparisons and consider their relevance to each other. The Hadar hominid collections were infinitely superior to ours from Laetoli, in quantity and far more importantly in quality. To me and to Richard, it seemed that they included a considerable range of variation, such that there must be at least two hominid types present. Lucy herself was a very small creature and seemed to us distinctive in several morphological details. The jaw and teeth, for example, had many primitive features, although the leg bones seemed to show that she had been fully bipedal. In contrast, several of the other Hadar hominids were much larger and seemed to us far more *Homo*-like than australopithecine. There was nothing unusual in the idea that two different kinds of hominid should be contemporary in one region: at Olduvai, we have *Homo habilis* and *Australopithecus boisei* in Bed I, while in Bed II *Homo erectus* appeared before the australopithecine line had died out. At East Turkana, Richard has an early *Homo erectus* which is demonstrably contemporary with a late robust australopithecine.

In their assessment of the hominids, however, Johanson and White not only took a different view but they used the material to make what they called a systematic assessment of the overall picture of hominid evolution. They claimed that all the Hadar material belonged to a single species, and went further by saying that our Laetolil Beds hominids belonged to this same species too. The species in question, they said, was a new one – an australopithecine, which they decided to call *Australopithecus afarensis*. When a new species is claimed, it must have a 'holotype' or type specimen: that is, a reference specimen on the basis of which it is to be defined. And was their holotype Lucy, or some member of the First Family, or one of their other well-preserved fossils from Hadar? No: as holotype they chose our Laetoli Hominid 4, one of the broken mandibles containing an incomplete set of teeth, which we had found before our first field season, back in 1974. With this arrangement, Johanson apparently expected me to be pleased, and he had even added my name to the authorship of the 1978 paper, the other authors being himself, Tim White and Yves Coppens.

This document, which first gave the news of the new species to the world, was to appear in 1978 in *Kirtlandia*, the house journal of the Cleveland Natural History Museum, where Johanson worked. Both Johanson and I attended the Nobel Symposium in Sweden in late May 1978, on the Current Argument on Early Man, where he was to speak, with me immediately following him. To my amazement, he devoted a large part of his paper to an account and assessment of the Laetoli hominids, which was something I was there to talk about. It was in the course of his talk that he mentioned for the first time *Australopithecus afarensis*, indicating that the paper giving full details of the new species was already in press, and acknowledging Tim White's major role in the classification that had been decided upon. This was the paper I was supposed to be putting my name to!

Tim White was with us at Laetoli in 1978, so it was not so long before I was able to take the matter up with him, and I told him very clearly that I wanted my name removed from the list of authors. The paper was so near publication that a cable had to be sent and the title page re-set; but my wishes were met. Before they were, however, I had to listen in the workroom at my own camp at Laetoli to a long harangue from Tim White in an attempt to get me to change my mind.

I do not want to go here into all the technicalities of my disagreement with Johanson and White over their views on *Australopithecus afarensis*. It seemed to me unjustifiable, and also scientifically quite wrong, to choose for a species named *afarensis* a type specimen that came from a site something like 1,000 miles away from the Afar Triangle and one which was also at the time supposed to be about half a million years older than the main group of material. Not only that, but surely no one should choose as type specimen a fragmentary mandible when there is a fossil as complete as Lucy to hand, to say nothing of upper and lower jaws much better preserved than the specimen from Laetoli. Any of those would have been preferable since the selection of a type fossil is supposed to help define as many aspects of the species as possible. One reason given for using L.H. 4, the Laetoli jaw, was that a published description had already appeared, but Johanson's main reason for not choosing Lucy appears to have been that she was rather atypical of the proposed new species. Indeed she is; many people still feel that the Hadar hominids are far too diverse to belong to any single species, whatever new or old name it might be given. As I remember that was also Johanson's own belief for the first few years, but Tim White appears to have converted him to the view that was eventually published. And over and above all this, I found myself in strong disagreement with the general reassessment that Johanson and White went out of their way to make, in which they said their new species, *Australopithecus afarensis*, was ancestral not only to the other australopithecine species but also to *Homo habilis* and hence the whole *Homo* line. Very few of their colleagues seem to have accepted that idea, and Richard and I are certainly not among them.

In 1979, the new reading for the age of the Hadar hominids at about 3.5 million years seemed to remove at least one of my misgivings by bringing the Laetoli and Hadar hominids into approximate contemporaneity, but even that has not lasted: papers published in 1982 have returned the date to the time-range 2.9 to 3.2 million years. Though the South African australopithecines to which *afarensis* was being claimed as ancestral are not themselves firmly dated, some are certainly quite early and it seems likely that the Hadar fossils are too young to occupy an ancestral position, even if they were otherwise appropriate.

Much of this long controversy is of a highly technical nature and has accordingly been conducted in the pages of scientific journals. If that were all, I should not have devoted nearly so much space to it here, even though it is all highly relevant to the preceding account of our work at Laetoli. But there is also Don Johanson's book *Lucy: the beginnings of humankind*, written with the assistance of Maitland Edey and published in 1981. Many of those who are reading these pages may well have read *Lucy* too, and I can hardly omit a few comments upon it.

I'm sure I must have read, or at least glanced through, *Lucy* when it was first published, but I thought it best to refresh my memory. I remember that when the book came out, various people were of the opinion that some of the statements either made directly by the authors or attributed by them to Tim White reflected on our professional competence. But really, one has too much work to do to get involved in this sort of thing, and it doesn't seem to me the way to conduct oneself in disagreements whose basis lies ultimately in the holding of different scientific opinions. All the same, in the days when Louis used to argue so vigorously with his colleagues, in print or at conferences, it all seemed to be done in a much more gentlemanly manner than is the fashion today.

Important discoveries concerning Early Man invariably arouse great public interest, and I believe it is very important that popular accounts of events should be clearly separated from serious factual reports. It is for this reason that *Lucy* gives me such cause for concern. A great deal of verbatim conversation is quoted in the book; some of it even purports to have taken place in my camp at Laetoli. Now, I know Don Johanson quite well, and have also met his co-author, and I am sure that I would have been aware had either of them been present at the incidents so graphically described, when the supposed conversations took place. But wherever these pseudo-quotations come from, the fact that I know so many of them to be inaccurate is bound to throw grave doubt over the rest of the account. To give just one example: I was the only person present to hear what Louis said when I showed him my find of the *Zinjanthropus* skull, and it certainly was not, as needlessly quoted in *Lucy*, 'Nothing but a God-damned robust australopithecine'.

According to *Lucy*, life on the Hadar expeditions seems to have been an extraordinarily eventful and colourful experience, what with people 'scrambling madly' in 'a near frenzy', on the discovery of the 'First Family', picking up the fossils which 'seemed to be cascading, almost as from a fountain, down the hillside'. It really does seem hard to picture a professional archaeological expedition behaving in such a manner.

183

Finally there is the bizarre episode of the removal of a modern human femur from a recent Afar burial mound, described in detail in the text. Unwisely, one might think. According to recent reports, when, in 1982, the Ethiopian authorities placed a ban on all foreign expeditions entering the country to carry out research on Ethiopian prehistory and palaeontology, one of the factors that influenced them was the text of *Lucy*. One report also drew attention to the fact that certain changes in the text were made in the British edition from the original American edition, perhaps to soothe ruffled feelings in Ethiopia, and it is interesting to note that this involved the alteration of at least one of the supposed verbatim quotations.

It is certainly to be hoped that this enforced stop to field research in Ethiopia is not permanent. The principal reasons for it are concerned with the very right and proper desire of the new Ethiopian state to retain control of the exploitation of the country's marvellous repository of scientific information, and to see that properly trained Ethiopian scholars are deeply involved in the work. With these provisos, the Ethiopian authorities are not, as I understand it, opposed to the deployment of international expertise at their sites. Given Johanson's important role in showing just how excellent is the material awaiting discovery, it would be sad indeed if an essentially lightweight book like *Lucy* were instrumental in delaying such progress. Meanwhile, for my part, I do not think the time has yet come to form a final view of the order of events in hominid evolution, or to adopt any inflexible attitude regarding the precise status of the hominid remains we found at Laetoli.

15
People and places

I SAID EARLIER that in any given year after Louis's death I was kept busy on a number of fronts, and of these the fieldwork was only one. We might in a long season be out at Laetoli from, say, the end of July to the beginning of October, but that is only a small part of the year. Sometimes, too, I had to leave the work in the care of my assistants, or break the season into two parts in order to attend a conference. For example, in 1976 there was the big conference in Nice, and in 1977 there was the Pan-African Congress in Nairobi. During the 1970s, and indeed since, travel has taken up quite a major part of my time. Most of it is done in the late winter or early spring, and my usual destination is the USA, via Britain. Lecturing is the main commitment, and there may be a dozen or twenty speaking engagements of one sort or another. But usually there are also opportunities to consult colleagues on the progress of research or to enlist the help of specialists in tackling some of our fieldwork problems. Often there are meetings and symposia to attend, and it has often been my privilege to receive special honours, including medals and honorary degrees, in recognition of the work done in East Africa. Perhaps best of all, at the personal level, there is usually sufficient time to visit old and valued friends.

Since – to the despair of those who ask me about past events in my life – I have never kept a diary or journal, I don't think it would actually be possible for me to give an accurate record of all the trips I have made. Better, I think, to let the memories merge, except where dates are important, and just pick out the highlights.

Ten years of experience has enabled me to get down to a fairly regular routine. I leave Olduvai at dawn in an attempt to get through to Nairobi the same day: the distance from my Olduvai camp to my house at Langata is exactly 300 miles, but nowadays one can count on an eleven- or twelve-hour journey. To begin with, the first 30 or 40 miles of the road from Olduvai is liable to be so deep in dust or mud, according to the season, that one can only drive very slowly. Frequently, between Olduvai and Ngorongoro, it is so bad that many vehicles bypass the road and travel part of the way across country. Formerly the stretch from Makuyuni to Arusha, about 60 miles, was tarmac and good going, but during the Tanzanian war with Uganda at the time of the Idi Amin regime, heavy army vehicles destroyed the surface, and huge potholes developed. From

Arusha onwards the road is tarmac and good, but one usually has some business to transact in Arusha, and then, of course, there are the customs and immigration formalities at the Tanzania/Kenya border. Before the border closed this was a relatively simple matter, but in recent years it could be lengthy and tedious, despite the courtesy and kindness that the border officials have generally displayed towards me and the members of my staff. Perhaps the most irritating part of the entire journey, even if not the most arduous, is to arrive in Nairobi during the evening rush-hour, only to be forced to crawl the ten miles out to Langata in a long line of slow-moving traffic.

Once in Nairobi there are the usual arrangements to be made before travelling on, but all this is made easy for me these days by my secretary Hazel Potgeiter. Departure for London from Nairobi is always about midnight and one reaches London in the early hours of the morning. From Heathrow Airport I make like a homing pigeon for Hampstead and the home of my regular, long-suffering and infinitely kind hosts, Michael Day and his wife Micky. Over the years, on account of my frequent visits, they have even given me a key to their house so that I can let myself in and quietly go to rest without disturbing anyone.

I first met the Days many years ago, when they came out to East Africa with their son Jeremy, then I suppose about nine or ten. Michael was to study two skulls Richard had found at the Omo, probably belonging to an early form of *Homo sapiens*, and has been involved professionally with many of our hominid finds since the discovery of *Homo habilis* at Olduvai in 1960. His wife Micky is an immensely hard-working doctor, but likes to find time for research if she can, and during their many subsequent visits to East Africa she has been studying the level of cholesterol in the blood of certain Masai groups. Because of their diet of milk mixed with blood, their cholesterol levels ought to be dangerously high; but for some reason not yet understood, this is not the case.

But these outward and homeward visits to England are brief and restful affairs compared to the hectic programme that has to be completed in America during the intervening weeks. It is one matter to travel between two cities in England, and quite another in the States, where they may be a couple of thousand miles or more apart; and there are time changes to be coped with. I found these very difficult and tiring at first, just as I did the effects of the transatlantic flight itself. In the States I may have to make several long flights in various directions in the space of a few weeks, and not until at least ten days have passed do I become accustomed to the time changes. In due course I learned to insist at the planning stage of a tour that I must have at least 24 hours to rest between arriving anywhere and lecturing – a stipulation which I am sure Louis would never even have dreamt of making.

Up to the time of Louis's death, I had made only two or three visits to the States, and none had been by myself, since I had gone either with Louis or with Richard. After Louis died, I did not at first go as a paid lecturer on tour, but simply to attend symposia, first in San Francisco and afterwards in New York. In the States, a symposium is often a big event attended by a very large number of interested members of the public, and I therefore became used to speaking to that kind of audience. As a result of these symposia, I was approached by the Leakey Foundation to undertake a lecture tour of the kind Louis used to give every year during the last period of his life. I agreed and the tour was successful enough for the Foundation to want it to become an annual occurrence: this really established the pattern of my visits to the States since 1977.

As regards the Leakey Foundation, I have in a previous chapter mentioned that our friend Allen O'Brien had founded it in 1968, in honour of Louis and to help him in raising funds for his research projects. The lectures that Louis gave under its sponsorship had been enormously popular and many people probably regarded them as the Foundation's *raison d'être*, though this, of course, was not the case. There was a Board of Trustees, mostly wealthy people, who were in charge of the fund-raising side (and expected to lead the way by example), and to control the spending of the money raised there was a hard-working finance and research committee, which received and passed judgement on grant applications from all over the world. Louis's lectures had been important and profitable occasions for the Foundation, and his death had left a gap that it was hard to fill. Hence their approach to me. On most of my lecture tours I would stay for a short while with Ethel and Melvin Payne, whom I have known for even a little longer than I have known the Days, and they have been equally kind and hospitable to me: I know that I am welcome to stay at their home whenever I go to Washington. My original contact with them came when the National Geographic Society first decided to support the work of Louis and myself at Olduvai, after I found *Zinjanthropus*, and I actually met them for the first time soon afterwards when Louis and I went to Washington to receive the joint award of the Hubbard Medal. Mel Payne has now retired from being President of the Society, but still plays an active role as President of the Board of Trustees and Chairman of the Research Committee. It was on one of my visits to Washington that I finally got to see somthing I had often heard about but had always previously missed: the blossoming of the famous cherry trees, of which hundreds were given as a gesture of goodwill by the people of Japan, and planted around the tidal basin in that part of the city where the national monuments stand. Whenever I arrived in Washington in the winter, sometimes fighting my way through the snow storms, I was told to come back in the spring next time to see the cherry blossom; but whenever I arrived in the spring I was always a week or so too early or too late. I forget in which year I did eventually get the timing right, but the sight was so beautiful that all the waiting was worthwhile; everything the Washingtonians say about it is true.

The next stop after Washington might be absolutely anywhere, but at some stage I would find myself in California. One of the pleasures of the regular visits to Southern California was the chance to visit my friends the O'Briens, Allen and his wife Helen. After Louis died, Allen transferred to me all the kindness he had afforded Louis on his California visits, and performed all the same practical services, including driving me in his car on those terrifying freeways wherever I needed to go. That particular example of his generosity was perhaps a mixed blessing, because he was a very fast driver whose style was rather in the mode of Henry de Lumley, and the California freeways are perhaps an even less appropriate arena for that sort of thing than the road from Laetoli to Olduvai.

Allen O'Brien was one of those people with the marvellous gift of perceiving a need and immediately taking practical steps to supply it. I can give no better example than his help in seeing me through the receptions that followed the lectures I gave. The usual programme on all these occasions includes a dinner given by the hosts, a lecture (given by me) and a reception at which the audience gets a chance to meet the speaker. The dinner is fine, the lecture I can cope with, but the reception! Louis used to love all the socializing that receptions entail, and perhaps the Leakey Foundation thought I would be the same. At some receptions, whether for reasons of economy or (perish the thought) principle, the beverage on offer would be a non-alcoholic fruit cup. Allen had the knack of finding this out in advance, and he had a little basket which he would produce from behind the scenes and quietly provide me with a tot of the right stuff, Jack Daniels, after the lecture and before the reception. After that, I felt revitalized. It may be that the news of this admirable system spread in California, because it was certainly followed with some success on a later occasion at San Diego by Sheldon Campbell, Assistant Director of the San Diego Zoo. He, however, did not use the basket technique, preferring to stock his pockets with miniature bottles, so that he clinked quite audibly when he walked. From time to time he would sidle up to me during the reception. 'Ready for another yet, Mary?' (Clink-clink.)

It was through Allen and Helen O'Brien too that I first went to a place which I have found attractive to a quite extraordinary degree, Baja California, in Mexico. For the sheer beauty of its desert scenery, and incredible variety of cactuses, I think I prefer it to anywhere in the world except Tanzania in the region of Olduvai. The year after Louis died, Allen decided I needed a break and he invited me out to stay with him at Newport Beach, paying my fare himself. I stayed with him there several times afterwards. I think it was in 1978 that he introduced me to his friends Don and Dorothy Koll. Don was a 'realtor', a property developer, and he had a charming family with six children. It was in Don's executive jet that we all flew down to Baja California. Sonia Cole and Bob Drake were also in the party. On that occasion we went right down to the tip of the Peninsula, where at San José del Cabo there is a tourist hotel, the building of which Allen helped finance. Allen was, as ever, on the quest for Early Man in California, and we all went fossil hunting, but the fossils there are almost all of marine origin, sharks' teeth and the like, so he came away with his hopes unfulfilled. Since Allen's death in 1980, Helen O'Brien has carried on the tradition of their generous hospitality to me. In 1981, she and I went again to Baja California as guests of the Kolls, this time to stay at Rancho el Barril, the delightful old Mexican ranch house that they own, along with four miles of coastline, on the Gulf of California. This was a marvellous place to visit, immediately across the peninsula from Scammon's Lagoon, where the California grey whales have their breeding ground. We were able to fly across in Don Koll's plane and go out in a small boat, right among the whales, and it was wonderful to see their complete lack of fear of man; just friendliness and curiosity. The Kolls took me back again in 1982 and on that occasion we actually watched the whales mating. On that visit they also took me to see some of the well-known rock paintings of Baja California. It is indeed a very special place for me, and one to which I certainly hope to return.

There was one other visit Allen O'Brien arranged for me which I must mention. After we found the animal footprints at Laetoli, my friend Patti Moehlman, now at Yale University, told me of the Miocene fossil footprints in Death Valley, California, which I was accordingly anxious to see. She had first seen them when carrying out her doctoral research on wild donkeys in that area. In 1977, Allen arranged for a friend to fly me down in a light plane, which I found to my horror entailed landing in the Mojave Desert on a highway lined with telegraph poles. When we had accomplished this unlikely feat, I was taken on in an army helicopter, which Mel Payne had arranged, to Copper Canyon, in Death Valley. At the time I still had a very weak ankle, having broken it earlier in the year, and the helicopter ride was to save me a rough walk of two miles. The footprints, mostly those of camel, were very interesting, though not in the event quite as useful for comparison with ours in Tanzania as I had hoped. Death Valley, however, is certainly the most spectacular place I have ever seen: unbelievable colours, and the extraordinary contrast between the great desert heat and the view of the high snow-capped mountains of the Sierra range just across the valley. By chance, I also saw the desert flowers blooming after one of the extremely rare showers of rain the area receives, by no means every year.

The way in which Allen arranged this trip for me was completely typical of the way he liked to look after his friends. His early death was a terrible tragedy. In memory of him, his widow Helen endowed the Allen O'Brien Memorial Lectures, and I had the great privilege of giving the first of these in Washington on 25 September 1982, at the Smithsonian Institution.

Americans seem to be among the most hospitable people in the world, and their pleasure in visitors is quite unfeigned. Accordingly, in so many of the places I have visited for the purpose of lecturing, little colonies of friends have sprung up, which always makes my return visit a real pleasure. It is sad that I have room to mention only a few of them here. Just occasionally some of the people visit East Africa, and I get a chance to make a token repayment of hospitality at Olduvai, but more often I am visiting them on their home ground and receiving their kindness.

I went twice to Arkansas, and at Little Rock there is Sandy McMath and John and Marge Pauley. Sandy is a lawyer, whose father had been Governor of the State, and he had visited East Africa in 1977, calling at Olduvai, which deeply interested him. It was he who arranged for me to lecture at Little Rock, to an audience at the Medical School there. The Pauleys were my hosts on my two visits to Arkansas: John was Chairman of the Department of Anatomy in the University of Arkansas. After I had lectured at Fayetteville, he took me on one of the happiest excursions I have ever made in the States, a drive through the beautiful Ozark Mountains, which had a special appeal for me because this is limestone country, strikingly reminiscent of the Dordogne in France, with the same kind of limestone cliffs and meadows on the flood plains below. There are also many large limestone caverns, very like those containing some of the very best of the French cave paintings: but alas there are no cave paintings in the Ozarks.

My lectures are not generally regarded as controversial, but in 1981–82, in Arkansas, I did encounter some good-natured heckling and a lot of questioning about Creationism – an issue that was, at the time, receiving widespread publicity. A bill before the Arkansas State Legislature aimed to make it lawful to teach Creationism as a science in schools, in place of evolutionary theory. Judge Overton was the person who had to rule on the proposal, and in the end his decision was that Creationism counted as religion, not science. But in giving this verdict he went out of his way to produce a long document which was in effect a brilliant destructive criticism of the Creationists' views, and this more or less silenced them.

Such special issues apart, I have never failed to find my American lecture audiences friendly, often well informed and almost embarrassingly enthusiastic. Applause at the end is one thing, but I just do not know how one is expected to cope with a standing ovation.

The 1982 tour also took me to St. Louis – a city I would have been delighted to visit if only because it was the home of Charles Lindbergh. I had been invited there to give the 1982 Mildred Trotter Lecture, and it was one of several occasions on which I have found myself the third member of the family, after Louis and Richard, to address a particular prestigious meeting. After the lecture I was taken sightseeing by my hosts and was shown the soaring metal arch by the Missouri River that symbolizes the city's proud claim to have been the Gateway to the West.

That same year provided an opportunity to visit Florida, where once again I have many good friends. They include Walter and Elinor Auffenberg, Pierce Brodkorb, Peter Meylan and Diana Matthiesen, who are all at Gainesville, where I was to address an audience at the University and where, incidentally, I added to my list of experiences that of giving a lecture in a baseball stadium. The people I have just named were colleagues as well as friends. Walter Auffenberg and Peter Meylan are herpetologists, and Pierce Brodkorb is an ornithologist. I had first been in touch with them when I wanted people to take on the study of the fossil tortoises and birds from the Olduvai excavations. The bird remains from Olduvai constitute the largest known single collection of such material of Pleistocene age anywhere, and the sheer volume of it had eventually defeated Pierce; Diana Matthiesen had taken on the task, and after some years of work she has now got the whole lot numbered and catalogued – a formidable effort since there are very nearly 30,000 items. The chief memory I brought away from Florida was that of the flowers – one can see how easy it was for the Spaniards to find a name for the place, when they first reached it. I wonder if they arrived as I did, in late spring? Though the dogwood was already over, the abundance of flowers was incredible, and the woods seemed to be full of flowering shrubs. I particularly remember the wisteria that was festooning the trees, rather in the way that bougainvillea does in East Africa, but so very much more beautiful.

I suppose that to some extent my very favourable impressions of America and Americans are biased by having stayed so often in private homes, where I was made so welcome. However, it does one no harm to be brought down to earth occasionally, and that too has happened to me on my travels. I can give an instance which in fact came right after my visit to Florida. I went next to Morristown in New Jersey, and when I arrived there I succumbed to a sharp gastric upset, which I suspect had to do with eating an airline snack that had spent more time in the steamy heat of Atlanta, Georgia, than it had in a refrigerator. I have twice stayed in motels in New Jersey, and each time I have discovered an awful truth about them. For five days only in the week do restaurant service and room service operate: on a Saturday and a Sunday there is no way of obtaining even so much as a cup of tea or coffee. What I desperately needed in my sick condition was something like a warm drink, perhaps some hot soup. All I had was an enormous basket of luscious fruit, a kind thought by my hosts, but utterly unsuitable in the circumstances.

Another extraordinary episode occurred on an earlier tour, when I attempted to get what seemed to me quite an ordinary kind of medical attention, in Minneapolis St. Paul. When I arrived there in the evening I had for some reason lost my voice and could manage only a rather feeble croak. Visits to various pharmacies produced only offers of lemon drops or mild cough lozenges; anything stronger and more effective was 'only on prescription', and I was directed to the local hospital. There I had to fill in several forms and wait interminably before finally being taken to see a young and, I suspect, not very experienced intern, who proceeded to wrap gauze round my tongue and jerk it downwards with a series of violent tugs in order to see my throat. No amount of argument would get him to desist from this pastime, and I would have been shouting with anger if I had been capable of it. Finally, I refused to submit any longer and the young man flung out of the room in a rage: I wonder what he said of the British? An older doctor then came in, grinning, and quietly asked me what the matter was. Almost speechless by then, and with my tongue numb from the treatment thus far, in addition to the lost voice, I explained as best I could that I had been travelling and lecturing for several weeks and that not only was my voice tired, but so was I. He understood at once and went off 'to look up the correct medicine'. Whatever it was he gave me proved to be a miraculous mixture, which saw me safely through that night's lecture and several others. There was even enough over to rescue Peter Jones, who, next year, was also in the States with some lectures to give, and found himself with a similar affliction in Los Angeles.

Perhaps these pages will have given at least some flavour of my travels in America. For me, it all adds up to an important episode in my life. The distances covered were vast, but because of that and the kindness of so many people who looked after me, I got to see many interesting and beautiful places that I could not otherwise ever have hoped to visit. I also had a chance to experience the American way of life in different parts of the States – and, incidentally, to renew my acquaintances with American food, much of which I greatly enjoy. The 'junk food' is awful, and I don't at all care for hamburgers; I also dislike the Californian habit of serving at the beginning of dinner a heaped plate of what I took to be rabbit food. But with those reservations, the rest is very good indeed. American lamb chops are unbeatable and American ice cream is delicious, while the sea-food makes my mouth water even to think about, especially soft-shelled crab, Alaska king crab, lobsters and clam chowder. Then, of course, there are American wines, especially in California, and

The final cleaning of the hominid trails at Laetoli. To the right, running diagonally, are the tracks of a three-toed horse, *Hipparion*, and its foal.

ABOVE: Measuring one of the hominid footprints in the trails at Laetoli.

LEFT: After gently easing it away from the surface, Peter Jones removes one of the many latex casts we made of the Laetoli footprints. On the left of the cast can be seen the line of four mysterious prints which at first were thought to be hominid.

RIGHT: A pause for contemplation and a cigar while excavating the Laetoli footprints.

LEFT: This aerial shot shows the Laetoli camp site shortly after all the surrounding grass had been destroyed by a bush fire.
ABOVE: The fossil termitaries at Laetoli – the earliest known workings of the higher termites.
RIGHT: The Laetoli deposits yielded a great variety of fossils, including these beautifully preserved guinea-fowl eggs.

ABOVE: Supervising the work of some of our African assistants, searching for fragments of a fossil hominid skull trampled by Masai cattle.
RIGHT: George Dove, who helped me rediscover the Laetoli deposits and build the Olduvai camp.
BELOW: All the soil from an excavation is sieved for fragments such as teeth and chips of bone.

RIGHT: Searching for new places to dig at Olduvai, accompanied by Simon and three of my Dalmatians.
BELOW: The procession during the Encaenia ceremony at Oxford in 1981, when I received my honorary D.Litt.

that is a great treat to a visitor from East Africa, where wine growing is minimal.

Not all the official functions in America during these years were lectures. After we had discovered the hominid footprints at Laetoli, I twice found myself giving major press conferences at the National Geographic Society's headquarters, in the presence of very large numbers of journalists representing papers all over the world, not to mention television cameras and a whole battery of microphones. I felt very nervous about this, especially on the first occasion, though I afterwards decided that this had been unnecessary. Those who asked me questions were friendly and nice, and they made no attempt to trap me or make me say more than I wished. I had the impression of people who were genuinely interested in what I was saying and who in many cases were prepared to go to great lengths to ensure the accuracy of what they wrote.

There have also been the numerous occasions on which I have been the recipient of some special mark of recognition; an Honorary Degree, a learned society medal, or some similar honour. I will not list them, but I am particularly proud of my Yale DSSc and my Chicago DSc, and my Honorary Foreign Membership of the American Academy of Arts and Sciences. These honours have an importance far beyond the purely personal pleasure they bring. I have been fortunate in having played a part in many quite spectacular and important discoveries, and I take a certain pride in what I have achieved, but the many marks of recognition that have been made have also been accepted on behalf of the many other people who have contributed to the work. The fact that there have been so many such honours is itself a fitting tribute to their achievements.

One of the more forbidding of these formal occasions was when I received the Gold Medal of the Society of Women Geographers in Washington, a high honour. There was a certain undercurrent of Women's Lib among some of the very large number of women present, and Women's Lib is something for which I carry no banner, though quite often people seem to expect me to do so. What I have done in my life I have done because I wanted to do it and because it interested me. I just happen to be a woman, and I don't believe it has made much difference. In fact, I dare say that particular occasion was more testing for Melvin Payne, who was there as President of the National Geographic Society, than it was for me: he was the only man among, I believe, 200 women. There was a rather grand formal lunch, and it transpired that for lunch women geographers drink water. Mel and I conferred rather desperately and then, with his usual aplomb, he asked the President if he and I might possibly have a gin-and-tonic each.

I called this chapter 'People and places', and I must not give the impression that all my journeys were to or within the United States. A catalogue of all my travelling would be of little interest, so to end with I will select just a few trips I have made during the past ten years for official functions in Europe. One of the first was to Burg Wartenstein in Austria, to a conference sponsored by the Wenner-Gren Foundation.

The Burg Wartenstein conferences were highly unusual and imaginative events, and it is sad that they have now long ceased to take place. In the days when the Wenner-Gren Foundation was at the peak of its prosperity the then Director of Research, Paul Fejos, persuaded the Trustees to purchase from Prince Lichtenstein a romantically situated hill-top castle in Austria, and to adapt it to make a lavishly appointed conference centre. Paul Fejos was Hungarian by birth and a man of excellent taste and diverse interests, the latter reflected in the wide range of conferences which were held, the first in 1957. The rules were quite strict: twenty was the maximum number of invited participants, and no wives or husbands could come unless on a professional basis, invited as colleagues in their own right.

Louis and I first went to Burg Wartenstein in 1965, for a conference entitled 'Background to Evolution in Africa'. He attended as a palaeontologist in the first week, and I as a prehistoric archaeologist in the second.

The oldest parts of the castle dated from the twelfth century and were in ruins, but the renovation of the rest provided excellent facilities and a high degree of comfort. Superb Austrian food and fine wines were served: indeed, the lunches were such large affairs that afternoon sessions tended to be very somnolent. All sessions were held round an enormous circular table, whose cover was a green baize cloth which had been specially commissioned for it and locally woven. I was terrified that one of my cigars would burn a hole in it, but fortunately I managed to avoid this on both my visits. Generally speaking, the delegates remained in isolation in the castle during the conferences, unless there was an organized excursion on an official day off, which there usually was, since a ten-day conference with no break was thought too long.

In 1967 I was very keen to see the Hungarian Lower Palaeolithic site of Vertesszölös, and the other delegates thought this was a good idea, so for our excursion we all went in a coach to Budapest, spent a night there and went out to the site; we also visited the museum at Budapest. I remember being impressed by the great formality at the Museum, where we all drank apricot brandy, sitting in high-backed chairs round a long table; by the bullet holes in buildings all over Budapest; and by the fact that the famous Blue Danube was anything but blue, more a muddy brown.

In 1973, the conference I attended at Burg Wartenstein was concerned with the Middle Pleistocene, and Africa was only one of the regions considered. The subject was generally referred to as 'The Muddle in the Middle'. Many discoveries and advances had been made in prehistoric archaeology since 1965, but at Burg Wartenstein not everything had changed. The rule about wives was the same, for example, so that when Dorette Curtis turned up, having insisted on accompanying Garniss, she was abruptly packed off by Lita Osmundsen to find herself lodgings in the village of Gloggnitz, which did not please her at all. Dorette was rather an advocate of Women's Lib.

This conference proved a useful one and even achieved general agreement on defining and dating the start of the Middle Pleistocene at the transition from the last major period of reversed to normal polarity, dated at 700,000 years ago. Quite an achievement. It was also a good chance for a reunion with several old friends I had not seen for a while, and to meet some new ones. One of the old Burg Wartenstein traditions still current in 1973 required that on the last evening of any conference the participants should produce an entertainment of some sort – playlets, charades, or the singing of specially composed songs or ditties to well-known tunes. On this occasion one of the items was a song with a chorus, which went as follows. (I still have the original typed copy, bearing sixteen distinguished signatures; the tune is 'Clementine', and it sounds much better sung than read in cold prose):

In a valley in die Alpen in neunteen-hundred neun
Oh, there werkte Penck and Brückner, carving up the Pleistoceun.
They had Günzes, they had Würmses in the Stages on their list,
But the biggest and the Grösstest – Interglacial Mindel-Riss.

CHORUS (repeat after each verse)
Correlation, constipation. Oh, now what are we to do?
All these bedses without dateses. Oh, we're really in the stew!

In the wastes of Central Europe, Jiri Kukla split the loess
With magnetic machinations into normal and reverse.
And the soils, he's embroiling, soliflucting down the hills,
Come from spatial interglacials, but they can't be linked with tills.

In some very dirty brick-pits, which they say were stone age bogs,
There sit Turner and Janossy counting pollen, mice and frogs,
They report that interglacials were a beastly nasty mess
And point out as the Stützpünkte, it was raining mud not loess.

There were structures, heaps and rubble, where our *Homos* sat and chipped,
Munching yarrow, meat and marrow, saying little, too tight-lipped.
Fires a'plenty swept the forest, lit by hunters chasing game.
Little pieces, flakes and faeces help interpret pollen rain.

Lots of tool types, groups and classes, much too many have we found,
But our 'abbos' cannot help us, for they have so few around.
Can't believe it. Can't believe it. We have found a boundary line.
Most of us agree t's a good one, for our Pleistocene mid-time.

In 1967, the counterpart song had been to the tune 'Waltzing Matilda' and is too long to quote here. Bill Bishop had been present on the occasion, and he was a great expert at these ditties, and would often perform them solo; he had a fine voice, and used to sing in amateur opera. Bill was the organizer of a major conference in London in 1975, sponsored by the Geological Society of London, to which I have already referred; Richard and I were both speakers at it. In 1976, there was Henry de Lumley's Sixth Prehistoric and Protohistoric Sciences Congress at Nice, preceded by excursions in southern France, and in 1980 there was a large symposium in London in March, jointly organized by the Royal Society and the British Academy, to discuss many aspects of human evolution against its geological and palaeontological background. These will serve as examples of the kind of functions which took me to Europe in the course of my travels. On each occasion, most of the leading figures in relevant East African research were there, and the principal papers were afterwards published in special volumes. During these meetings, at various receptions, lunches or dinners, and less formally in the evenings, one got a chance to exchange news and gossip with one's friends. Since by the end of the 1970s it had become very difficult for colleagues to make visits to Olduvai, this became more important than ever in helping me to keep in touch.

Yet another of these occasions provided me with the chance of a delightful genuine holiday in France. Following the success of the big conference at Nice in 1976, Henry de Lumley decided to organize another, not quite so large, in October 1982, entitled the First International Congress of Human Palaeontology. When I was in Berkeley earlier that year, Dick Hay and I found that we were both going to it, and Dick was taking his wife Lynn. We thought how nice it would be to combine the conference with a visit to the caves of southwest France: it was many years since I had visited the paintings, and Dick and Lynn had never seen them. At the end of that visit to the States I was once again in Washington, staying with the Paynes, and I suggested to Ethel that she might like to join us. She jumped at the idea. So it came about that the four of us met up in Bordeaux before the conference and hired a car, driving down through the Dordogne to the Lot and visiting all the main sites. Richard at that time had recently completed his major television series *The Making of Mankind* for the BBC, and in the course of the filming had taken the cameras into Lascaux, the first time the famous paintings had ever been televised. For many years the cave had been closed while the invasion of algae, which had so seriously threatened the paintings, was dealt with. Richard was able to arrange for us to have a private visit to the cave, which we duly made, and I was enormously relieved to see that the paintings were as clear and fresh again as I remembered them many years before: the rescue operation seems to have been a brilliant success, and once again I found the paintings overwhelmingly affecting and impressive. At Périgeux, Dick and Lynn turned back and made their way to Bordeaux through the famous vineyards. Lynn had to return to the States, and Dick flew to Nice from Bordeaux. Ethel and I used the remaining days by hiring a small Peugeot car and driving ourselves towards Nice in easy stages, going just where the fancy took us, wandering through little villages by small roads, and putting up at any hotel we happened to find towards the end of each day. Ethel was exactly the right companion for such an unhurried tour, and our tastes for the quiet by-ways and simple enjoyments seemed to coincide exactly. It was the nicest and most relaxing holiday I have had in years.

A very special occasion for me among my attendances at conferences and symposia in Europe took place in 1978, not in London this time, but in Sweden, when I received an invitation from the Royal Swedish Academy of Sciences to attend the symposium organized by the Nobel Foundation entitled 'The Current Argument on Early Man', and the Secretary-General of the Academy, Professor Carl Gustav Bernhard, further informed me of my selection for the award of the Linnaeus Medal, which was to be presented to me during the symposium by King Gustav of Sweden. Richard was also invited, and many other friends were there, including Glynn Isaac, Henry and Marie-Antoinette de Lumley, Phillip Tobias and Yves Coppens. I flew from London to Stockholm for this meeting, and remember being surprised to find all the cars with their lights on at midday, according to Swedish law. After a night in Stockholm we drove out to the conference venue, and we stayed in the Bofors Company official guesthouse at Karlsruhe. The medal was duly presented by King Gustav, and I also had the honour of meeting Queen Sylvia, who is a most charming person. I also had the privilege of flying back to Stockholm in the Royal plane with the King and Queen and with Carl Gustav Bernhard and his wife. Some parts of the whole occasion I found extremely formal, especially the dinners given by the Royal Academy of Sciences in Stockholm, when each lady was taken in on the arm of a gentleman, in correct order – an entirely new experience for me. Things were more relaxed at the dinners in Karlsruhe. On one occasion, aquavit was mentioned, something that I had never tried, so I suggested at once that we should have some. As it happened, Richard and I were at opposite ends of the very long table, and I could feel the waves of disapproval extending all the way up to me. 'Mother,' said the waves, quite clearly, 'I cannot have you breaking out like this!' But there was nothing he could do about it, and I noted that my end of the table seemed to become a lot more animated than his.

I will end this chapter with another rather special occasion, this time not attached to a lecture or symposium, which was the award to me of an honorary degree by Oxford University in June 1981. Here I was again following in Louis's steps, and at Oxford I have several close friends, most of whom were able to attend the ceremony. Unlike the award to Louis in 1950, my honorary degree was conferred at the Summer Encaenia, which is the principal full-dress academic occasion of the year, when honorary degrees are conferred by the Chancellor himself on six or seven people chosen from many fields, before a packed audience in the seventeenth-century Sheldonian Theatre. Accordingly I found myself in very distinguished company. Before the ceremony itself, in mid-morning, the 'honorands' join the Chancellor and the higher echelons of the University's academic staff and administration in a college hall for 'Lord Crewe's Benefaction' – Lord Crewe being a very right-thinking seventeenth-century bishop who left a sum of money to provide champagne and strawberries for this very occasion. Everyone is in full academic dress, with scarlet the dominant colour. There is then a short procession through the city streets to the Sheldonian Theatre, led by the Chancellor, who was then Mr Harold Macmillan, now the Earl of Stockton a former Prime Minister of Britain. In deference to his great age, the pace of the procession is necessarily slow. I found myself next to Lord Soames, a Cabinet Minister, and we encouraged each other, having established that neither of us had attended a university.

At the ceremony itself, long stretches of the proceedings are in Latin, and at Oxford they speak Latin as if they understand it. In due course, each honorand in turn stands before the Chancellor dressed in the robes appropriate to the degree that is being conferred, and the Public Orator delivers a speech in Latin about him or her. For members of the general audience on these occasions, a key to success is the ability to laugh in the right places, and therefore everyone is discreetly provided with a copy of the Latin text and an English translation (or paraphrase, as they insist on calling it). I must say these speeches are very well done, and indicate considerable homework on the Public Orator's part. I will quote here the one about myself.

'The best Latin authors tell us that Africa is a land rich in triumphs and that it is always producing something new. Here is a scholar who keeps on bringing back very ancient things from Africa, the triumphs of a woman of peace. There is a place in Tanzania, Olduvai Gorge, where the earth gapes in a deep fissure. The ancients would have called it the jaws of Hell: we using more exact methods know that it is one of the thresholds of human life. Imagine our honorand, working over this terrain like Diana the huntress with her Dalmatian hounds, searching for traces of early inhabitants. As she probes the ground most scrupulously there suddenly appears part of a skull, then two teeth akin to molars: here now, making their debut in the clear light of day, are those famous remains of *Australopithecus boisei*, who used tools of stone. When I tell you that these are very ancient, you must not think that this is a gentle inflation of the truth, such as one might expect from an Irish Public Orator. Instead, ask the scientists who can date things by measuring the changes in potassium and uranium. They will tell you that these finds are 1.7 million years old.

'She is not content with finding bones. She also hunts footprints in the manner immortalized by Winnie-the-Pooh and Piglet. At Laetoli (near Olduvai Gorge) she has found fossilized footprints of an animal which must be a biped, standing erect. I must apologize to our learned guest for confining myself to telling the story of her most famous discoveries, which are merely the tip of an enormous iceberg of patient labour, "excessive work" as Virgil put it. For in her digs it is the routine to mark all finds with the utmost care. After a day working in the blazing sun there is time only for a light supper, for the evening must be devoted to "writing up" and labelling.

'Dr Leakey has anthropology in her blood: one of her ancestors was John Frere, who published an article on the flints he found in Suffolk in 1797, the year before Nelson won the Battle of the Nile. So she is descendant, wife, and mother of anthropologists, but she has not been infected with the arrogance one might expect. She is like the modest Archedice

"Unto whose bosom pride was never known
Though daughter, wife, and sister to the throne."

She takes no part in those public controversies to which the life of an archaeologist is prone. She joined this profession because of her remarkable skill in drawing, which caught the eye of a certain Louis Leakey, her future husband. I must finally reveal something which will encourage many people and be a salutary lesson to us in the universities: Dr Leakey has already two honorary degrees; she has great skill in an academic discipline; but she never went through any university course. I present Mary Douglas Leakey, a Fellow of the British Academy, for admission to the honorary degree of Doctor of Letters.'

When the speech was over, I had to climb some rather steep steps, shake hands with the Chancellor, who actually conferred the degree in a further brief outbreak of Latin, and then take a reserved place. The worst was over, and there was a chance to look discreetly around the audience to see if I could pick out the faces of any of my friends.

The degree ceremony was very colourful and I quite enjoyed it on balance, but the whole occasion also involved other official events, some of which were much less to my taste – a formal dinner at Christ Church, a lunch at All Souls College after the ceremony, and a garden party at Merton College later in the afternoon. The lunch was a most pleasant occasion, and I enjoyed talking to Cardinal Hume and Lady Soames, but I did not enjoy the dinner at Christ Church nearly so much. Not having been warned in advance, I had to borrow a suitable long dress at short notice and I was suffering from a stomach upset and a viral eye infection, which didn't help. The tone of the Dean's remarks welcoming ladies to the College in the course of his speech was probably not intended to suggest that it was a privilege the College would rather have withheld, but that was how it came across to me. Worse was to follow. When cigars were handed round after dinner, the ladies were carefully excluded from the offer: I quickly solved that problem with the help of a sympathetic college servant, doubtless to my hosts' disapproval. And then they had the nerve to offer me a soft drink when the dinner finally ended at 11.30pm. It was a great relief to get home at last to the Faggs' house, where I was staying, and give Mary my views on the evening. As a delightful contrast, next day, I dined at St Anne's College, which had honoured me by electing me to an Honorary Fellowship. The Principal, Mrs Trenaman, introduced me to other Fellows of the College and we had a quietly enjoyable evening and intelligent conversation on a wide range of topics.

16
A time of change and reflection

Although the years since Louis's death have involved me in a great deal of travel, our work in East Africa continued throughout, with many new developments and the now-familiar succession of visitors. It has also been a time of great change in the countries that have been my home for all these years, and some of these changes have had profound repercussions on our personal and professional lives. The camp at Olduvai has been the principal background for most of these events, so it is with Olduvai that I will begin this final chapter.

I recorded how, through the kindness of George Dove and Gordon Hanes, the new stone building and the water storage tanks were added during 1973. In due course we built a large laboratory and store next to George's building. This was adequate for all our Olduvai material, but when we began to bring back large quantities of finds from Laetoli, not to mention the casts of the footprints, it very soon got hopelessly over-crowded. To ease this problem the Tanzanian Antiquities Department built for us another new work-room with storage facilities, and also put up two huts for visiting workers. Meanwhile, Gordon Hanes had placed us further in his debt with the generous gift of an electrical system for the camp: there were two tall windmills to generate the electricity, and an array of storage batteries housed in their own shed behind the camp. Gordon himself came over from the States with two of his friends to install this system, and they worked very hard on it with great skill, though I got the impression from Gordon that for them the trip had some of the features of a light-hearted schoolboy outing. Grateful though we were for the electricity, the system proved to have certain shortcomings which Gordon himself recognized too late. It hadn't occurred to him, for example, that American voltage was quite unsuitable for English appliances, so an inverter had to be installed, although we could use the electric light system without any problems. He also had not realized that the windmills would need governors or cut-outs to prevent them going round too fast. At first they were highly dangerous, and one blade did in fact break and fly off with such force that it cut down a substantial comiphora bush within a few feet of where I was standing. Also, the siting of the two windmills close to the edge of the Gorge behind my hut made them a serious hazard to birds: there is a considerable turbulence and up-draught along the steep edges of the Gorge, and two young ravens were caught by this, hurled into one of the working windmills, and killed. After that happened, I resolved never to use the windmills again during the day, and they are still only used at night, after the ravens have flown home at dusk to roost. Fortunately the nights are often windy at Olduvai, and we are able to store enough electricity to maintain our lighting in the camp, though not enough for refrigeration and for other uses Gordon had had in mind.

Gordon seems to have taken a philosophical view of these reverses, because he afterwards sent me what he called *The Parable of Olduvai*, which reads as follows:

'In a faraway place there lived and worked a lady motivated in the highest by the love of and thirst for knowledge. She heeded not her lack of creature comforts, for within her burned the God-given need-to-know and all other needs faded into nothingness in its celestial radiance.

'From far away there came three not-so-wise men, thinking to bring her some small comfort, for she numbered her years nigh unto three score. They raised two towers half way to heaven, but like the tower of Babel in olden times, confusion and at last disaster was the result.

'Now this lady numbered among her friends the birds of the air. She loved them and they repaid this love with trust. The ravens were her special friends (as their ancestors were to Elijah when he hungered in the desert) and it came to pass that the ravens, having no fear of man and his engines, were destroyed by them and grief for her friends came to Mary. Forthwith the machine was closed down and darkness settled upon the land.

'And God looked down from heaven and he said: "This is an example and a parable for this generation. If man refuseth to make a sacrifice of his own comfort for the lives of his friends, his vision will grow dim and his lungs will labour in vain in the air which he has polluted.

'"As surely as my stars move in their assigned orbits, man will end his days in a second great flood, not from the waters of the earth, but from his own excrescence."'

This mention of the ravens leads me naturally to the subject of the Olduvai birds and animals, for one cannot live at such a place without there being always something of interest to see. The birds have become one of my great pleasures, and the bird-bath we built for them at the front of the camp ensures that there are always plenty of them about, with many different species, some resident and some passing migrants according to the season of the year. Many become quite tame, including scrub robins, who will perch on a chair to ask for cheese, and bulbuls who will eagerly pounce on anything edible the moment one's back is turned. But the white-naped ravens are particular favourites, and quite an institution in camp for we have had a pair of them for as long as I can remember and they are now in the second generation. They come to be fed, when they cannot find food of their own, on pieces of dog-biscuit softened in warm water. When the young ravens have learned to fly it is not long before the parents bring them into camp, raucous creatures not much smaller than the adults, but inclined to miss their target when landing, or to land down-wind so that they unwittingly turn head over heels. Usually there are two, but in 1983, for the first time, four were successfully reared. One year, one of the fledglings fell from the nest, which was a couple of miles up the Gorge from camp, and we happened to pass by and see it, helpless on the ground at the bottom of the cliff face, not yet able to fly. Peter Jones climbed down and rescued it, and we took it back to care for it in camp. It lived in one of the guest huts for a week, but was let out whenever the parents came into camp so that they should not forget it was theirs.

At certain times of the year the raven family, particularly the young birds, will indulge in remarkable aerobatics as they soar along the Gorge, apparently for sheer high spirits. But far more remarkable are the three occasions we have witnessed when in April there has been a great 'convocation' of ravens at Olduvai – sixty or seventy of them, soaring along the Gorge together and performing all sorts of aerobatics. They will even take up tufts of grass and toss them to each other and catch them. These convocations seem to be the occasion for pairing off and finding mates, though all the birds take part in the flying displays, young or old, single or already paired. Since ravens are highly territorial, such a gathering must represent the raven population of a very large area, and I cannot begin to guess how the word gets round as to the time and place of the meeting. We do not see it every year, so presumably there are venues other than Olduvai Gorge.

One can always find animal stories to tell about Olduvai, though in fact even these are now dwindling, thanks to the loss of some species through poaching, and the sharp reduction of others apparently through disease. To retain a little privacy from the Masai we made a low thorn barrier round the camp area which does keep out the cattle, goats and sheep but is no obstacle to most of the wild animals who wish to visit the camp at night. Giraffe of course can easily step over the fence when they wish, and come in during the night when there are young green shoots or seed pods on the camp acacia trees for them to eat. Occasionally they bring down our overhead electric cables or catch one of the radio aerial supports with their long necks.

A few years ago we were visited, or perhaps I should say adopted, by a cheetah, Lisa, who one morning walked into camp and drank from the dogs' water bowl, after hanging around watching us for about a week. Lisa was desperately thirsty, starving, and in very poor condition, besides being covered in lion-flies and suffering from chronic diarrhoea. She was also wearing a heavy radio collar, weighing perhaps as much as six pounds: it was a particularly cruel handicap for an animal that depends chiefly on its speed for success in hunting.

Lisa's story, as we gradually discovered it, was that after her mother had been killed by poachers, she had been hand-reared by Skip Leavitt and his wife, who ran a safari lodge at Fort Ikoma on the western Serengeti. But the authorities had ordered Skip to release her. Lisa was hardly ready by then for life alone in the wild, and in due course she had come to the notice of George Frame, one of the people at the Serengeti Research Institute. He was said to be studying cheetahs, but was experiencing some difficulty in keeping track of them, and had therefore attached a radio collar to Lisa, who was entirely tame.

We wanted to care for Lisa and see her cured and able to fend for herself before returning her to the wild, but how to achieve this in camp presented insuperable difficulties, since she hated the dogs and they feared and hated her. With the permission of Mr Mgina, the Ngorongoro Conservator, Jonathan kindly took her to Kenya for veterinary treatment at the Kabete Veterinary Clinic and later to convalesce at his Lake Baringo home. George Frame heard of this and set out to make a major row, accusing us of illegally exporting a Tanzanian cheetah, but since Mgina knew the true story we did not get into trouble and in any case we had no intention of releasing Lisa until she was in good health. On her return from Kenya, Lisa again chased the dogs and Masai goats, so we knew that she was in danger of being speared by the Masai. We therefore took her to the Ngorongoro Crater and released her. For a time we would go back and look for her, taking her a leg of beef from the Ngorongoro butchery until she was reported to be catching Thomson's gazelle for herself. Finding her was not easy and we eventually became oblivious to any other large carnivores we might encounter as we searched for hours on foot through the long grass and scrub on the crater floor. So much so that I remember quite seriously reminding Michael Mehlman, a young American archaeologist who was helping me, not to go up to any tawny animal he might see lying under a bush without first calling to it. This was not the end of the story, however, because one day several months later, Lisa suddenly reappeared at our camp, purring with delight at seeing us again and pleased at being back; but we could not keep her, for the same reasons as before, so we took her out onto Serengeti as far as Ndutu and released her there. Since then she has not been seen again.

During the 1970s I always had a team of Dalmatians with me at

Olduvai, usually four of them at any one time. Sam, Smudge, Sophie and Janet are all now gone. I have lost the three older ones during the last year and Sam was poisoned years ago, so now I only have Matt, five years old and one of the most handsome and intelligent Dalmatians I have ever had. He has an uncanny knack of knowing by instinct when I have taken a dislike to someone, and has even been known to go quietly and bite them when he saw an opportunity, even if I have given no outward sign. With Matt I have at present an adopted stray mongrel who formerly belonged to a local Masai group but was abandoned when they moved away. He answers to the name of Brown Dog, and while the Dalmatian tolerates his company, he leaves him in no doubt of his slightly inferior social status.

Matt, I am glad to say, does not share his predecessors' love of illicit hunting. There are far too many predators in the area for such unaccompanied canine expeditions to be safe. I never did find out how they exchanged their secret starting signal, but there can be no doubt that they had one. One moment the four would be lying in the sun, sleepy and comatose; the next, there would be a thunder of feet as they streaked from camp, oblivious to our shouts: later, perhaps, there would be joyous barking somewhere in the far distance. Because of the danger to them I always dropped what I was doing whenever this happened and took off after them in my car, while others would set out in different directions on foot to help. Many a visitor during that period, engaged in earnest conversation with me, would suddenly find himself looking at a couple of skid marks instead: speed was essential if one hoped to catch up with the dogs. Sometimes these chases could be long affairs, with the searchers widely scattered, so we devised a system whereby if the dogs were brought safely back to camp, or made their own way home, a white sheet would be hoisted on one of the windmills as a general recall signal. The other thing I must record about the Dalmatians of that period was that a tourist once went quite seriously to the Conservator at Ngorongoro to report seeing a new species of predator on Serengeti – white, with black spots. It was my pack of Dalmatians, doubtless in full cry at the time! It is remarkable that in fact no harm ever befell any of them on such an expedition, though each of them in old age suffered badly from arthritis. I suspect this was the result of falls, and all the rough going they encountered while out hunting.

Up to 1977 I had many visitors at Olduvai. I do not only refer to individual colleagues who came, as they so easily could from Nairobi before the border closed, but also to the more serious kind of tourist parties, mostly from the USA, who would arrange in advance for me to show them round the main sites and give them a short lecture, in return for a very welcome contribution of $200 to the Olduvai Research Fund. It was that kind of lecturing, early on, which got me accustomed to public speaking and to addressing non-professional audiences. Many of those who came assured me – and even went to the extent of writing afterwards to say so – that their visit to Olduvai was the highlight of their East African tour. The groups came mostly from colleges, museums or zoos: I remember, for example, the New York Zoological Society, the San Diego Zoo, the California Academy of Sciences and the American Museum of Natural History, among many others. Members of these parties had often clearly done a great deal of homework before arriving and their questions were highly intelligent.

Many visitors came to stay in camp because the 1970s were very busy from the point of view of fieldwork, and there was always material to be studied in our laboratories. The visitors were well looked after by my excellent staff, notably Kitetu and Kabebo, and it was only while Kitetu was away and I had a temporary cook that there was any difficulty. There was nothing wrong with the cooking itself, but I recall two different temporary cooks whose fondness for drink was their undoing. The drink in question was no ordinary beverage, but *changaa*, a raw spirit distilled by the Masai at one of their nearby *manyattas*, where members of my staff seemed to be welcome as drinking companions. The effects of *changaa* could be terrible, and one Sunday afternoon when I was alone in camp with one woman visitor, the cook returned so far gone that we could hear him shouting and yelling when he was still at the far side of the Gorge. When he got nearer we could see that he was actually frothing at the mouth, and we fled to our respective huts and locked ourselves in: he was quite mad with drink. He came and battered on our doors, but could not get in, and I was very relieved when people from the guides' camp heard the noise, and came across and overpowered him.

The other incident was more hilarious than dangerous. This time another temporary cook had not waited till off-duty hours to go in search of drink: it had apparently been brought to him in a gourd by Masai women during the morning, with the result that the task of carrying in the lunch and putting it on the table for me to serve proved just too much for him. He staggered in with the dish and by a somewhat meandering route arrived beside me, where he hesitated and then, before he could get the dish down safely on the table, sat down in my lap. There were quite a lot of visitors for lunch that day, too. Just occasionally, I have had this problem with members of the excavating staff, and I have always had to get rid of them, for their own safety as much as for any other reason. I have often been sad, in the process, to lose people who were really good workers and sometimes very skilled. But I could not have my vehicles driven by men in that condition, and also people who are going to come back to camp across the Gorge at night, totally drunk, are liable to fall victim to prowling lions, for whom it is a favourite place after dark.

The stream of visitors ceased abruptly in 1977 when, without any warning, the Tanzanian Government decided to close its border with Kenya, which meant not only that people could no longer drive down, but also that direct flights from Kenya to Tanzania or vice versa ceased. The reason for Tanzania's action was apparently dissatisfaction with Kenya following the break-up of the East African Community: Kenya was thought to have retained the lion's portion of the formerly shared facilities, but it may be that fundamental differences in political ideology also played a part. I was staying in Nairobi when it happened, but by chance on that very day I flew down to Olduvai for a few hours' visit with my cousin, Michael Norton-Griffiths, in his aeroplane. In the morning we called, as was customary, at the Manyara airstrip in Tanzania to collect a permit for the visit and fortunately the usual practice for a day trip was for the 'in' and 'out' clearances to be given at the same time, so that one did not have the trouble of a second stop at Manyara on the way home. While we were at Olduvai the border closure took place, and all Kenyan planes and vehicles in Tanzania at the time were impounded. Many tourists were stranded as a result of this, though the Tanzanian authorities did make a special effort to get them on to their destinations by other means. We, meanwhile, flew home direct from Olduvai to Wilson Airport in Nairobi, blissfully unaware of what had happened, and caused amazement by our arrival. Had we needed to go back to Manyara, we should not have been allowed to leave. We must have been the very last to fly back to Kenya, and by a strange coincidence when the border reopened on 17 November 1983, mine was the first car through after President Moi when he returned to Kenya following the meeting in Arusha of the three East African Heads of State.

Through the kind understanding of the Tanzanian Antiquities Department and the good offices of Amini Mturi, the Director of Antiquities, I have had no difficulty since 1977 in obtaining the permissions I have needed to remain and work in Tanzania, or to travel to and from Nairobi when I have needed to do so. This courtesy has extended to members of my staff, and others working within my research projects, and has been greatly appreciated.

One effect of the enforced isolation in Tanzania has been to strengthen the ties of friendship and the bond of mutual reliance between those of us who live on or near the Serengeti. George Dove had left three years before the border closed, and since his departure my closest neighbour has been Margaret Kullander, who has been a wonderful friend. She was born in Tanzania, though of British parents, and has spent most of her life in the country. When I first met her, Jim Gibb, her first husband, was still alive and they ran a coffee plantation at Karatu, a village on the road from

Ngorongoro to Arusha. After Jim's death, from a stroke, she married Per Kullander, a Norwegian who had been farm manager while Jim Gibb was alive. Gibb's Farm, as it is still called, has become a highly successful tourist lodge and has a fine kitchen garden from which Margaret and Per have generously supplied my camps with superb fresh vegetables, so essential to our well being.

One of the most unfortunate results of the 1977 closure of the Kenya/Tanzania border was the increased isolation from the other members of my family. I could still travel to Kenya to visit my sons and their wives and children, but the closure made it impossible for them to come and spend holidays with me at Olduvai, and this I greatly regretted. My sons' careers were flourishing and by now I had ten grandchildren, but the travel restrictions meant that I was seeing far less of them than I would have liked.

My youngest son Philip is now 35. I always suspect that he would have made a good scientist had he so chosen, since he is always overflowing with interests and ideas and practical skills. But by the early 1970s his interests had turned to politics. He lost his first election in 1974, but next time round he was successful and he became MP for Langata, the only white Kenyan Member of the Kenya Parliament. In due course he was appointed Assistant Minister of Natural Resources. By coincidence, on the very day that I wrote these words, news reached me at Olduvai of his victory in the 1983 election, when he was re-elected to the Langata constituency. He has now been appointed Assistant Minister in Foreign Affairs, with special responsibilities for the selection and implementation of foreign aid programmes.

Amidst the general success of the family there was one shadow whose length grew as the 1970s progressed. Richard's health began to deteriorate: the original cause seems to have been a throat infection many years before. He concealed from us for as long as possible the fact that he knew his kidneys must one day fail; but by 1979 the crisis had come, and in due course he had to go to London and be kept alive by dialysis until a transplant operation could be arranged. Both his brothers at once offered to donate a kidney, and when tissue tests were made it was found that Philip could provide an ideal match. Philip was already deeply involved in his election campaign and it was agreed that the operation could not take place till the election was over. I went to London too and stayed as usual with Micky and Michael Day, who looked after me with the utmost kindness during the anxious time. After the operations Richard and Philip quickly became lively enough to reject the hospital food, and Meave would twice a day cook fresh meat and make a salad and bring it to the hospital for them. All seemed to be well with Richard, but shortly afterwards he picked up a virus and as a result his body made strong efforts to reject the new kidney. He was rushed back to intensive care and for a while it was touch-and-go whether he would live: but he pulled through. Since then he has returned to robust health, and Philip has shown no ill effects. Jonathan continues to live at Lake Baringo, commuting to Nairobi several times a week in his Cessna 206. He and his second wife Janet, who used to work with me at Olduvai, have two baby daughters born within a year of each other.

Having not long recovered from the stress of our near-tragedy with Richard, 1982 was to have a nasty surprise in store for me too. I was feeling fit and happened to be alone at my camp at Olduvai. I usually rest and perhaps sleep for a while during the hottest part of the day, after lunch. On this occasion, when I woke up, I found I could only see out of my right eye. This was very frightening and alarming and I had no idea of the reason. Next morning there was no change and I knew something must be done. We have at Olduvai a radio transceiver, and as luck would have it I had hardly got the machine connected up to a battery and made my call-sign, when I heard the voice not of Radio Control in Nairobi but of Jonathan in Baringo: 'Good morning, Mother, how are you?' He had been about to make a call of his own and had recognized my voice. 'Jonny!' I said, 'Thank goodness. Listen, I seem to be in real trouble....' Within moments he was making the necessary arrangements for me to fly to Nairobi for medical advice.

A specialist examined my eye and was soon able to tell me what had happened: I had suffered a thrombosis. The blood clot, which could have gone anywhere, including to my heart or brain, where it might have proved fatal, had settled behind my left eye. It was highly unlikely that I would ever have effective vision in that eye again.

Things seem very different now to what they did in the immediate aftermath. At first, when I heard from the doctor that the affliction would be permanent, I was very depressed and sorry for myself. Richard and Meave were kindness itself: they insisted that I should stay with them while I was in Nairobi, instead of moping at Langata. Richard skilfully extracted me from my low state by alternately giving me pep talks and spoiling me with his choicest wines and specially cooked meals – real *haute cuisine*, prepared by his own expert hands, for Richard is a most gifted cook among his other talents. The treatment worked. I spent part of the Christmas holiday at Baringo with Jonathan, Janet and various of the family and by mid-January of 1983 I was back at Olduvai, grappling with the early stages of the writing of this book. At first, I thought I might never be able to write or draw again, let alone drive a car. But it is amazing how one can adapt. Now I can even draw again quite successfully, so life goes on much as before.

Times change – and with them one's feelings and attitudes. For many years I dreaded even the thought of leaving Olduvai and moving back to Langata. A very large part of my life has been spent there among its rocky gullies and cliffs, surrounded by birds and animals of every sort, and with the distant hills forming a familiar backdrop to my work. Leaving it all behind seemed barely conceivable. Yet the Tanzania I knew has changed, and over the past few years life at the Gorge became increasingly difficult – indeed it became a battle for survival. Food supplies have always been a major concern, and keeping the camp provisioned took a good deal of time and effort. That was when petrol was fairly easily available. When fuel supplies dwindled almost to nothing – despite the generosity of the personnel of the Ngorongoro Conservation Authority who gave me all they could spare – the problems became insurmountable. In the end, my decision to move back to Nairobi came very easily: what I had earlier thought would be a terrible wrench was actually a great relief. The main attractions were the prospect of being able to continue my work without incessant problems, and, of course, the thought of being closer to my family. I still have a great deal to do, and can look forward now to getting on with it in comfort and with the facilities I need.

As any archaeologist will know, there comes a time when the main fieldwork and laboratory studies have been completed and the results have to be written up. So it is with me now. Over the past five years or so I have been involved in a great deal of writing – both with colleagues and on my own. A major item has been the Laetoli report, and I have also been working on a large monograph that will bring together all the results of my work at Olduvai on Beds III and IV. The Laetoli volume has now been completed and I look forward to seeing it in print by 1985. And within the past few weeks I have received the first bound copies of my book on the rock paintings of Tanzania: it is a beautiful volume and has brought me immense pleasure.

The Olduvai camp is being handed over to the Tanzanian Department of Antiquities although it is my intention to return there from time to time, particularly to set up a Laetoli exhibit in the Museum and to receive the Trustees of the L.S.B. Leakey Foundation when they visit Kenya and Tanzania in 1984. For the present, a caretaker staff will look after the camp, and the guides will continue to show visitors sites in the Gorge, but it is the aim of Mr Mturi, the head of the Antiquities Department, that the camp with its existing laboratories should become a research centre for prehistoric archaeology and the study of fossils. This project will necessarily require quite substantial funding from overseas and I most sincerely trust that this will be forthcoming: the venue would be ideal.

Having spent the best part of sixty years trying to increase our knowledge of man's past, ranging in time from the Miocene and the earliest known bipedal hominids, who lived 3·5 million years ago, to people of the Iron Age, only a few hundred years old, I owe those who have read thus far some explanation of my motives and a few words about what has been achieved. Basically, I have been impelled by curiosity. Unlike Louis, I have never believed that knowledge of the past would help us to understand and possibly control the future. As I see it, the future is wholly unpredictable and what may happen to the world in general, including mankind, will be incapable of control to any significant degree. Nature, the process of evolution, or whatever other term we use, will take its course, and man's activities will follow an irreversible pattern. But the past is different in that what has happened has left traces in the geological record, in the animal kingdom and in man's activities. Small pieces of the record have been preserved and can sometimes be found, but it cannot be stressed too strongly that they are indeed small parts and what we uncover may give us a biased view of the picture as a whole.

Man's early tools and any insights we can get into the lifestyles and activities in succeeding stages of human evolution have been the aspects of the past that I have found the most absorbing, more so than the anatomical features linking or separating one fossil hominid from another – a subject that sparks off more heated debate than any other aspect of man's past. My preference of stones to bones may seem strange since I have personally been responsible for finding a number of significant fossil hominids and certainly on each occasion I have been excited and delighted. But the ensuing arguments, not always conducted in the best of taste, have rather tarnished my enthusiasm for these discoveries.

Before embarking on a brief account of what I consider to have been my most significant achievements I must stress that whatever finds I have made would have been valueless without the close co-operation and unstinted help of many colleagues, particularly in the fields of geology, dating and palaeontology. Prehistoric archaeology is wholly dependent on these sciences if it is to contribute to the general picture of the past.

When I first came to Kenya, and for a number of years afterwards, I had a lively interest in the Neolithic and Iron Age, following my training in England. Hence my digs at Hyrax Hill, the Njoro Cave and my study of the Dimple-based pottery; but my interest in these periods has waned and been directed further and further into the past, culminating in the Pliocene site of Laetoli. In fact this was really no place for an archaeologist since it had no stone tools, but I was not to know that when I embarked on the project. Both Louis and I hoped that the skull of *Proconsul africanus*, which I found in 1948, might be the long-sought Miocene ancestral hominid. One must have existed at that time, about 18 million years ago, and we thought we had found it; but alas, it proved to be more ape-like than hominid. For all that, it was the very first skull of a Miocene ape known, and for that reason was of considerable importance.

Perhaps the most significant of the discoveries for which I have been responsible was the trails of hominid footprints at Laetoli, 3·5 million years old. Anthropologists had for some time postulated that *Australopithecus* walked upright, basing their conclusion on the conformation of the thigh bones and pelvis. But here was incontrovertible proof, and moreover it was earlier than the australopithecines that had been studied. The footprints are so similar to those of modern man that they demonstrate this was by no means the beginning of bipedalism. It was all the more surprising, therefore, that no trace of tools was to be found in contemporary deposits. Of course this is negative evidence but I find it hard to believe that if stones were used at the time, in whatever form, no trace at all would have been left: stones are virtually indestructible. In fact the first well-documented evidence for working stone came over a million years later in the form of some rudimentary chips found in the Omo Valley of southern Ethiopia. Nothing is known of what may have happened in the interval. But by two million years ago the Oldowan stone industry existed. Louis had found some of these tools before I ever went to Olduvai, but in those days there was no means of ascertaining their age, and the full extent of this early tool kit was not appreciated until I excavated several living-sites during the 1960s. By that time the geology of the Gorge was beginning to be fully understood, and isotopic dating had come into being. But I remember the incredulity among my colleagues when they were first shown such a diverse assortment of tools belonging to that early period. It was a breakthrough in understanding the early Stone Age.

Laetoli has shown that bipedalism and tool making were probably quite separate developments in the mosaic of human evolution: Olduvai Gorge has given us vital clues in understanding the different aspects of the Acheulean hand axe culture, the most widely distributed and longest in duration of all Stone Age traditions. When I first began my archaeological career these tools were classified into many successive stages based on their shape and the nature of their trimming, which was believed to have become increasingly refined as time went on. But when I excavated hand axe sites at Olduvai Gorge at different levels, in a sound geological context, I found to my great surprise that some of the most refined and highly finished tools were earlier than crude and apparently less skilfully made ones. This was very puzzling until I began to relate the numbers of flakes knocked off in shaping the tools to the types of rock that had been used. I found that tools made from fine-grained rocks like phonolite had many more trimming flakes than those made from coarse-grained, tough rocks like basalt. The reason is simple. A sharp and serviceable cutting edge, to my mind, was without doubt the purpose of a hand axe, and the type of stone used would necessarily affect the nature of the edge. My assistant Peter Jones had found that a thin edge of fine-grained rock would be too brittle to withstand wear, and that it was therefore necessary to strengthen and reinforce it by delicate trimming flakes. But the edge of a tough, coarse rock would stand up to wear and, moreover, become too blunt to be useful if further trimmed. It is now clear that the old idea of hand axe typology becoming more and more refined through time no longer holds good. Although my work at Olduvai has shed some light on why such different types of hand axes are to be found, we still have no valid explanation as to why this particular tool was so widespread and remained the unchallenged tool type for over a million years. Why should there have been no new ideas or new activities to promote new tool types during all this time? Possibly the hand axe was such an efficient all-purpose tool that no others were required or, alternatively, if *Homo erectus* was indeed the maker, he was perhaps too slow witted to be capable of new inventions, in spite of his relatively large brain size.

In Africa, the hand axe culture did eventually give place to a surprisingly uninspiring group of industries lumped together under the term Middle Stone Age; a stage in prehistoric archaeology for which I have never been able to feel any enthusiasm. In fact it is true to say that my interest flags during the whole of the later part of the old Stone Age and is only reawakened when prehistoric man – now *Homo sapiens* like ourselves – had developed artistic ability. These early paintings and drawings have fascinated me from childhood. The European paintings in dark caves are awe-inspiring, but many of the African paintings have great artistry of a rather different character. These sites too, particularly those used for painting over and over again for hundreds of years, have an aura which I sensed when I worked on them in 1951 and which was recognized also by the local people in the Kondoa area of Tanzania.

If the Laetoli footprints were the most significant of the finds for which I have been responsible, although it was Paul Abell who actually found them, the *Zinjanthropus* skull perhaps attracted even more publicity and at the time of its discovery was a most important step in the study of early man. A number of robust australopithecine skulls had been found in South Africa but their age was unknown. *Zinj* could be dated by the potassium-argon method and proved to be 1·75 million years old, very much earlier than anyone had anticipated. Not only was the date important but the excavations also showed that Zinj was contemporary and living side by side with another type of hominid, *Homo habilis*. Until then the idea that two hominids could occupy the same area at the same time had been unacceptable to most scientists. For a while Louis and I fell into the trap of believing Zinj was the maker of the Oldowan tools since the skull was found on a living-floor where they were abundant. But this idea was soon abandoned when parts of the skull of a juvenile *Homo habilis*, found at a nearby site, showed that his brain size was substantially larger than that of Zinj. Not only was his brain bigger but the hand and foot bones also showed that he was capable of a precision grip and an upright bipedal gait. This was the first clear evidence of bipedalism at such an early date. Needless to say the term *Homo habilis*, the inference of manual dexterity and of bipedal gait, all attracted the storms of protest that usually ensue after any discovery that upsets the accepted scenario of hominid evolution. Louis was at the centre of it – and loved it.

Zinj's position was soon established. He and other robust australopithecines were relegated to a side branch of the main evolutionary stem that gave rise to ourselves, a branch that proved unsuccessful and died out approximately one million years ago at Olduvai and elsewhere. The position of *Homo habilis* was more contentious. Many people felt that he was an advanced form of *Australopithecus africanus* and that the term *Homo* was unjustified, but it seemed to us that his bigger brain and association with a diverse tool kit merited the term. Subsequently, when chimpanzees were discovered to use 'tools' for certain purposes, some doubt was again cast on whether tool making could be used as one of the criteria for *Homo*. But in my view the objects used by chimpanzees are in a very different category from the stone tools of *Homo habilis*. They are merely grass stalks and other things modified for their required use by biting or breaking by hand, and cannot be compared to a diverse tool kit requiring considerable manual dexterity to shape each tool to a preconceived pattern. However, since the days of the *Homo habilis* controversy we have learned that the great apes are indeed our cousins and it is likely that human tool-making began in a similar fashion to theirs.

Many of my colleagues expend a great deal of time and mental energy in reconstructing trees of hominid evolution. They juggle with Miocene apes, the various australopithecines, and with types of early *Homo*, sometimes making a simple evolutionary pattern and sometimes ones that are extremely complex. It is good fun, and an entertaining pastime if not taken too seriously, but in the present state of our knowledge I do not believe it is possible to fit the known hominid fossils into a reliable pattern. There are too many gaps, and some of the specimens are not sufficiently well dated for their position to be determined with accuracy. Added to this there is the matter of nomenclature. Given an entire skull it is likely that most anatomists and anthropologists would agree on what type of being it represented, but with incomplete specimens, sometimes mere scraps of bones or a few teeth, the position is very different. Moreover, the circumstances attending the discovery of many fossil hominids have often been far from ideal. Some have been surface finds that have been attributed to the deposits on which they were found without sufficient emphasis being given to the possibility that they might have been derived from another level and therefore not be of the age claimed for them.

If there were more specimens to fill the gaps, and better-documented evidence, there would certainly be much closer agreement about the evolutionary pattern. Needless to say, on my lecture tours I am often asked to express my opinion, but I invariably decline. My reply is that we require a great deal more evidence before we can hope to formulate a reliable reconstruction. We do not know, for example, whether some of the fossils we have are in the main line of hominid evolution or relics of unsuccessful side branches like the robust australopithecines. This factor alone is of vital importance in arriving at a correct solution. For the present we would do well to concentrate on discovering new, firmly dated specimens and spend less time in putting forward our own, personal interpretations.

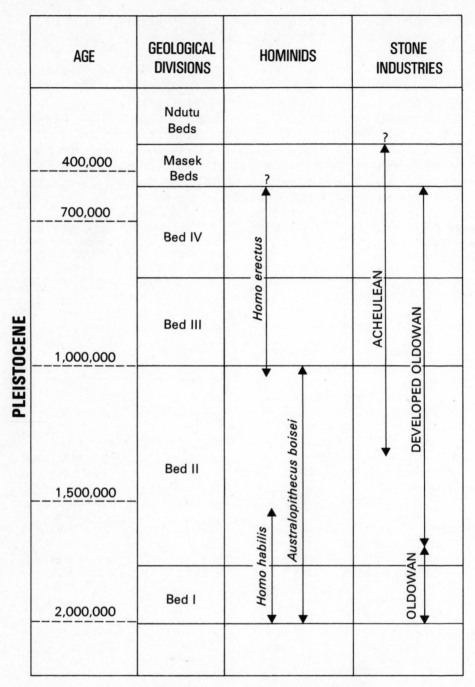

The geological succession at Olduvai

Glossary

Acheulian An early Stone Age culture characterized by large, almond-shaped tools known as hand axes.

Anthropology The study of mankind.

Australopithecus A genus of extinct East and South African hominids, to which 'Zinj' (*A. boisei*) belongs. The name means 'Southern Ape'. The various species within the genus are known collectively as the australopithecines.

Basalt A dark-coloured volcanic rock.

Baulk An unexcavated strip left between two areas of excavation in order to provide a reference point for the various levels.

Bipedalism A two-legged upright gait.

Burins Stone tools with chisel-like working edges.

Calcite A crystalline form of calcium carbonate.

Calcrete A hard layer of surface limestone often found in desert areas.

Chert A rock consisting mainly of silica. It is easily flaked to give stone tools with very sharp cutting edges.

Cleavers Large tools characterized by having a straight working edge at right-angles to the long axis, rather like an adze.

Hominid A member of the family Hominidae, which includes *Homo* and *Australopithecus* but excludes the apes.

Homo The generic name given to the hominid group containing fossil and modern man.

Inselbergs Small hills consisting of basement rocks projecting up through younger sediments.

Knapping (flint or other stones) The process of shaping stones by striking or pressure-flaking to produce tools.

Mandible The lower jaw.

Manyatta A Masai homestead, enclosed by a thorn fence.

Maxilla The upper jaw.

Mesolithic The Stone Age period between the Palaeolithic and the Neolithic. The prefixes indicate 'Old', 'Middle', and 'New' Stone Ages.

Miocene A geological period dating, approximately, from 25 million years ago to 5 million years ago.

Neolithic The 'New Stone Age' during which agriculture, pastoralism and pottery were developed.

Oldowan An early Stone Age industry, first recorded at Olduvai Gorge. A later industry, derived from the Oldowan, is known as the Developed Oldowan.

Palaeoanthropology The study of early hominid fossils.

Palaeolithic The 'Old Stone Age'.

Palaeontology The study of extinct animals and plants.

Pleistocene The geological period following the Pliocene, spanning the period 2 million years ago to 10,000 years ago.

Pliocene The geological period between the Miocene and Pleistocene, 5 million years ago to 2 million years ago.

Phonolite A fine-grained volcanic rock, believed to ring when struck.

Quartzite A silicious metamorphic rock, fine-grained varieties of which were widely used for making stone tools.

Rock shelters Overhanging rocks used by prehistoric man as living-shelters, and in some parts of Africa for mural paintings.

Scrapers Stone tools with curved spoon-like edges, believed to have been used for preparing animal skins.

Stratigraphy The branch of geology concerned with the relative positions of deposits, and the sequence of events associated with them.

Tuff Consolidated volcanic ash. Aeolian tuff refers to wind-transported ash.

Zinj (*Zinjanthropus*) The generic name originally given to *Australopithecus boisei*, and meaning 'The man of East Africa'.

Further Reading

Readers wishing to learn more about early man, his origins, evolution and way of life, or about the work of the Leakeys and others in East Africa, may like to refer to the following:

Leakey's Luck, The Life of Louis Seymour Bazett Leakey 1902–72 by Sonia Cole. (Collins, London; Harcourt Brace Jovanovich, New York, 1975)

Origins by Richard Leakey and Roger Lewin. (Macdonald & Jane's, London; Dutton, New York, 1977)

The Evolution of Early Man by Bernard Wood. (Peter Lowe, London & New York, 1978)

Evolution by Colin Patterson. (British Museum (Natural History) London; Cornell University Press, Ithaca, 1978)

Olduvai Gorge: My Search for Early Man by Mary Leakey. (Collins, London, 1979)

The Illustrated Origin of Species, Charles Darwin, abridged and introduced by Richard Leakey. (Faber and Faber, London; Hill and Wang, New York, 1979)

Secrets of the Ice Age by Evan Haddingham. (Walker, New York, 1979; Heinemann, London, 1980)

The Making of Mankind by Richard Leakey. (Michael Joseph, London; Dutton, New York, 1981)

Human Origins by Richard Leakey. (Hamish Hamilton, London; Lodestar, New York, 1982)

Missing Links by John Reader. (Collins, London; Little, Brown, Boston, 1981)

Africa's Vanishing Art by Mary Leakey. (Hamish Hamilton, London; Doubleday, New York, 1983)

One Life by Richard Leakey. (Michael Joseph, London, 1983)

Picture Credits

Sources of photographs are credited in the photographs' order of appearance, page by page, within the four blocks of illustrations.

Photographs between pages 48 and 49
M.D. Leakey; M.D. Leakey; M.D. Leakey; Howard Carter; L.S.B. Leakey; M.D. Leakey; M.D. Leakey; L.S.B. Leakey; M.D. Leakey; M.D. Leakey; L.S.B. Leakey; Rainbird Publishing Group; British Airways.

Photographs between pages 96 and 97
Peter Jones; Rainbird Publishing Group; Rainbird; Rainbird; Rainbird; Hugo van Lawick; Hugo van Lawick; Des Bartlett, National Geographic Society; Hugo van Lawick; Hugo van Lawick, National Geographic Society; Hugo van Lawick; Michael Day; National Geographic Society.

Photographs between pages 144 and 145
M.D. Leakey; British Airways; Des Bartlett; M.D. Leakey; Des Bartlett; Bob Campbell, Armand Denis Productions; Hugo van Lawick; Melville Bell Grosvenor, National Geographic Society; Des Bartlett; Michael Mehlman; Yale University; John Reader.

Photographs between pages 192 and 193
John Reader; Bob Campbell, National Geographic Society; M.D. Leakey; Peter Jones; John Reader; John Reader; John Reader; Melville Bell Grosvenor, National Geographic Society; John Reader; Anthony Edgeworth Inc.; Hugo van Lawick; John Reader.

Map on page 10 drawn by Eugene Fleury.

Index

HOCKESSIN PUBLIC LIBRARY
HOCKESSIN, DE. 197.07.

301.092 Leak
Leakey, Mary D. 1913-
Disclosing the past

12/84

NEW CASTLE COUNTY

DEMCO